Cooking for One

1st Edition

by Jennifer Fisher

A Wiley Brand

Cooking for One For Dummies®

Published by: **John Wiley & Sons, Inc.,** 111 River Street, Hoboken, NJ 07030-5774, www.wiley.com

Copyright © 2023 by John Wiley & Sons, Inc., Hoboken, New Jersey

Published simultaneously in Canada

For general information on our other products and services, please contact our Customer Care Department within the U.S. at 877-762-2974, outside the U.S. at 317-572-3993, or fax 317-572-4002. For technical support, please visit www.wiley.com/techsupport.

Wiley publishes in a variety of print and electronic formats and by print-on-demand. Some material included with standard print versions of this book may not be included in e-books or in print-on-demand. If this book refers to media such as a CD or DVD that is not included in the version you purchased, you may download this material at http://booksupport.wiley.com. For more information about Wiley products, visit www.wiley.com.

Library of Congress Control Number: 2023930255

ISBN 978-1-119-88692-1 (pbk); ISBN 978-1-119-88695-2 (ebk); ISBN 978-1-119-88694-5 (ebk)

SKY1004863_012625

Contents at a Glance

Recipes at a Glance

Healthy Smoothies, Parfaits, and Breakfast Puddings

Salads for Every Season

Soups for Singles

Sandwiches, Personal Pizzas, and More

Chicken Dishes to Cluck About

Beef Dishes that Can't Be Beat

Fish and Seafood Dishes That Make Waves

Meatless Meals for Everyone

Grains, Beans, and Beyond

Fruits and Veggies to Brighten Your Plate

Savory and Sweet Snacks That Satisfy

Single-Serve Desserts: Automatic Portion Control

Smaller-Batch Desserts: Sure, Have Another

Table of Contents

Introduction

Congratulations, if you've opened the book and come to this point, it means you're at least tossing around the idea of cooking a meal for yourself real soon! Perhaps you've recently flown the nest and been binging on reality cooking shows while eating take-out meals straight from the Styrofoam boxes, and now you've had that light bulb moment. Maybe you can take ownership of your own meals, too! Or maybe you're a little further down the path of life, divorced, widowed, or as Mom might say, "still single," and want to improve your skills in the kitchen and clean up your diet a bit. It doesn't matter if you're young, old, a first-timer, moderately experienced, or a little more "seasoned." If you can read and follow along with basic instructions, you should be good — no license or special credentials needs. Cooking is a practical endeavor that can turn into an enjoyable pastime, even a passion, regardless of your age or stage of life.

Don't be intimidated by cooking or fret if you're a late bloomer in the kitchen. Julia Child, the famous chef who brought French cooking techniques to American homes in the 1960s and 1970s, didn't take up cooking until her 30s and didn't land her first TV show until after turning 50. She was a big believer that fear should not keep you from cooking. She wasn't afraid of her own failures and freely admits to many mishaps in the kitchen. You've likely heard that saying, "The master has failed a thousand times more than the student." Honestly, if you haven't messed up something significantly yet when cooking, then you probably haven't tried hard enough!

Some people are intimidated by cooking because they think it must be fancy to be phenomenal — and this is absolutely *not* the case. Some of the best, most incredible meals are those that are the simplest, even humble. Recipes with very few steps that do not require much time but focus on delicious, fresh ingredients will likely become some of your favorites. And, sitting back for a second to pat yourself on the back and treat your senses to the smells and sights before taking that first amazing bite of a meal that *you made — ahhhhh!*

You'll find useful information in this book to help you set up your kitchen with the appropriate gear and gadgets, plan for and secure ingredients like a pro, and whip out recipes day after day to savor and smile about — all from the perspective of the single home chef.

About This Book

Cooking for One For Dummies is the perfect cookbook for anyone interested in feeding themselves! We all need to eat to live, and if you're a "party of one" it can often seem like chore . . . but eating the same old take-out can be a bore while it also drains your wallet. In this book, you'll learn the steps to plan, shop, prep, and execute a delicious and responsibly priced meal for one. With over 145 single-serve and small-scale recipes at your fingertips for any meal of the day, plus snacks and dessert, you can't go wrong!

Here are guidelines to keep in mind about the recipes in this book:

>> It is standard operating procedure to read a recipe from top to bottom before starting. This is to account for any necessary marinating time, chilling time, and so on, as well as to round up any special equipment, gadgets, or cookware sizes that the recipe may require.

>> All temperatures are Fahrenheit (see the appendix to convert Fahrenheit temperatures to Celsius).

>> Ingredient weight measurements are in pounds and ounces (see the appendix for metric conversions).

>> All microwave cooking is on *high* unless otherwise noted. Please note that microwave cooking times can vary a good deal based on the appliance's wattage, brand, and age.

>> All dry ingredients should be measured in measuring cups that are for dry ingredients, which are leveled at the top with a knife, not heaping full.

>> For accuracy, all liquid ingredients should be measured in a measuring cup designed for fluids. The headroom, handle, and spigot also ensure that nothing sloshes out before adding to the recipes.

>> All flour in recipes is all-purpose white flour unless otherwise noted. You may substitute a cup-for-cup, gluten-free blend of flours specifically labeled for baking, but be aware that the results may vary a bit.

Foolish Assumptions

We make a few assumptions in this book about you as the reader:

>> You're cooking for yourself, either on a daily basis or just occasionally, and are looking for single-serve and smaller-batch solutions to big family-sized recipes.

>> Your kitchen is set up with the basics including refrigerator, oven, stovetop, microwave, and a few entry-level pots, pans, knives, and other prep implements. If your kitchen is already set up with entry-level essentials, this book will help you decide which extras would be helpful to purchase for small recipes.

>> You're looking for easy, quick, tasty recipe ideas to make at home to help minimize drive-in, take-out, and delivery food consumption.

>> You're concerned with minimizing food waste and avoiding excessive packaging disposables when possible, to leave a "greener" footprint in your path.

>> You're looking to optimize your meal budget or at least make smarter choices to help save money.

>> You want to make better decisions for your health and take conscious control over what you put into your body.

>> You're eager to try new dishes, develop your cooking skills, and celebrate the rewards of self-sufficiency.

Icons Used in This Book

The icons in this book are like sticky notes, pointing out more details that may be important to you. Here are the icons you will encounter and the kind of information they point out:

TIP

When you refer to the Tip icon, it's like a backstage pass for someone who's been there and done that. Here, you'll discover additional practical information and functional strategies that help save time, energy, money, and your mood.

REMEMBER

When you've become busy, gotten side-tracked, and forgotten the bigger picture of a chapter, look for the remember icon and skim the content for a quick refresh to get back on task.

TECHNICAL STUFF

The information marked with this icon is a much deeper dig into the topic. It may be interesting to know, but it goes beyond what's essential for your basic understanding.

WARNING

Watch out for this icon! Think of it as a little alarm that warns you about potential problems and common pitfalls of shopping for, prepping, and cooking smaller-scale recipes.

Finally, a little tomato icon (🍅) is used to highlight vegetarian recipes in the "Recipes in This Chapter" lists, as well as in the "Recipes at a Glance" at the front of this book. If you are a *lacto-ovo* vegetarian, the recipes are compliant as written. However, if you do not eat dairy or eggs, please be aware that you will need to find suitable plant-based alternatives.

Beyond the Book

In addition to the abundance of information and guidance related to cooking for one that is provided in this book, you can access even more help and information online at Dummies.com. Check out this book's online Cheat Sheet. Just go to www.dummies.com and search for "Cooking for One For Dummies Cheat Sheet."

With the Cheat Sheet, you'll be privy to important information for your cooking-for-one journey that has been distilled down into a quickly digestible read. You'll discover how to stock your kitchen space with the right equipment, gear, and gadgets. You'll develop efficient food hunting and gathering strategies that are suited for a single lifestyle. And, you'll be able to tap in to the successful habits of single-portion chefs, including stocking a pantry for one, scaling recipes up or down, embracing leftovers, and making the most of your freezer space (it's prime real estate)!

Where to Go from Here

Where to go from here depends on your immediate needs — or cravings! Is the next meal of the day breakfast, lunch, or dinner? Simply head over to the book section that matches your mood and dig in to the chapters and individual recipes. When in doubt, the dessert and snack chapters are sure to get you running to the kitchen and inspired to cook. The super functional thing about picking up a cookbook is that you can jump straight into any section and chapter and understand what's going on without needing cumulative information from past chapters. However, there is great information on the front end about how to shop and prep and store from the vantage point of riding solo on the experience. And, near the end of the book, you'll find the "Part of Tens" that provide actionable steps to help you make the most of your freezer space and learn how to take advantage of leftovers. Grab some colorful sticky notes to mark the recipes you want to try first, throw on an apron, and let's get cooking!

1
Savoring Cooking When You're Single

Discover the joys and benefits of cooking for yourself that go beyond just simply "making food."

Embrace a dedicated space within the kitchen for gear and gadgets that help support your "cheffing" success.

Hone your food hunting and gathering skills to optimize time, save money, and reduce waste.

Develop strategies to scale recipes up or down on demand and to deal with unexpected (or on purpose) leftovers.

Chapter **1**

Digging Into Cooking for One

I f you've picked up this book, you have joined countless others in the quest to learn or hone "cooking for one" skills and to discover a treasure-trove of delicious, single-serve recipes in the process. Literally, you're not alone! Over the last seven decades, America has gone through a historic transformation in household living arrangements. Today, one in seven adults lives alone, which represents more than one-quarter of all households in the United States.

Whether you're a college student and have just set up your first apartment, a young working professional, or a newly single individual (widowed or divorced), who is learning the cooking for one ropes in the kitchen you've called home for years, this book can help! Heck, I'm married with kids, but individual portion recipes have become my best friend with a husband who travels frequently and three older boys who often grabbed a burger or pizza with friends after sports practice when they were still living at home.

No matter your age or stage of life, this book will serve as a practical resource to help you set up and organize your kitchen, shop smartly, and improve your cooking skills and repertoire with over 145 tasty dishes that are sure to please your mood of the moment. You'll find a meal to meet almost every need, whether your goal is to save money, eat more nourishing meals, reduce food and packaging waste, tap into your creativity in the kitchen, feel self-sufficient and empowered — or all of the above.

Eating What You Want When and Where You Want It

Do you dream of kicking off the weekend with burgers and brats grilled right in your own backyard? Do you crave a warm, homemade cookie or salty, sweet bowl of kettle corn to power you through a couch-bound movie marathon? Perhaps you'd like to level up your lunch hour at work by packing something wonderfully fresh and exciting that will make dining at your desk feel like a delight? Whatever you do — you do you! No need to be at the whim of someone else deciding where, when, what, and how you eat!

Learning how to shop, prep, and cook your own food will give you the freedom to decide where, when, what, and how you'll eat without being at the mercy of restaurant hours, limited menus, and travelling around town more than necessary to score a meal that's decent. Plus, when you cook for yourself, there's no special dress code. You can indulge in a five-star restaurant quality dinner of steak and seafood while wearing fuzzy slippers and a robe and not a single head will spin. Or, flip your hair back and get glammed up in cocktail attire for yourself — again, you do you!

Sustaining yourself after shift work

Perhaps you work the graveyard shift and are hungry for dinner at an uncustomary hour. Or you may awake pre-dawn to run or work-out and need a high-performing breakfast to get you out the door quickly and keep you going for the long haul. Growing a skill set of methods and having access to a resource of proven recipes for one means you can be well-fed 24/7 without having to rely on "open all night" establishments, convenience stores, or another person to make and serve your breakfast, lunch, dinner, and snacks.

Brown bagging like a boss

Before you get post-traumatic stress from a childhood lunchbox flashback of a smooshed peanut butter sandwich paired with a mealy apple and tiny box of extra dry raisins, know that brown bagging as an adult can be vastly more tasty and varied. Depending on your access to a microwave at work, you can prepare a hot meal (even leftovers) or a gourmet salad or sandwich to eat at your desk — or better yet, a nearby park! Getting outside for lunch on a nice day is a proven mood boost.

Do-it-yourself meals and snacks you take to school or work save a substantial amount of money over the course of a week, compared to picking something up in the work cafeteria or nearby take-out every single day. With just a little bit of effort in advance on the planning and packing, you can save time in the long run (who wants to wait for delivery or stand in a big ordering line) and also hit your exact nutritional goals for the meal. Of course, you don't *actually* need to put the meal in a brown bag. In fact, there are far better insulated containers on the market in a variety of sizes and fun (or distinguished) designs to suit your personal needs and style.

Transcending from Survival Mode to Creative Mode

For most, it's a simple matter of survival to learn basic food sourcing strategies, food preparation skills, and cooking methods. Starving is not a sustainable option (wink-wink), and getting "hangry" is a regrettable state of mind and body. That's why obtaining the know-how to execute a simple recipe from prep to plate is a life changer.

But man (and woman) can't really live happily ever after on never-ending meals of hard-boiled eggs and toast, or whatever you classify as the emergency "I don't really cook" form of basic sustenance. At some point, you just want *more*. More variety, more colors, more texture, more flavors, and more "Wow, I made *that*!"

Cooking is an art

Just like playing the guitar or painting a canvas, cooking requires you to open your mind to the endless possibilities, relationships, and harmonies between foods and the ways they are married together. Transforming raw materials (the ingredients) into a nourishing meal is itself the work of an artist, even if it's not something that would ever be displayed in a museum. And, honestly, could your taste buds give up that eating opportunity?

Your creativity can compound daily

If you are the type of person who follows the recipes here and elsewhere to a "T," you may find yourself beginning to experiment with the spices, seasonings, sauces, garnishes, and plating to suit your mood. That's fabulous; go for it — that's creativity! One day you may find yourself hooked enough on the creative process of cooking to write your own recipes — or cookbook!

Eating Fewer "Heat and Eat" or Food Kit Meals

Even if you're not officially dining out in the physical "I'm sitting in a restaurant booth" sense, raise your hand if you've subscribed to a meal kit service or pick up "heat and eat" prepared foods from the grocery store frequently! Sometimes this type of option is a lifesaver, but on a regular basis, you're still letting someone else do most of the heavy lifting of food preparation!

The popularity of meal kit services and prepared foods, many of which are marketed to the solo diner, is sky rocketing. They are marketed as a quick and easy meal solution for people pressed on time, cooking skills, or both. Learning how to cook dishes for one can help you dial back this expensive habit while providing you an amazing feeling of self-sufficiency. You have to admit that taking off a lid and hitting the microwave's 1-minute button can start to feel a little sad and boring day after day.

In addition to acquiring new skills and saving money, waste and over-packaging are additional considerations that may make you want to reduce a habit of "heat and eat" and food kit consumption. At first glance, you might say these options minimize waste. You receive the precise amount of "this and that" to make the given recipes, or the dish is already made and packaged up in its entirety to be heated, as needed, and consumed. No bits and pieces of waste to toss away or rot in the produce drawer; it's food for you to eat. So, yes, high marks on reducing *food* waste, but what about those insulated shipping containers and ice packs that come with each delivery, pick up, or take-out? These types of packaged convenience meals create a mountain of unnecessary trash with environmental ramifications.

Catering to Your Nutritional Needs

Chances are you consciously try to avoid some type of food or beverage; most of us do. Maybe you require a dairy-free latte and a gluten-free sandwich for breakfast or a plant-based pasta (nix the mushrooms, please) tossed with a low-sodium sauce and a nut-free brownie for dessert. Learning to cook for yourself provides full control over what's on (and off) your plate. Scoring exactly what you want in a restaurant or delivery situation and trusting the waiter to accurately relay that message to the line cook is much more difficult and limiting.

Allergies and intolerances

More than 10 percent of U.S. adults have at least one food allergy or intolerance, with the spectrum of severity ranging from disrupting daily health and well-being to being life threatening. Top food allergens include milk, soy, eggs, wheat, peanuts, tree nuts, sesame, fish, and shellfish. If you have an avocado or chocolate allergy, I am grieving for you. But, all jokes aside as this is a serious topic.

Other medical and health concerns

In addition to food allergies, people have many medical, philosophical, lifestyle, religious, and other reasons for varied nutritional requirements. Diabetes, pregnancy, weight loss, sports nutrition, vegetarian, keto, Paleo, sugar-free, low-fat — this list could go on and on!

Personal taste

Let's take into consideration personal preferences, too. Do you abhor the taste of cilantro (it's a genetic thing) or get a gag reflex when thinking about blue cheese? Maybe you can't get enough quinoa or clams or key limes and want to see more in your meals. I personally pick out every bit of bell pepper in dishes, and it was a light bulb moment, years ago, when I realized that if I cooked for myself I would never have to see, smell, touch, or taste another bell pepper again.

Religion and belief systems

Making your own meals can make it easier to keep specific dietary protocols in check for religious reasons, including kosher, halal, and others. Also, in a world with many ethical, moral, and philosophical belief systems, taking charge of your personal meal making allows you to eat according to your mindset and be part of the larger collective action within that community.

Having Less Waste When a Recipe Flops

When a recipe doesn't turn out as expected, it can be a big disappointment and a wallop on your wallet — especially if it's a huge recipe that serves a crowd. One benefit of single-serve and small-batch recipes is that if there is a lackluster result, the emotional and financial loss is lessened. Most scaled-down recipes just call for a tablespoon of this and a couple ounces of that. Your meal might have gone up in smoke, but at least your food budget won't get burned to a crisp!

Why a recipe might flop

A recipe can flop for many reasons. It's too spicy, too salty, or too sweet for your preferences. You went "off-recipe" and made a substitution that didn't work, accidentally missed an ingredient or step, the oven temperature was improperly calibrated, or the pan size was too big or too small. Sometimes even when a recipe is executed perfectly, you honestly just may not care for the texture, taste, or even the appearance. Remember, if a recipe turns out looking a little less perfect than the cookbook photo or your preconceived mental image, it probably still tastes fantastic. Always do a taste test; looks can be deceiving!

Salvaging a lackluster result

It's easier to say "yes" to the small risk of trying a new dish or experimenting with recipes when an "oopsie" just means tossing out one serving of food, not a massive, family-sized feast. Instead of just throwing flopped recipes in the trash, add to a personal compost pile or compost bin if your trash pickup offers the service. If the recipe in question is still edible, consider repurposing it, if possible. For example, you could pick out the shrimp in a too spicy sauce, rinse them off, pat them dry, keep them chilled, and use them later on a salad. Or, if the recipe just misses the mark with your taste buds but is still perfectly fine otherwise, there is always a neighbor hungrier and less inspired to cook than you.

Plating Like a Pro to Really Savor the Results

Nothing wrong with throwing a chicken breast and a pile of rice on a paper plate and calling it dinner. But, since all of our sensory systems are closely interconnected, "eating with your eyes" becomes an undeniable part of the process. That's why plating your recipe with at least a moment of thought and consideration can really transform your dining experience from "just grub" to "just absolutely gorgeous."

Even if setting a table for one, you should still celebrate your finished recipes with a proper plating. Hey, make your plating social media worthy; snap a photo and show off your new skills — you never know where all that creativity and exposure could lead! The following are things to consider when plating:

» **Choose your plate.** It seems so obvious, but the plate (or bowl or mug for that matter) is often given no regard. A white plate is like a blank canvas; it can really make the colors of food pop and is the choice of most food stylists. Dark plates also can work, adding moody drama for the right food situation. Typically, patterns are to be avoided, unless you are trying to capture some sort of particular niche look — blue-speckled country plates or even cutesy mugs with clever sayings can be just the thing at the right moment.

   The convenient thing about single-serving recipes is that you don't need an eight-piece serving set of the same dish; you only need one! Visit thrift shops or garage sales to inexpensively stockpile your cabinets with plates and serving pieces that speak to you.

» **Drizzle or garnish.** A drizzle of sauce, sweet or savory depending on the dish, lends a welcomed visual vibe. It can be as sophisticated or carefree as you like, depending on how you drizzle. Use a spoon for organic results or a squeeze bottle to be more precise. Garnishes add bits or a pop of color that can also whet the appetite — a lemon slice cut and twisted atop a fish filet, fresh herbs sprinkled on eggs, or chocolate shavings and powdered sugar speckling the top of a dessert. Functional garnishes that add to the recipe's flavor work the best. But really there are no rules, just your personal tastes — edible and visual!

» **Prepare an odd number.** For whatever reason, an odd number of items, say three objects clustered together are more appealing that an even number displayed symmetrically. The "magic of three" is also a design trick that interior decorators use to create visual interest and draw the eye where they want. Lay three huge shrimp (or another odd number like five) on a pile of grits. Or arrange three distinct food groups on your plate, like steak slices, sweet potato, and broccoli — with a drizzle or garnish, of course!

» **Skip it.** If fancy plating seems like a burdensome step, then just skip it. It only adds extra pleasure to the meal if you enjoy doing it. Plating for one can vary wildly through breakfast, lunch, and dinner, day to day. And, don't forget that plating can be extra special and fun for various seasonal holidays, Sunday dinners, and other celebratory events.

No-Wait Cooking (Almost)

In most cases, you can sit down to a satisfying, homemade meal faster than picking up take-out, waiting for delivery, or getting acknowledged by the hostess at that trendy restaurant that opened down the street. Of course, there is wait time involved with cooking for yourself — baked goods have to puff up and become set, meats and seafood need to be cooked to their required internal temperature for safety, and other recipes might need to be chilled, frozen, or allowed time to cool down or rest. Also, many recipes for one are suitable for the microwave or air fryer, which will make cooking time fly by.

REMEMBER

However, please note that it's always a smart idea to read through recipes, top to bottom, before jumping into the making action. This is not just to ensure that you have all the ingredients, understand the instruction steps, and use the right cooking appliance, but also to confirm that you have enough time to commit to making the recipe. Trust me, you can't pull a cake out of the oven half done, leave to run an errand, and then return to finish cooking it. That just doesn't work!

Buying Smaller Amounts of Ingredients

Sometimes you just need a pinch of this and a couple tablespoons of that when cooking for one. Based on your previous shopping trips (and stuff later thrown in the trash), this might seem like an inconvenience, considering that many items in the store are packaged for families or at least multiple servings. But in upcoming chapters, you'll be introduced to the wise ways of shopping for, one including hitting the bulk section for mini-portions, separating items in the produce department (yeah, you don't need to buy *all* the asparagus rubber-banded together if it's sold by the pound), unleashing the hero powers of your freezer, and using other advantageous tips and tricks to make your cooking for one journey smooth sailing.

Prepping and Cleaning Up in a Snap

Slicing, dicing, chopping, and other recipe prep steps can be tedious and time consuming in full-size recipes. The great news is that with smaller-scale recipes, the workload is minimized. Think about it; there's really nothing to cry about when you only have to dice a tablespoon of onion instead of the entire big bulb! Additionally, many recipes incorporate a convenient swap like using preminced garlic from a jar or ground onion powder to lessen the chore and also efficiently address the tiny amount required.

Also, many recipes in this cookbook minimize the use of multiple pots, pans, and cooking utensils just to create a single dish. You'll even find recipes that are mixed right up in a mug that you can eat straight from — how's that for prep and clean-up efficiency! Even when a recipe requires a pot, pan, or baking dish, the very nature of the smaller surface area means less to clean up. For example, a family-sized 9 x 13–inch casserole dish offers 117 inches of bottom surface to scrub (and *more* if gunk sticks on the sides), while a mug or one jumbo muffin pan will become your new best friend with hardly any area to clean up in comparison. Bigger means more to clean up; smaller means less — the same goes with houses and that's why some days I'd trade my big suburban house for a tiny downtown apartment in a snap!

Celebrating Your Self-Sufficiency

If you think it seems silly to make a big deal out of making a meal for yourself, think again! Human brains are wired to respond to rewards and then strive for more rewards and larger rewards, that's how we tick. So, celebrating the successful completion of a small accomplishment like learning how to crack an egg without getting shells in the bowl can lead to mastering a mug muffin, which can lead to making a layer cake, which can lead to becoming the best baker on the block! You don't know until you try something out and toot your own horn for a job well done.

Of course, eating the finished recipe is the ultimate reward! Nothing quite like smelling something sizzling on the stovetop or baking in the oven and knowing that in just a short time you will be digging into an amazing creation that you made.

Here are a few ways to celebrate your recipe successes:

>> Fun plating: Make the meal a special experience and not just an eat-on-a-TV-tray kind of day.

>> Style your food and snap photos to share in a scrapbook on social media or text to family to show how your skills are progressing.

>> Start a journal, personal cookbook, or vlog documenting your recipes, steps, swaps, and experiences.

>> Make an extra serving of your recipe to share with a friend, family member, co-worker, or neighbor.

» Buy some fun dish towels, kitchen gadgets, or special fancy ingredients to level up your home kitchen.

» Branch out to new cooking methods and recipes; treat yourself to a new cookbook or cooking class, online or in person.

Reflect on your cooking journey to date and how it has impacted your life for the better. At a minimum, you likely are benefiting from improved nutritional choices, eating a more varied and balanced diet with ingredients you have a say-so about choosing (or not choosing). Chances are you have saved money by dining out less frequently. And come on — it feels good to feed yourself, and it can even be fun!

Chapter **2**

Gearing Up to Cook

Setting up a kitchen may sound like an overwhelming task, especially if you're a cooking newbie. But, honestly, it's not a difficult undertaking at all and most likely will be a very satisfying experience because the final product is (fingers crossed) a nice, home-cooked meal.

Of course, if you've watched any home decorating or cooking shows, you're bound to have seen showstopping kitchens that leave even an experienced chef's mouth wide open in awe. Remember, though, excess and superfluities in the kitchen do not equate to skill. No need for top-of-the-line equipment and the most expensive tools to get the job done. However, you do need decent-quality basics — a fridge, an oven, a microwave, better-grade cutlery, appropriately sized pots and pans, and other cookware necessities.

Focus on a few good pieces over sheer quantity of kitchen "things" because you will be using these items for years to come and want them to last. Do research before making purchases because high quality doesn't have to mean the top-of-the-line, most expensive items! Sometimes inexpensive is fine, like a nonstick skillet. Why spend big bucks on something that needs to be replaced every couple of years?

However, on the flip side, you might find a kitchen item that is well worth the price, paying off dividends in the amount of time it lasts, its inherent functionality, or sheer convenience. You can look at it as a price per use, not splurging. If you are going to be using the item a lot, you can justify spending more. A lot of this kitchen gear will be tied to your particular interests as a cook, chef, and maker of food. Grilling enthusiasts may want to splurge on a meat smoker or grill with all the bells and whistles, while a baking aficionado would get mighty good use out of a high-quality stand mixer.

In this chapter, you will learn how to select the kitchen gear you need to make your kitchen-for-one start humming like a finely orchestrated back-of-the-house operation in a fancy restaurant. This includes picking out pots, pans, and kitchen gadgets that are essential or nice-to-have for churning out cooking-for-one recipes. You'll also learn more about which countertop appliances are worth the money and space expense.

Selecting Pots, Pans, and Kitchen Gadgets for the Single Chef

A huge hoard of kitchen stuff isn't needed to create the recipes in this cookbook and most other culinary delights. As tempting as it is for those of you who like to load up on new shiny things, hoarding pots, pans, and gadgets just creates a chaotic cooking space. Cluttered cabinets, countertops, and drawers ultimately become a distraction to finding and sustaining the joy in cooking.

However, having a small collection of multitasking tools and the "right-sized for one" bakeware, pots, and pans will make your time spent in the kitchen productive, yielding positive results and personal satisfaction. For example, a single portion of rice cooked in a standard 4-quart sauce pan is going to create a burned-to-the-bottom disaster, while cooking that same portion in a smaller 1-quart saucepan makes your rice nice!

Tools for basic recipe prepping

Ingredients for recipes don't typically come premeasured and prepped, unless "kit" cooking — and by reading this book, it's my hunch that you're trying to level up from that! To get slicing, dicing, mixing, and all that tasty jazz, you'll need a collection of basic recipe tools. The good news is that kitchen tools aren't typically very costly and can be found in most home goods stores, grocery stores, or online. To save space in a small kitchen, nesting or accordion-fold tools store nicely. Also look for tools that are multifunction, such as a can/bottle/corkscrew combo or simple box grater with a micro-shredder on the side. Quality basics are best bets when setting up a kitchen for one, but every now and then it's fun to treat yourself to a frivolous gadget to amplify the joy of cooking. My most recent joyful kitchen acquisition was a set of colorful silicone pot "lid lifters" shaped like farm animals that sit on the edge of a pot to keep one side propped for steam release. A must have? Definitely not, but the little lid lifter herd always makes me smile and whistle while I work!

The following are items you'll need for kitchen prep:

>> **Knives:** A good quality 8-inch chef's knife, a serrated knife for bread, and a small paring knife.

>> **Cutting boards:** For food safety, get one board for veggies and one for meats. If you don't have the space, one cutting board will do, just mark the side for each with a permanent pen and flip sides as needed. Here are some options you can choose from:

- **Wood cutting boards:** Most chefs agree that the best cutting boards are made from wood. They are nicer to knives and provide the best food safety. Wood is naturally antimicrobial and pulls harmful bacteria away from food as you prepare it, including meat, poultry, seafood and even produce. Select a board made from a hardwood like teak, maple, or beach and that is constructed from a single sheet of wood rather than a pieced together or composite construction. Also, remember to clean wood boards thoroughly after each.

- **Plastic cutting boards:** Inexpensive and convenient, plastic cutting boards are great to have on hand but not quite as germ-resistant as you'd imagine. The inevitable nicks, gouges, and scrapes that come from use end up being hiding places for harmful bacteria, even from fruits and veggies, unless they are cleaned properly and replaced after noticeable signs of wear. Plastic is a little rougher on knifes, and boards with slick surfaces can cause potentially hazardous food slipping during prep.

- **Glass boards:** Glass cutting boards, as well as those that are any type of stone, aren't typically recommended. They dull knives very quickly, can cause the blade to roll while cutting, and make food slip around undesirably while prepping. If you already have a glass board, it can be repurposed into a lovely charcuterie or serving tray!

- **Flipping boards:** If prepping both meats and produce one after another and you need to use the same cutting board, just flip it! One side is for meat, one side is for fruits and veggies!

TIP

To clean any type of cutting board, use a diluted chlorine bleach solution (1 table-spoon per gallon of cool water). Be sure to rinse it well with warm water and set upright to dry. You can also remove stains before the cleaning step by rubbing the board with baking soda or coarse salt and a half-cut lemon and letting it sit for 5 minutes before washing with the bleach solution and rinsing. The dishwasher is also a fine method to sanitize plastic boards, but it will warp and damage wooden boards.

» **Dry measuring cups:** A nesting set for dry ingredients that includes a separate 1 cup, ½ cup, ⅓ cup, and ¼ cup is most versatile. If drawer space is an issue, some sets are *nesting,* specially designed to stack compactly on themselves. Don't get an all-in-one combination measuring cup (where you just fill up to a marked tick line) because this can make it difficult to get a precise measurement, an issue in small-batch baking.

» **Liquid measuring cup:** Make sure to get a 2-cup glass measuring cup for liquids that can withstand the microwave and oven. Look for a handle and spigot for easy pouring, plus a little headroom over the 16-ounce capacity to allow for cooking in the microwave.

» **Measuring spoons:** A nesting set that includes 1 tablespoon, 1 teaspoon, ½ teaspoon, ¼ teaspoon, and ⅛ teaspoon will serve all your needs.

» **Instant-read thermometer:** A food-safety and quality-ensuring essential for all roast, steak, and pork or lamb chop recipes, especially single portions, which can cook faster than intended.

» **Colander:** A huge colander for draining pasta or rinsing lettuce is not necessary when cooking for one, but a 1- or 2-quart colander is just right.

» **Mesh strainer:** A 6-inch wire mesh strainer will make it simple to rinse quinoa, drain cans of tuna fish, and pour extra liquid from any ingredient. A smaller 3-inch strainer works beautifully to rinse just a few berries or beans.

» **Wire whisk:** Look for a smaller-scale tool, about 6 to 8 inches; anything larger makes it difficult to use on a small-scale recipe.

» **Spatulas:** At least one soft spatula for stirring and scraping and another firm spatula for flipping. See Chapter 20 to help you select the right spatula for the job at hand.

» **Wooden spoons:** Choose a wood known for its durability and high quality, such as beechwood, maple, olive, cherry, bamboo, oak, and teak.

» **Can and bottle opener:** An electric can opener is not necessary, instead look for a manual version that cuts a safe, smooth edge and features an ergonomic handle and bottle opener function.

» **Cheese grater:** A four-sided box grater offers grating, shredding, zesting, and slicing options. Look for one with a non-skid rubber bottom. If you don't have storage space, a simple flat-lay grater does simple jobs and can be kept in a drawer.

» **Oven mitt and potholders:** Traditional, suede, or silicone, it's really your preference! If you're looking for full hand and wrist protection that also allows for dexterity, check out oven gloves. This is your chance to pick out something practical but fun that adds personality and color to your kitchen.

Pots, Pans, and Cookware

Pots and pans and baking sheets, oh my! Don't worry, it's not as intimidating as it sounds to pick out the essential kitchen pots, pans, and other cooking stuff needed for single–serve and small–batch recipes. Discover the essentials that will send you off on any cooking journey set up for maximum success, and delve into important stuff, like the difference between a frying pan and skillet and the never–ending uses for ramekins (after you find out what one is)!

Here is a list of cookware and bakeware essentials you'll need:

» **Skillets/frying pans:** Choose a 10- to 12-inch frying pan with lid, a 6- to 8-inch oven-proof skillet, and an oven-proof 3.5-inch skillet (perfect for one egg or a single-sized dessert).

TIP

Frying pans and skillets — aren't they the same thing? They look pretty similar. That's a yes and a no, depending on who you ask. Today, the terms are used fairly interchangeably. The only significant differences between the two are that skillets are traditionally a little deeper, heavier, and thicker than fry pans (to retain heat) and come with a lid for braising and simmering. A frying pan is lighter, flat on the bottom, and has sloped sides designed to spread heat evenly and faster. They are used for frying, searing, and browning over high heat, and as such, don't typically come with a lid. Most skillets are oven-safe, but you should give your frying pan a double check. If your frying pan has a ceramic or other nonstick finish (like Teflon), you *may* be able to put it in the oven between 350 degrees F to 500 degrees F (depending on manufacturer). And this is only if all the other parts of the pan are heatproof, like the handle and sides and not just the bottom part that sits on the stovetop burner. Never use a nonstick pan under a broiler.

» **Sauce pots:** An oven-proof, 1.5-quart saucepot with lid is perfectly sized for the single chef to boil pasta or make small-batch grains and soups. Also, a mini sauce pot, less than 1-quart, is so handy to prepare true single-serve portions and also heat syrups.

>> **Grill pan:** A cast iron, ceramic, or nonstick grill pan (in a 6- to 9-inch size) is a great way to sear and caramelize food indoors when you don't have access to a grill. You won't achieve that smoky flavor, but the raised ridges of the pan create sear marks and allow the food's natural juices and fat to be collected underneath, without creating a greasy or steamed result you might get in a skillet or frying pan.

>> **Baking sheets:** You'll want a standard-sized cookie sheet and a smaller rimmed tray that can fit in the toaster oven.

>> **Muffin pan:** Look for a 6-count standard-sized muffin pan that will fit into either a traditional oven or a toaster oven. Another option for a metal muffin pan is a set of silicone muffin baking cups. Perfect for times when you're just making one or two muffins, these reusable cups stand alone on a baking sheet (no muffin pan needed). A mini muffin pan with 12 smaller openings is great for small-batch muffin recipes and also for freezing little portions of sauces, juices, pureed fruits, and other excess ingredients to use later.

>> **Cake and pie pans:** A standard 8-inch diameter metal cake pan is useful for making a single layer cake and also for oven baking items other than desserts. There are also many vessels available for smaller batch recipes, including 5- to 6-inch diameter cake pans, miniature pie pans, mini loaf pans, tiny Bundt pans, and single-serve tart pans.

>> **Ramekins:** Collect a few ceramic, oven-proof ramekins in at least 4-, 6-, and 8-ounce sizes for baking, puddings, and mini-casserole type recipes. I also like to use mine as a portion control bowl to hold my snacks like nuts or pretzels and also to keep at the ready my prepped ingredients for more efficient recipe making.

>> **Mugs:** Larger microwave- and oven-safe ceramic or stoneware mugs can also be used for baking everything from coffee cakes to mac-and-cheese. Mugs 15 to 25 ounces work best and help prevent overflow and mess during the cooking process.

>> **Glass canning jars:** Sometimes called Mason jars or jelly jars, these glass jars are old-school, originally used for canning at home as a method to preserve food. No pickle-making in this cookbook, but glass jars are super handy to have on hand for meal prep and storage. When available as an option, choose wide mouth jars over regular jars. The larger opening makes the jars easier to load with food, clean up afterward, use as an eating vessel (like jar salads and overnight oats), and stack more compactly for storage. These sizes of glass jars are useful for single-size portions: 4, 8, 12, and 16 ounces.

Choosing Must-Have Countertop Appliances

Choosing countertop appliances for your kitchen really comes down to how the device will jive with your space, cooking vibe, and lifestyle. In kitchens everywhere, especially for singles, very well-loved (and well-used) appliances seem to consistently be microwave, blender, and toaster oven. That's the winning trifecta! These three tools help prepare quick-and-easy meals for one quickly and efficiently, while also standing in as a trusty sous chef who knows all the special shortcuts when you want to tackle a more complicated recipe.

Microwave oven

A microwave gets named as a "can't-live-without" countertop (or built-in) appliance in home kitchens serving just one to restaurants serving 101, and every circumstance between. When my trusty microwave died last year and I had to go without a replacement for two weeks, I quickly realized just how much I relied on it for quick reheating and some simple cooking tasks.

Microwaves are compact, cook quickly in mere seconds or minutes, and use less energy, which keeps my bills lower and Texas kitchen cooler. I really appreciate how a microwave lets me prepare the smallest portions of food and reheat my homemade leftovers and take-home meals from restaurants. That's not to say there aren't a few drawbacks like the potential for uneven cooking and the challenge of getting things crisp. But, still, the utility of a microwave far outweighs any disadvantages. And with the proper microwave cookware, technique, and trial-and-error, you can overcome much of these minor issues.

If you live in a newer home or apartment, your kitchen is most likely outfitted with a microwave, either built into a cabinet or over the stove. If not, don't fret! Many economical countertop microwave options are out there, and a reliable one with sufficient functions can be scored surprisingly inexpensively. To free up countertop space, set your microwave on a sturdy kitchen cart or in a door-free cabinet outfitted with a trim kit to make it look built in. Another upside with countertop microwaves is that if you move to another home or apartment, the microwave moves with you! Let's take a look at a couple of categories to consider when buying a microwave:

>> **Size matters.** While there is some leeway in the size of your countertop microwave, you want it to match your needs and fit into its designated nook or counter space. Measure the height, depth, and width of your space before shopping. Also consider how you'll be using the microwave. If just for popcorn

and reheating coffee, you won't need a huge model. But if you want enough interior space to reheat plated dinners, measure your plates and add a couple of inches as a buffer. For reference, the standard dinner plate is 10 inches in diameter. If you are using the microwave for more heavy-duty cooking tasks, then go for the bigger microwave.

>> **What about wattage?** When it comes to microwaves, wattage equals power and generally how fast your appliance will cook food. A 1,000-watt microwave will cook quickly and efficiently, so it's a great baseline model. Although microwaves with 700 watts or less can be inexpensive, they are slower and may cook even less evenly.

Blender

Blenders make margaritas — and healthy smoothies. Need I say more about their relevance in living the good life? Kidding aside, and after much consideration based on my own personal usage of small appliances, I declare the bender a definite must-have in the cooking-for-one kitchen.

A high-powered blender crushes ice, purees, frappes, liquifies, grinds, and even dices veggies by pulsing the motor. It's a very versatile small appliance for making frozen adult drinks, healthful smoothies, soups, sauces, and salad dressings, and even for whipping up easy-to-pour pancake and waffle batter (that's one of my favorite uses)! A high-powered blender can even make nut butters from whole nuts!

The biggest conundrum concerning blenders is that most blenders seem to be sized for a crowd, not those rolling solo. Making a single-serving sauce in a big blender can be a real problem when the ingredients poured in don't even rise to clear the blade.

Thankfully, personal-sized blenders have become all the rage, and they typically accommodate about 16 to 20 ounces of ingredients. Some even operate on batteries or recharge alongside your cell phone. You can get a small blender for chump change that can handle basic blending needs. They won't last forever and are somewhat limited in scope (like they're not powerful enough to make nut butter), but they are actually quite resilient. I used an off-brand small blender *twice* a day for about five years (mainly to make smoothies) before the motor died — just a fraction of a penny per use considering I only paid ten bucks!

However, it is useful to have a larger-capacity and/or higher-powered engine blender if entertaining, making bigger-batch recipes, or meal-prepping. My advice is to get the best of both worlds with a blender that features different-sized pitchers that can be swapped out on the same motor base; they are more pricey but worth it in my opinion.

Toaster oven

Countertop space is prime real estate in most apartments, smaller dwellings, and kitchens for one. Keeping space limitations in mind, the number one countertop appliance to have in your kitchen is a toaster oven. At a minimum, this toaster oven should bake, broil, toast, warm, reheat, and defrost. These are all pretty standard functions on toaster ovens. You can spend next to nothing on one of these lower-end toaster ovens, and if that's all your budget allows, then at least you have an entry-level tool on hand to help! But, be aware that the less expensive models are limited, don't last as long, and importantly, they rarely heat evenly, meaning that you are subject to less reliable results. If you have a more robust budget or are being treated to a special gift, consider a toaster oven that has additional bells and whistles like convection baking, air frying, slow-cooking, and dehydrating. These larger-sized countertop units perform more like a built-in oven and retain and circulate heat more accurately than the smaller options. Plus, the extra features, like air-frying, become a blessing of convenience when making quick meals or reheating leftovers on a busy day.

While a toaster oven could be called a "mini-me" to a much more sizeable, built-in oven, don't underestimate its ability to efficiently help you cook grown-up meals and learn new skills. Specially made "toaster oven bakeware sets" with perfectly sized pans are available in most homeware stores and online, and some "big oven" cooking pieces, like cake pans and mini-muffin pans, fit in the smaller oven space just fine. Here are some reasons why you'll love a toaster oven:

» **Versatile:** You can scratch cook an entire meal in a toaster oven or bake up single-portion servings of your favorite goodies. You can use this countertop appliance to give new life to leftovers or as a warming oven while the rest of the meal cooks. Heck, you can even toast up some bread when you get a craving!

» **Skill-sharpening:** It seems less intimidating to level up your cooking skills in a toaster oven. You'll find that gourmet tasks you may have shied away from or skipped over, like toasting nuts and spices or broiling sugar on a crème brûlée, seem more welcoming in a toaster oven.

» **Preheats quickly:** Smaller in size than a full-size oven, a toaster oven is able to heat up more quickly. That translates into getting your meal on the table faster!

» **Uses less energy:** A 2011 report from Energy Star, the U.S. government program that provides the standards for energy efficient appliances, noted a toaster oven uses between a third and a half less energy than a conventional oven. This also keeps a small kitchen cooler in warmer months!

>> **Heats more evenly than a microwave:** Microwaves are notorious for hit-or-miss heating, leaving some areas of the food over or under done or soggy. A higher-end toaster oven or multifunction countertop oven can help you get that browned, crispy, or crunchy finish you desire.

>> **Simple to monitor:** Because a toaster oven sits at counter height, near the hub of kitchen activity (or wherever you want to put it), it's easy to keep an eye on. This accessibility, along with the front window, encourages frequent check-ups on cooking progress to make adjustments as needed.

>> **Easier clean-up:** Even if you make a mess in your toaster oven, it's easier to clean up. Thanks to being smaller, there is less room for splattering, and most removable parts can go in the dishwasher. The bottom crumb tray and wire racks slide out for scrubbing, and some models have removable doors and other parts for deeper cleaning.

Buying Nice-to-Have Countertop Appliances

While there is no need to accumulate a mound of appliances to prepare a great meal for yourself, sometimes it's fun to add something shiny and new to the kitchen as a way to inspire current and future cooking adventures. A microwave, blender, and toaster oven have already been mentioned in this chapter as must-haves, but there are so many more extras to choose from. If you're a coffee drinker, an espresso machine would be a dream or maybe you'd get good use out of a carbonated soda machine. On the flip side, maybe coffee and bubbly drinks are something you look forward to enjoying out of the house! See, it really comes down your lifestyle and personal taste. Check out these small appliances that are popular across the board with cooking for one enthusiast.

Air fryer

When you're cooking for one and trying to be mindful of your health, an air fryer makes it easier to stick to the plan. I seriously flirted with making the air fryer a must-have countertop appliance because I use mine so much. Air fryers are touted for making certain foods taste fried without any added oil, and it's true! Just imagine crunchy tater tots and fries or breaded fish and chicken tenders that are crispy on the outside yet still moist and tender on the inside! So much better for you than hitting a fast-food drive-thru for the higher-calorie, higher-fat coun-terpoints. Comfort foods aside, you can cook so much more in an airfryer and even express your gourmet side. Air fryers are basically just smaller-scale convection ovens that circulate hot air around to lessen cooking time. My favorite easy fixes in the air fryer are salmon, cauliflower-crust pizzas, and the world's best baked potatoes made in half the time.

Most complaints about air fryers center on the small capacity size of the basket that holds the food. The most commonly purchased air fryers are 2- to 6-quarts; consider the 6-quart one (or even larger, they are available in up to 20 quarts or more) for sheer convenience and versatility. Mainly, that's because overcrowding food in the air fryer should be avoided. Food needs to stay in a single layer for it to brown and crisp evenly. This could definitely be a problem for a family of four, causing you to have to cook things inefficiently in batches. But when it's just you, the space limitations are not as much of an issue, but it's still nice to have a little extra space (even if it's just so that you can crisp up a couple of slices of pizza leftovers at once). In fact, you end up saving energy by not heating up more than you need. To minimize on the number of countertop appliances you have, consider hybrid appliance like a toaster oven with an air-fryer feature or air-fryer/pressure cooker combinations. These multifunction units are usually the airfryers that have the largest capacity.

Multi-cooker

A multifunction pressure cooker or *multi-cooker*, like an Instant Pot, can be useful if you decide to get into the type of meal-prepping that focuses on make-ahead meals to kept in the fridge or freezer. Typical functions of a multi-cooker include pressure cooking, slow cooking, rice and grain cooking, yogurt making, sautéing, and more. The beauty of this appliance is that you get the utility of multiple stand-alone countertop appliances all rolled into one, so it's very space saving — only if these are the types of cooking methods you will use. Multi-cookers come in a range of sizes, with a 3-quart version being on the small end, perfect for small batch recipes, or a larger 6 quart — accommodating recipes to serve about four people and good for batch-cooking for the single person. So, if you're cooking in the big one, and you're cooking for just yourself, you'll need to be ready and willing to eat leftovers, stockpile in the freezer, or share the bounty with family and friends.

Slow cooker

Slow cookers are ideal for "fix it and forget it" type meals; they are low-maintenance workhorses that can render even the toughest cut of meat fork tender. Whether you have a roast, casserole, or soup in mind, just dump the ingredients in the ceramic crock and set the temperature, and at night return to a home-cooked meal! However, like multifunction pressure cookers, these countertop appliances can be in sizes that are better suited to cooking for an army — at least for more than a lone ranger! The largest slow cookers on the market hold a copious 10 quarts (that's 320 ounces!) and even "standard" size models accommodate a generous 5 to 7 quarts.

So, if mass-feedings aren't your battle, a large slow cooker might exacerbate stress and storage issues, unless you are into batch cooking and stockpiling single portions in the freezer. Consider a smaller 2.5- to 3.5-quart version, which is perfect for smaller-scale soups, stews, and all-in-one dinners. But, if this still sounds like too much, get something even smaller; you can find them in most housewares departments and online shopping sites. I have a mini slow cooker that holds 20 ounces, ideal for single servings of beans, keeping queso dip warm, and for fondue for one!

Mini waffle maker

There's something undeniably nostalgic about enjoying a golden-brown waffle with syrup oozing out of every crook and cranny. As a kid, you probably fought over this comfort food with siblings (hey, leggo my Eggo!), and as an adult it's an out-to-brunch item that's anything but basic. With a waffle maker at home, you can enjoy restaurant-quality breakfasts and revisit good memories. Waffles are simple to make, easy to freeze, and can be topped in so many ways to please — whether savory or sweet. These days, waffle maker enthusiasts have found clever ways to cook almost anything in a waffle maker, from eggs and burgers to hash-browns, chaffles, and s'mores.

There are several types of waffle makers available from larger 4-square waffle makers, to Belgian waffle makers, to single waffle makers, to models that "flip" halfway through cooking, touting more even cooking. With limited space and just a solo plate to fill up, check out the mini waffle makers that fit easily into a cabinet or even a kitchen drawer. Very inexpensive and often designed with cute waffle "pocket" designs, these gadgets make a single, round waffle about the size of a frozen waffle in just a few minutes.

TIP

Stovetop rice is nice, but a mini rice cooker makes the whole process even nicer. Perfectly portioned and so fun, a 2-cup capacity mini rice cooker turns out up to 4 cups of cooked rice easily and with little mess. It can also be used creatively to make banana bread, omelets, small cakes, and more!

SMALL OUTDOOR GAS GRILL

If you grew up with family barbecues and backyard cookouts, you may be pining away for the robust, roasted, and (sometimes) pleasantly charred taste and caramelized crust of foods grilled over open fire. Grilling for one, especially with charcoal and/or wood chips, isn't the quickest and most efficient task. After all, it takes some skill and patience to get those briquets burning just right and that might seem like an excess of work for a burger or steak. Yet, nothing shores up a feeling of self-sufficiency in feeding oneself than cooking meat (or veggies, for that matter) over fire. Grunt, chest pound!

If grilling speaks to your soul, then by all means get a charcoal grill — there are many smaller-scale models that can efficiently distribute heat for a meal being made for one or two. Even a simple Hibachi grill can do the job. One caveat to consider is your living environment. Some apartments do not allow the use of open flames on patios, and grilling over fire indoors is *always* a no-no!

Small gas grills are also available for use on decks, patios, and to take camping (it's what I use) and run-on small propane tanks. Just ignite the grill with the push of a button, and you can whip up endless meal ideas for meat and veggies, sensational sandwiches, and more in less time and with easier prep and clean up than with charcoal.

Countertop Appliances You Could Live Without But Are Still Cool

You can live a great life and eat well without any of these extra countertop appliances. But if they spark joy, then by all means get yourself set up with one or all — or use the recommended substitutes. Really the point of cooking for yourself, aside from basic human nourishment, is to enjoy the process and have fun.

TIP

Many countertop appliances are novelties and quickly become clutter with the original owner. Visit a thrift shop or garage sale and pick up something fun for your cooking journey at a small fraction of the cost. When the novelty wears off for you, donate it again or pass it on to a friend.

The following is a list of countertop appliances that you can avoid buying:

>> **Indoor grill:** Why bother with the expense and space considerations if you don't get the coveted smokey flavor that outdoor grilling imparts? A stovetop grill pan accomplishes the same results with no hassle or headache.

>> **Quesadilla maker:** A 12-inch all-purpose skillet can do the same job.

>> **Juicer:** Unless you are into fresh juices and "cleanses," these juice-extracting machines take up a lot of storage real estate. In a pinch, a high-powered blender works sufficiently, and, if needed, the juice can be drained through a mesh strainer to remove pulp.

>> **Popcorn maker:** Forget this little machine and make your popcorn easily the old-fashioned way in a pot (with a little oil) on the stovetop. Also, you can toss kernels in a brown lunch bag and microwave on high for 2 to 3 minutes for a no-fat, no-fuss solution.

>> **Food processor:** They chop, dice, grate, and slice along with many other food-prep options. But, a blender, knife, box grater, and other simple gadgets noted in previous sections are actually better suited to smaller-scale recipe making than a large food processor, which can be hard to fill up and is more difficult to clean. However, a mini food processor can be worthwhile to make food prep tasks like chopping onions or garlic more pleasant and hands-off.

>> **Stand mixer:** Unless you are baking all the cookies for your office holiday party or are on-the-rise as an artisan bread maker with tabletop space to spare, you can most likely live without a stand mixer. Even many pastry chefs will agree that a whisk, spatula. and mixing bowl with a non-skid rubber ring attached to the bottom will work just fine for a baker of any skill set. And, honestly, I consider all the whisking and mixing a solid arm workout — but you may not! In that case, consider a hand-held mixer as a space-saving, money-saving compromise.

>> **Electric skillet/griddle:** An electric skillet or griddle can give the small space kitchen an extra cooking boost. Sure, a regular skillet or fry pan can do the same job, but an electric version can offer a little more cooking surface area to perhaps griddle up pancakes and eggs at the same time. Also, it is a real lifesaver if you don't have a working stovetop.

Chapter **3**

Hunting and Gathering Groceries for One

Just think about how much easier gathering and hunting for food is today than it was for our nomadic ancestors thousands of years ago. You just hop in your car, drive to the market, and select from a dizzying array of consumer goods and convenience products. No power walking a marathon in search of a few sparse berries, seeds, and, if lucky, a wild critter to roast over an open flame. Heck, from the comfort of your home, you can order up a week's worth of top-quality nibbles and nourishment online and have it delivered straight to your door.

But shopping in contemporary times is not without certain issues. While you're not fending off predators and other life-ending dangers like poisonous mushrooms, you *are* facing legitimate, annoying problems like giant-sized cereal boxes big enough to feed an army, cream that curdles before you can finish the carton, and cuts of meat packaged for a full-sized family of four or more. True, these are first-world problems, but by being more mindful and intentional in your choices, you can create a positive ripple effect for others.

Limited time and endless distractions can also complicate finding groceries for meal-making. That's why learning how to make and shop with a list, how to get in and out of a store efficiently, what to stock up on and what to pass by, convenience products and hacks, where to find food other than at the local Piggly Wiggly, and why you should share when you can are all impactful to your overall sustenance strategy as a "single."

For the Love of a List

Committing a grocery list solely to memory is risky business —or at least it is for my corn kernel-sized brain! With dozens of "tabs" open in my head, I often find myself standing in the center of the store with a sparsely filled cart and no solid recollection of my original food-hunting mission. Was I here to get ingredients for dinner tonight, breakfast tomorrow, to fulfill some special craving, buy tooth-paste, or all of the above?

That's why I rely on a well-made shopping list for each grocery-sourcing experi-ence, whether I am stocking up for an entire week online or just grabbing in-store items to see me through a couple of days. As you get accustomed to making and sticking with a shopping list, you will quickly understand what a helpful and effi-cient tool it can be for saving valuable resources including your time, your money, and your sanity.

Keeping more money in your wallet

If you've experienced sticker shock with your shopping experiences, you're not alone. With food prices rising steadily and increased costs of getting goods on the shelf expected to continue, even those who have never worried about the bottom line of their food budget are looking for ways to save on their grocery costs.

Creating and being committed to stick by that shopping list is a great technique to reduce food expenditures. A list puts in print exactly what you need to create deli-cious meals and snacks and, by omission, eliminates unnecessary frivolities. Sticking to my list has helped me avoid regretful and expensive impulse purchases like bakery items I don't really need (but smelled so good at the time) or an over-priced cold bottle of soda in the cooler at checkout.

Most of a store's floor plan, product displays, and promotions are designed to elicit physiologic responses that subconsciously (or even intentionally) spur you into spending more. Higher priced brands or items stores are actively promoting get more visible display real estate, like the center shelf on aisles or end caps. That wafting aroma of warm French bread right out of the bakery oven can make me put a loaf in my cart without thought. Even when I do aim to shop smart and keep my eyes, nose, and stomach on good behavior, those BOGO (buy one get one free) deals lure me into rationalizing purchases. That's why I, regretfully, have way too much quinoa and enough batteries to light up the Empire State Building. BOGO offers you can't use up within a couple of months are a gateway to hoarding! I jest a bit, but when you spend too much on stuff you don't really need, you often find yourself strapped to make essential purchases or cover unexpected expenses. Thankfully, having my list on hand, however, keeps me out of trouble and focused!

Even marketers in the digital shopping arena are implementing more and more tactics to lure you into impulse purchases. With online shopping history and demographic information at their disposal, you may be even more targeted. Just think about those lists of convenient or happy-mood-making extras that are magically presented to you. Hey, how did they know you wanted guacamole? Personalized "buy it with" recommendations and special offers driven by time exclusivity (hurry, this deal ends in 24 hours!) are also popular impulse purchase tactics. Low stock warnings are also used to elicit the fear of missing out and trigger impulse purchases (hurry, only 2 left in stock)!

Thank goodness for my list! Spending five minutes at home making a shopping list keeps me productively on task, stops me from wandering around aimlessly without a goal (virtually or in-person), and becoming prey to these clever up-selling tactics. Don't you think you need a list, too? The correct answer is yes! According to a study at Rutger's, planning meals in advance and making detailed shopping lists can cut your grocery spending by 20 percent or more.

TIP

When making a list, find your store's weekly mailer or online update of sale items. Most stores have phone apps and reward programs where you can learn about sales and "clip" online coupons. By simply familiarizing yourself with the products being promoted each week, you have more time to make better-informed decisions when making your list and shopping from it. Using these sales as inspiration for your upcoming recipe selections can save a significant amount of money.

Optimizing your time

Light bulb moment: A minute I spend doing one thing is a minute I can't spend doing something else. It sounds so obvious to say that out loud, but most of us don't consider how a little bit of time here and there can add up and diminish the free time available to pursue life's passions or just relax from being so stressed out. Spending just 20 minutes longer in the store than intended means I've unintentionally squandered the time it takes me to jog a couple miles, read a chapter of a book, play with my dog in the backyard, or actually roll up my sleeves and make a meal in the kitchen — all things I would most definitely prefer to be doing over shopping.

No doubt you've heard the metaphor, "Time is money." It's an idea often attributed to Ben Franklin in his short essay "Advice to a Young Tradesman," although the concept also dates back to Greek philosophers. The notion is that wasted time is wasted money — being idle or wasting time means the opportunity to make money (during that time) is lost. Good advice to a point, especially if your sole income is based on an hourly wage. But, in the 21st century, most of us can always try to make more money later. However, I can't name one person who has made more time than the 24 hours allotted per day.

Since time is such a limited resource, deciding how you want to spend your minutes, hours, and days is pretty important. Lists for all aspects of your life can help you optimize what you get done throughout the day and not overlook something important. I've found that spending five minutes making a shopping list gains me back more than 5 minutes in times savings on in-person grocery trips as well as digital shopping experiences. I'd estimate a shopping list saves me 20 minutes at the minimum. If it takes 5 minutes to create a list, that's a net 15-minute time savings. Fifteen minutes saved might not seem worth the trouble, but that adds up to 780 minutes (13 hours!) saved over a year of weekly shopping trips — and more if you shop more frequently. Think about what you'd do with those hours and start making your list!

TIP

Categorize your shopping list to fit the layout of the store departments and aisles like Produce, Deli, Dairy, Snacks, Packaged Goods, Bakery, Bulk, Baking, and whatever part of the store you frequently visit. This "divide and conquer" technique will allow you to seek and snag desired items of the same type quickly rather than repeatedly circling back, wasting valuable time with a randomly ordered list.

Minimizing "forgets," frustration, and frequent trips

My mind gets overloaded and easily distracted, Heck, I can't remember if I took my vitamins in the morning, let alone every item that needs to be acquired on a shopping mission. Without my list, some of the hardest items for me to remember to pick up are spices, condiments, and esoteric recipe ingredients that I don't restock frequently. On the flip side, I will also forget something as basic as my weekly carton of milk. The point is, whether it's big or small, expensive or cheap, a necessity or extra, you will probably forget *at least* one thing on each trip without a list.

In the past, I tried mind games and tricks like memorizing the number of things I need (like ten things), making an acronym (like PETS — pasta, eggs, and tomato sauce), or recalling what the photo of my intended recipe looked like. Nope, none of it was as infallible as my trusty sidekick shopping list.

TIP

Categorizing the list in a way that is in alignment with store layout also helps tremendously with not overlooking an item and getting through the store quickly. All dairy products are in one column; all produce needs are in the next; packaged goods in another; and so on. Now I can zip through and grab everything in one department without backtracking, eliminating forgotten items and a potential, unscheduled return trip to the store — which is a total time waste!

The moral of the story here is always remember to make a list. Also, always remember to *bring* the list along — don't leave it at home, at work, in the car, or crumpled up somewhere where it is ironically of no help. Pen and scratch-pad lists work just fine but are so easy to lose, even in the middle of the store. A list kept in an app like "Notes" on your phone or a store app are trusty methods that will always be at your fingertips. When something runs out, immediately add it to the store list you shop at for that item. Sometimes I also just text myself the list, easy-peasy. If using any of these phone list methods, just make sure that your device is fully charged for the outing.

TIP

No need to pick up a pen or type out a list. Take advantage of a high-tech tool like Alexa voice assistant through your phone or an Amazon Echo or similar device to create a shopping list that can simplify your shopping experience. For example, just tell Alexa to add items to your list by saying something like "Alexa, add a half-pint of cream to my shopping list." When another need pops in your mind, tell Alexa again — and so on, and so on. Then, as long as you have your phone, you can access the list. Or, if you have a friend, neighbor, or personal shopper (lucky you!) able to swing by the store for you, you can voice share the list with them, too! "Alexa, share my shopping list with Fred." Fred will get an Alexa notification, be able to see your list, shop for you, and will probably want to be invited for dinner.

Not Too Much, Not Too Little, Just Right: Buying Groceries

Whether you're shopping at the grocery store or online, the goal is to hunt and gather good-for-you foods, quickly, conveniently, and in portions that are suited for single-portion recipes or small-scale pantry and freezer stocking. The following sections show you how to stock up on the right products in the correct quantities.

Tips for butcher, deli, dairy, produce, and frozen departments

When shopping for groceries for one, you may feel frustrated that package sizes or quantities are aimed at larger families or multiple servings. Here are some ways you can minimize waste and control costs in the various grocery departments.

At the butcher counter

Your store's butcher is on hand to prep and package exactly what you need, even if that need is just five or six shrimp, a single 3.5-ounce strip steak, or a single serving of ground beef (¼ pound, typically). Don't be shy to introduce yourself to the person behind the butcher counter and explain your situation. They are more than happy to oblige and fulfill special requests and often will give you some of the best and freshest portions. If purchasing meat, poultry, or fish already wrapped or packaged on foam trays in the cold case, it is likely prepared for at least two to four servings. Be prepared with the proper containers, wraps, and bags to repackage and freeze the extra at home.

TIP

Ground beef is a versatile and affordable protein choice with lean options. It is typically portioned in 1-, 2-, and 5-pound chubs (ground beef packaged in plastic tubes) or as 1 to 2 pounds on a foam meat tray or in a vacuum-sealed package. However, if you want to quickly divide ground beef into single servings, purchase a 1-pound chub. Then slice it (straight through the plastic packaging) into four 4-ounce portions and freeze in a freezer-friendly container. If you know the beef is going to be used for burgers, preform it into patties, layer with wax paper, and freeze in a freezer bag or container. As needed, pull a ground beef chunk or patty out of the freezer and defrost it in the fridge. Voila, you have ground beef ready to brown in the skillet or grill up as a burger.

In the deli department

At the deli counter, you can custom order the specific quantity of meat or cheese needed. I frequently ask for only a couple of slices of prosciutto, enough pepperoni for only a personal pizza, or a quarter pound of smoked turkey to see me through a couple of sandwiches. My frugalness really shows when I ask the deli clerk not to layer my meats and cheese with the wax paper in between each slice — that adds to the overall weight and cost.

On the deli refrigerated shelves, search out single serve, wrapped cheese selections like cheese sticks, little wrapped cheese spread wedges, and even more gourmet cheeses that have been sealed individually in wax. If you end up with more cheese than you need, it can be kept in the freezer in a freezer-friendly, air-tight container. Grated cheese will stay fresh for about three months and whole cheese blocks that are properly wrapped for about six to nine months.

Also in the packaged deli department, you can grab refrigerated personal-sized cups of hummus, smashed avocado, olives, salad dressings, and more.

In the produce department

The great thing about the produce department is that you can buy as little or as much as your appetite dictates. For example, if there is no way you can possibly consume a whole watermelon (like me, burp!), then select the cut-up chunks or a wedge. You may spend a bit more per ounce, but you won't be tossing spoiled stuff away later.

TIP

Feel free to reportion loosely, open-packaged produce sold by the pound into the smaller quantity that you need. I do this all the time! You don't have to buy the entire bunch of grapes in the bag; take a few out. The same goes for asparagus, green beans, Brussels sprouts, and the like. If in doubt about what you can and shouldn't reportion, ask the produce manager to help you out.

If your mood or recipe calls out for a little of this and a little of that, look toward prepackaged fresh bags of produce mixes (like broccoli, cauliflower, and carrots, or stir-fry mixes). You can cook them as a medley or pluck out piece by piece to incorporate as a single ingredient in recipes.

If your store has a salad bar, this is a genius venue to source ingredients — you don't actually have to make a salad! I zoom in on the chopped green onions, mushroom slices, and bean sprouts, along with various lettuces and greens. These are some of my favorite small picks from the salad bar as their full-sized siblings from the produce department can't be stock-piled in the freezer and tend to lose their freshness more quickly in the fridge. Often, too, you can pick up a small amount of diced turkey, ham, or tofu, which makes it easy to add impromptu protein to your recipes.

WARNING

With salad-bar scavenging, be wary of "heavy" ingredients. Often traditionally inexpensive items like cooked beans, roasted potatoes, or chopped carrots can weigh more than they're worth. You are better off buying ingredients such as these separately and finding a way to use them up over the week, freezing, or sharing.

In the dairy department

You can't go wrong with single-serving cheese sticks and individual yogurt cups. Many stores also now offer individual cottage cheese cups and smaller portion cream cheese and sour creams. Shopping online also provides many single-serve portions that you may not find in traditional grocery stores.

Look for eggs packaged by the half-dozen. However, depending on your penchant for eggs, which are also staples in baking, going for the entire dozen may make sense. If needed, you can freeze cracked eggs for about four months.

TIP

A great way to prep eggs into individual servings is to crack each raw egg, scramble it with a fork, and pour it into a muffin cup. Then freeze and transfer the frozen "egg pucks" to a freezer-safe container for use as needed. Eggs from a carton (also available in just egg whites) is another option ideal for solo chefs — just pour out what you need! Carton eggs can be frozen in 1 tablespoon portions to be thawed and used in a lot of the baked treats in this cookbook.

Got milk? You probably should, but go for the smallest carton available. Same goes with cream, half-and-half, and other dairy products, unless you're a confirmed frequent user. Another option for those who only need milk occasionally is to keep smaller shelf-stable cartons of alternative milks on hand for your needs. You can also buy powdered dairy milk and alternative milks (like powdered oat milk) that can be reconstituted in any amount needed, large or small, for baked goods and other recipes.

TIP

If you use half-and-half in your coffee but need milk for a recipe, just water it down. Use ¾ cup half-and-half and ¼ cup water as a replacement for 1 cup whole milk.

In the frozen department

Aside from pints of premium ice cream (for mood-boosting purposes), there are a few essentials from the freezer aisle to consider keeping on hand for actual recipe-making. Keep several bags of your favorite frozen vegetables on hand for quick-and-easy side dishes or to mix into recipes like omelets, casseroles, and more. Some of my favorite recipe-ready frozen veggies that I can portion out as needed are diced onions (no crying!), frozen mushrooms, peas (toss into pasta and fried rice or smash into guacamole), shelled edamame beans (extra protein!), frozen spinach, frozen kale, and frozen chopped herbs. And frozen berries are amazing and will let you enjoy a burst of sweetness in any season. Instead of buying a half gallon of ice cream, treat yourself to individually-wrapped, single-serve treats – perfect for enjoying yummy things but being mindful of portion control! Finally, if you love hot bread, buying a frozen bag of dinner rolls or biscuits can't be beat — just cook 'em up one at a time with no waste!

Buying in small-batch from the bulk department

When I first heard the word "bulk" department, I assumed it was for folks building a stockpile big time — large families, groups, pantry hoarders. True, you can buy as much as you want from the bulk department, which typically stocks staples like grains, flours, beans, spices, nuts, dried fruits, and more. But the true beauty of the bulk department is that you can also buy as little as you need — down to the ounce and gram.

Buying small-batch in the bulk department is a smart strategy for those cooking single-portion recipes. Purchase exactly how much you need for the recipe and eliminate excess in the pantry, which could potentially go to waste. Plus, if the taste does not end up suiting you, you're not stuck with a big stash. This removes a lot of the risk and expense out of trying new dishes and flavor profiles.

Additionally, the bulk department does not use traditional packaging methods, which creates less trash. Items fill up big bins or dispensers, and you take out what you need. Typically bags and plastic tubs are provided for the customer's use, but feel free to fly your earth-loving flag and bring in your own containers.

Here are some tips for buying in bulk for cooking-for-one recipes:

» **Bring along your own measuring cup if you are trying to purchase the precise amount of an ingredient for your recipe.** Most bulk departments just have a big scoop and scale, so you're always guesstimating unless you are experienced at eyeballing or a genius at dry good weight conversions. Remember, one cup of beans doesn't equal the same amount as one cup of popped rice cereal.

» **Avoid a pantry littered with barely used spice bottles by purchasing your spices in small batch in the bulk department.** Ground spices lose their freshness in about six months, so it makes sense just to buy a couple of tablespoons at a time if you are just cooking for yourself. My favorite spice hack is to store small amounts of ground spices in a seven-day pill organizer or even in small craft containers with small, divided spaces. Both of these containers fit nicely into a drawer near your stovetop, which is so much more convenient than in the pantry.

» **Purchase treats (like chocolate covered almonds or yogurt pretzels) in small amounts rather than having to buy a family-sized bag.** This is helpful if you are concerned about portion control or just are looking to try something you are not sure you will like.

» **Bring your own containers to reduce waste, even though the bulk department provides plastic bags and tubs to bring home purchases.** If the containers have weight to them, have a sales associate help weigh the item so that you are not paying extra for your own container. Just ask; they are happy to help in most stores.

Online shopping strategies

Over the last few years, I think everyone can agree that online grocery shopping is here to stay. It's a convenient and safe way to get virtually any food you may need, whether you are driving in for curbside pick-up or having it delivered to the door. From your local grocery chain to national big box stores and online-only retailers and aggregators, you can order what you need, when you want it, and from wherever you are. Follow these tips to make the most of your digital food hunting experience:

>> **Take advantage of subscriptions:** Sign up for reoccurring orders so that you never run out of your favorite items. My "auto-pilot" items would be coffee, protein bars, and kettle chips. If you choose this auto-reorder (or sometimes called a subscription), just make sure it's something you use quickly enough that you won't end up with a stale stash.

>> **Stay focused:** Remember, you are still just shopping for one! Sometimes when I can't physically see what I'm putting in my cart, I tend to over or under order. Two pounds of chocolate almonds — sounds reasonable! A half-pound of sweet potato never looked so tiny! Don't forget you can still ask for exactly what you want — like one medium apple or 4 ounces of beef — just be specific so that there is no question. Many personal shopping services also offer an option in which you can communicate in real-time if any questions or substitutions need to be made.

>> **Activate coupons:** Why not save a few bucks by "clipping" a digital store or manufacturer's coupon straight into your store app or website? In this stay-at-home economy, digital coupons are more frequently redeemed than paper coupons — and the benefit is that you can't lose them or find them later crumpled at the bottom of your purse. The discount is applied automatically at checkout, thank goodness!

>> **Inspect order:** As soon as you pick up your order or have it delivered, open the bags for a quick visual inspection. Have you received everything ordered and does it meet your quality expectations? Sometimes the personal shoppers just don't have enough experience yet or there is an ordering snafu that results in you getting grapes *and* tomatoes when you really just wanted little grape tomatoes. If not satisfied, immediately contact the website or store to make replacements or renumerations.

TIP

One of my favorite tips when still en route home from a trip is to order breakfast fixings online for next-morning delivery. As soon as the airline captain says we can get back on our phones, I send in my order for fresh fruit, bacon, milk, and waffle ingredients to be delivered in time for brunch making!

Tips to win the club shopping game

Shopping in a big box store like Sam's Club, Costco, or BJ's can be alluring. There's just something that feels like you're really taking care of business and preparing for the unknown by coming home with 32 rolls of toilet paper, 20 sticks of butter, and 10 pounds of pancake mix. However, a 2018 study, published in the *Journal of Market Research*, has shown that those who shop in club stores don't really come out ahead; they spend more money; they spend more time shopping; and they ultimately consume more calories. Plus, there is the sunk cost of $50 to $100 for a membership. But, that's not to say that you can't make it work for solo needs. Here are some ideas to weigh before walking in a big box club store:

>> Can I get a membership with a friend or family member to spread the "sunk" costs and to go "halfsies" on the mega-sized packaging?

>> Do I have the freezer, fridge, and pantry space to store enormous amounts of food and consumer goods?

>> Have I looked at the cost per ounce and compared it to my local grocery store?

>> What are the products I go through like crazy (like coffee and protein bars for me), and do they stock the brand I prefer?

>> How far do I have to drive and how much do I have to spend on gas?

>> What is the shelf life of the products I'm looking at, and can I use it up before it expires?

>> Are other items and services that are offered something that would benefit me? These could include pharmacy services or over-the-counter medications or vitamins you use daily, lower-priced gas, automobile tires and batteries, furnishings, home goods, name-brand clothing and footwear, and more.

If, after perusing the pros and cons of a big box club membership, you decide it's not for you — no worries! You can easily purchase everything you need to make meals for one at traditional grocery stores and through other alternative resources. If you decide the shopping format may benefit you, seize the opportunity without worry — memberships (and your obligation) expire after only a year.

Convenience products and pantry staples to have on hand

A well-stocked pantry will help you create quick, delicious budget-friendly meals even if you have only a few fresh ingredients on hand — or even none! Keeping shelves stocked with enough, but not so much that you can't stay ahead of your expiring stash, will also help minimize those dreaded, last-minute trips to the store or calling out for an unplanned pizza delivery.

The following are items to always keep stocked in your pantry:

>> **Grains:** Look for single-serve cups of rice, quinoa, pastas, and whole-grain medleys to cook up quickly in the microwave as needed. Also, ready-to-eat pouches of similar products are also available, typically on the same aisle.

However, if you have the pantry space, most dry rice, pasta, and grains last indefinitely, so you can stock up to meet your needs.

>> **Fruits:** Stock your pantry with single-serve cups of applesauce and other fruits like diced peaches, pears, and mandarin oranges. This is a no-brainer way to have fruit on hand at all times for snacking or to mix into oatmeal, add into mug cakes and cobblers, or to toss into your salad.

>> **Meats:** If you need to reel in a quick meal, you'll be thankful to have a can of tuna, salmon, or chicken in the pantry. Mix with mayo for sandwiches and salad toppings or toss into casseroles, soups, and other hot dishes.

>> **Spice packets:** Grab a few spice-mix packets like taco seasoning, chili seasoning, pumpkin pie spice, or Italian seasoning. These blends of spices are much more cost effective and space saving than the enormous number of bottles it takes to make your own.

>> **Cooking/baking staples:** Cooking spray and cooking oils; spices, salt, and pepper; garlic and ginger (fresh as needed or little single serve cubes found in the freezer aisle vegetable section); soy sauce and Worcestershire sauce; baking soda and powder; vanilla extract; flour and sugar for baking.

>> **Condiments:** Just go for the smallest bottle or package available, unless you are a certified addict of a particular condiment. Ranch dressing is my vice! Pickles, olives, and other relish-y things are now sold in single-serve, shelf-stable pouches.

>> **Take-out packets:** Maybe you have a huge stash of ketchup, soy sauce, and other condiments and toppings from take-out and delivery. No need to waste the unused ones, just save for your next cooking for one recipe. Check out these common single-serve packets and their approximate shelf life:

- **Honey, salt, granulated sweetener packets:** Most likely forever.

- **Tabasco, Sriracha, vinegar, black pepper, red pepper flake packets:** 3 to 4 years

- **Jelly packets:** 2 to 3 years

- **Olive oil, Parmesan cheese, mustard, soy sauce packets:** 1 to 2 years

- **Mayo, BBQ sauce, nut butters, salad dressing, ketchup packets:** 1 year

Exploring alternative food sources

Shopping in store or online are the most common ways to hunt and gather food today. But you can cut out the middle man and get the freshest of fresh foods at a local farmer's market. Or, take it one step further and get back to your ancestral roots by foraging for freebies or cultivating your own crops with a mini garden with yields for one:

» **Farmer's markets:** If you have a little extra weekend free time, seek out a farmer's market. Fruits, veggies, meats, and dairy products can be found as fresh as they get, straight from the source at the peak of ripeness with no middle man and no long-distance transportation to jack up prices. Plus, shopping farmer's markets gives you a chance to connect with community, support small-scale agricultural operations, get to know your farmers and ranchers, and have more appreciation for whom and where your food comes from, and be an informed buyer.

» **Foraging:** Consider foraging, at least for a few items, as a legitimate food sourcing strategy. Mother Nature is abundant, and many of her edible treats are overlooked. I've collected pounds and pounds of pecans off the ground and picked dandelion flowers and greens (a nutritious weed!), wild onions, and loquats that fall off my neighbor's prolific tree into my yard. The beauty of foraging for one is that you are not feeding the whole tribe, only yourself!

» **Grow your own:** You may not have the space for a full-on, green-acres garden, but growing your own herbs on the kitchen window sill or coddling along a cherry tomato plant on the balcony is a fun hobby, can save money, and instills a sense of personal pride!

Sharing with family and friends

When has too much food ever been a bad thing? You might say "never," but it's my pet peeve to see food get thrown away or spoil needlessly at home! Did you know that more than one-third of food goes to waste in the United States? According to the U.S. Environmental Protection Agency's *2018 Wasted Food Report*, food from an estimated 81 percent of American households was taken to combustion facilities or landfills. That's just shocking!

Single cooks seem to end up with more food than they need or can properly store. For me, the issues are that I grab a bigger-than-I-need box of whatever (because that's all there is); my eyes are bigger than my appetite; or life just happens and my plans change from eating in to dining out at that new hot spot with friends.

Of course, meal planning mindfully helps prevent waste. For example, if you have an excess of spinach, you could use up the remainder in a soup, salad, egg scramble, or smoothie. Also, sharing a bounty of groceries and leftover meals with family, friends, neighbors, and those in need can be a powerful action. Sharing food shows care and concern, builds relationships, passes on traditions, and shares the "wealth" — all while putting the brakes on waste. Here are a couple of ideas on how to distribute food when you have more than you need:

>> **Half a haul:** Going "halfsies" is one of my favorite single shopping strategies in stores overflowing with family-sized products. Partner up with a shopping buddy, agree on what to buy, and then divvy it up straight down the middle when you get home! Make sure to have storage containers and zip-top bags on hand for the repackaging. Who knows, maybe this cooking for one situation will turn into a cooking for two arrangement!

>> **Swapping with your squad:** Leftovers that you love but just don't have room to store can be shared with a co-worker, neighbor, or an individual in need. It's a great way to show off your new cooking skills while reducing waste and ensuring that someone who may not be getting a decent, square meal is being well fed!

Chapter 4

Scaling Up and Food Storage

Yes, this book is all about cooking for one, so why am I talking about making a recipe larger or smaller? Occasionally, you might want more servings from a recipe . . . or less! This "more or less" is called *scaling*, a simple method of adjusting the number of servings in a recipe up or down by multiplying ingredients (to increase) or dividing ingredients (to decrease). While you just need to brush up on basic math to scale a recipe, you should also take note of other potential issue areas like what size pot or pan to use for the adapted recipe or how to handle ingredients that are not easily split into fractions.

If you are anticipating leftovers (maybe you're scaling up for meal prep) or have come into excess food unexpectedly (you are sent home with the holiday leftovers), it's important for food safety, quality, waste reduction, and plain old saving money to understand and implement the best methods in which to store food for a repeat performance.

Cutting Down or Doubling Up Recipes

Most mainstream recipes are written to serve four, six, eight, or more people. Pretty annoying if you just want to serve yourself and avoid leftovers — and leftovers of leftovers! Or, perhaps a friend is dropping by at the dinner hour, and you need to convert your favorite recipe "for one" into "for two." Don't panic at the stated serving size of a recipe you've been drooling over; don't let the size scare you off because it's "too much" or keep you from sharing with that special someone. The majority of recipes are simple to scale up and down if you understand basic math and keep a few tips and tricks in mind.

Scaling down family-sized recipes

Going big might be a great way to tackle an important goal, but it isn't always the best strategy when cooking for one. For example, maybe you have an heirloom recipe from Great-Grandma, passed down through the generations, and you don't want it to get archived into oblivion. But her recipe serves a farmhouse-sized family of 12, and you are just flying completely solo. Scaling down by dividing each ingredient can help you reduce the yield, whether in half, in a quarter, or even more and better suit your modern situation.

Solve it with math

Reducing the serving size of a recipe calls for understanding basic math, implementing fractions and division. For example, transforming a recipe for six into a recipe for one would mean using only one-sixth of the listed ingredients. So, 3 cups of flour become ½ cup, and 12 ounces of cream cheese become 2 ounces — make sense?

Transforming ingredient quantities fractionally to suit your needs is all fine and dandy until you realize that you don't know how many cups are in a pint, ounces in a quart, or teaspoons in a tablespoon. And, for that matter, what is a "pinch" or "dash"? And don't forget about metric conversions, such as grams, liters, and kilos, which should be simpler because the measurements are based on multiples of 10. Instead of memorizing . . . measurement, see Table 4-1 for the liquid and dry ingredient conversions. (See the Appendix for metric conversions.)

TABLE 4-1: ## Conversions for Liquid and Dry Ingredients

Liquid Fluid Ounces	Cups	Pints	Quarts
16	2	1	½
32	4	2	1
64	8	4	2
128	16	8	4
Dry **Cups**	**Tablespoons**	**Teaspoons**	**Grams**
¹⁄₁₆	1	3	14
⅛	2	6	29
¼	4	12	57
⅓	5⅓	16	76
½	8	24	114
⅔	10⅔	32	152
¾	12	36	171
1	16	48	229

Note: *A pinch or dash is less than ⅛ teaspoon.*

TIP

You can "count" on a calculator for failproof results when the math gets complicated — for example, to solve the brain-exploding task of converting a metric measurement to an imperial measurement, like grams to teaspoons. First, do any fractional work on the metric number based on how much the recipe is being scaled down. For example, 100 grams of sugar in a 4-person recipe becomes 25 grams for a single serving. Then, unless you are a math genius, plug that number into a free, online conversion calculator (such as The Calculator Site at www. thecalculatorsite.com/cooking/cooking-calculator.php) to solve the rest of the problem. For this sugar problem, the online calculator tells me it's 5.97 teaspoons of sugar — just a scant under 2 tablespoons.

The great "egg issue"

Eggs can be one of the most onery and frustrating ingredients to scale down. If you've ever tried to eyeball a single raw egg into multiple, even parts, you are nodding in agreement! But if you understand that a large egg (with white and yolk) makes 4 tablespoons of whisked egg, on average, it becomes super simple to scale down. For example, when scaling down a four-serving recipe that calls for one egg to a single-serving, just fork-whisk the egg up and spoon out 1 table-spoon for your recipe, saving the rest for another use. Another idea that's even simpler: Forget about buying whole eggs by the dozen; use liquid eggs from a carton to have complete control of smaller amounts and to minimize waste and cleanup.

Also, alternative egg products like chia egg or flax egg can be useful to single-serve chefs, even if there is no specific egg-free dietary constraint. It's shelf stable, and you can mix up exactly how much you need on demand. To make this type of egg-free substitute, mix 1 tablespoon flax or chia seed with 3 tablespoons water and let sit for 5 to 15 minutes to set up and create the equivalent of one egg. Store any leftovers in the fridge or consider making less by scaling down the ingredients.

Turn down the volume

Smaller-scale cookware is typically needed to cook many converted-down recipes successfully. While it doesn't really matter what size skillet you use to pan-sear a single steak or sauté spinach, it will most definitely affect the cooking time and quality for small recipes in vessels like a too-big pot, casserole, or cake pan. This brings us back to math. With baked items, like muffins, it can be easy — you just pour the batter into the regular muffin pan, just filling up fewer reservoirs. However, other recipes can be fussier, and how high or low it fills the pot or pan will affect the final result. You'll need to convert the approximate area of the dish originally called for into a new measurement and keep figures crossed that you have that smaller-sized dish.

For example, for a recipe that needs a 9-×-13-inch pan, you first figure out that $9 \times 13 = 117$ square inches. Then, you can pick the appropriate pan from the following options:

>> For half of the recipe, use an 8-inch square pan or a 9-inch round dish:

- $8 \times 8 = 64$ sq. in.

- $3.14 \, [\pi] \times 4.5 \times 4.5 = 64.5$ sq. in.

>> For a fourth of the recipe, use a 6-inch round dish: $3.14 \times 3 \times 3 = 28$ sq. in. Another alternative would be to use 2 to 3 silicone muffin liners on a cookie sheet as an alternative to this size baking dish.

Don't overcook

When scaling down recipes, you'll want to keep an extra eye on the clock to prevent the meal from overcooking. This goes for all cooking in smaller batch recipes;
it just seems to get done more quickly! A smaller-size pan swap could affect the
cooking time as could the equipment. For example, toaster ovens seem to cook
and brown stuff more quickly than a traditional built-in oven, even using the
same pans and temperature. Over time you will learn how to tell visually when
recipes are ready, but until then, it's better to check often for doneness — you
can't unburn something if it's already been scorched!

SWAPPING INGREDIENTS IN A PINCH

Just because you realized that a specific "supporting cast" ingredient isn't on hand in the
pantry or fridge doesn't mean that your recipe-making mission needs to be abandoned.
There are many easy ingredient substitutions that perform beautifully when the listed
real deal isn't around. You may be swapping for dietary constraints, too. In fact, I should
probably make a *For Dummies* book just about swaps and substitutions in cooking.
Below you'll see some swap-ins that might come in handy for the recipes in this
cookbook, but it's by far not an inclusive list!

- Don't have whole eggs, use 4 liquid eggs for every 1 large egg.

- Don't have whole milk, use heavy cream and water in a 1:1 ratio.

- Don't have cream, stir ½ cup whole milk into 3 tablespoons melted butter that has
  cooled a bit. Use in creamy sauce recipes, not for whipping.

- Don't have Greek yogurt, simply swap out for the same amount of sour cream and
  vice-versa.

- Don't have vegetable or meat stock, mix together 1 tablespoon Worcestershire
  sauce per 1 cup hot water or use a bouillon cube.

- Don't have fresh herbs, substitute 1 teaspoon of dried herbs for every 1 tablespoon
  of fresh.

- Don't do gluten but need flour, then swap in an equal amount of specifically designated "gluten free baking blend."

- Don't have brown sugar, then use coconut sugar, date sugar, or granulated sugar.

- Don't have an egg, then use 4 tablespoons liquid egg or egg white from carton, or
  mix together 1 tablespoon powered flax or chia seed with 3 tablespoons water.

For more ideas, check out the list of common ingredient substitutions on the
Allrecipes website at www.allrecipes.com/article/common-ingredient-
substitutions.

Salt and season sparingly

When in doubt, always season food more lightly in a scaled-down recipe — a little goes a long way. After cooking, you can always add more salt, pepper, and other seasonings to suit your personal tastes, but it's almost impossible to fix too salty or too spicy soups, stews, and other meals.

Scaling up single-serve recipes to serve two or more

Again, it's math! Scale up single-serve recipes to serve more than one by using multiplication. If serving two, just double the ingredients. If serving three, then triple! But also keep in mind issues like pan-size conversions, cooking time (it might take longer), and weird ingredients to divvy up like eggs.

Exploring Meal Storage Solutions

When it comes to keeping food stashed safely and with the best chances of tasting amazing later, you have to dig deeper than just tossing a napkin on top of your plate and sticking it in the fridge. Still, the strategies aren't difficult or complicated. The best outcomes in food storage include using appropriate containers for the specific contents and storage environment; learning best practices in how long cooked and uncooked food stays safe in the fridge and how to best freeze it for optimal results; and keeping a "first in, first out" system for all food, fresh, frozen, or pantry staple.

Containing leftovers for later

Even when trying to avoid leftovers, sooner or later you're going to be faced with a few. Perhaps your eyes were bigger than your stomach and you weren't as hungry as expected, or the recipe just made a bunch. Don't toss leftovers away! With minimal effort, you can optimize the time you spent cooking to make another meal or two. Even small portions of leftovers can be repurposed as an ingredient to create a new meal. A few bites of leftover steak can be chopped up and tossed into a next-day breakfast taco, or leftover spaghetti sauce can be spread on a personal-sized pizza crust and topped with cheese for a quick-fix lunch.

To keep leftovers at their best and help prevent foodborne illness, immediately cover and wrap excess food in airtight packaging or seal into a storage container with lid. This helps prevent unwanted bacteria growth and also keeps strong-smelling foods from infiltrating other food being stored in the vicinity. Nobody wants to be sick or even have their overnight oats smelling of garlic. After properly packaging up, immediately place leftovers in the fridge or freezer. Sometime "immediately" is not possible, especially when you are bringing food home from a restaurant. As long as food begins the chilling process within two hours of being served, it should remain safe. Most cooked food can be stored in the fridge for three to four days and the freezer for three to six months.

To prevent foodborne illness, food that was once hot should be reheated to 165°F (74°C). Food kept at temperatures between the danger zone of from 40°F to 140°F (4°C–60°C) creates an opportunity for bad bacteria to grow quickly and make you sick. However, even when you think you stored it carefully, always use your senses as a guide — if a leftover doesn't look, smell, taste, or feel right, it probably isn't.

Freeze it, but don't get burned!

Freezer burn happens when water sublimates from frozen food. Sublimation is a process similar to evaporation, except water molecules don't turn into vapor; they turn into ice crystals. Ever stuck a loaf of bread in the freezer in the original plastic packaging to find it spotted with spots of powdery ice a week later? That ice was formed by water vapors as they were pulled out of the moist bread. Now your bread may taste a little dried out. Meat and every other food, especially those with a high-water content, can fall victim to freezer burn, too. Freezer-burned food will look shriveled, be discolored a dingy grey, or be covered in ice crystals. It is still fine to eat technically, especially if dehydrated parts are cut off, but freezer-burned food may leave you feeling disappointed about the taste and tough texture. Don't get burned by freezer burn, follow these tips:

>> **Use the correct containers:** Invest in freezer-proof storage containers of various sizes, from 4-ounce to 1-quart rigid-side freezer containers to specific freezer-safe baggies in every size. This small expense pays dividends by maintaining the taste, texture, and integrity of foods kept in the freezer. Plus, these heavier-duty vessels work beautifully in the fridge. Keep in mind that plastic take-out containers, Styrofoam trays with plastic wrap, or simple food storage baggies not specifically created for the freezer can contribute to freezer burn.

>> **Eliminate air:** Air is not your friend in freezing; it leads to freezer burn. However, when freezing foods, you must leave enough "head room" at the top to accommodate food increasing in volume as the liquids freeze. If not enough room, the "growing" food will push off the lid or crack the container, further

deteriorating the quality. When using freezer-proof zip-top bags, simple eliminate the air by squeezing out as much as possible or using a straw to suck it out before quickly sealing. Another option is a vacuum-sealing appliance, which does a first-rate job if you can justify the financial and storage-space expense.

>> **Minimize temperature fluctuations:** In an ideal world, frozen foods do best when they are kept at a constant temperature of 0°F (–18°C). So, when you need to open and close the door to retrieve and store items, do it mindfully and quickly! Other ways to help minimize temperature fluctuations are to

- Keep the freezer at least 75 percent full, which helps stabilize the overall temperature.

- Avoid keeping your stand-alone freezer or freezer-fridge combo in the hot garage.

- Defrost freezers that are not self-defrosting or frost-free when they get a build-up of more than ¼ inch of ice on the walls.

- Do a yearly deep clean of your freezer to remove gunk and keep it operating efficiently.

As a perk, all of these tips help save energy, which saves you money!

WARNING

Don't put warm leftovers into the freezer straightaway. The heat will raise the temperature of the freezer space and disturb the frozen foods inside. Instead, wrap warm leftovers properly and let chill in the fridge for a few hours before transferring.

First in, first out

First In, First Out (FIFO) is a classic accounting method, meaning assets purchased first are used first. Makes sense, right? Restaurants also use FIFO with their food inventory as do smart home cooks. With the price of groceries constantly on the rise, I think we can all agree that it's a good idea to use up food by the expiration date rather than finding it too late, shoved in the back of the pantry or freezer.

The following guidelines will help you manage your food inventory:

>> **Mark food with "use by" or "expiration" dates.** These should be machine-printed on the label but often are too small to read clearly when you're grabbing for things in a hurry. For items you use infrequently or have stocked up on in the pantry, use a permanent marker to write the date in a size that is readable from the shelf. I learned this from my mother-in-law, who does this with all the canned goods in her pantry. Do the same with fresh food and

leftovers you are storing in the freezer. Mark these with the date you made them or put them in the freezer. Most disposable freezer-safe bags have a pen-friendly label area. For containers use a permanent pen on masking tape and then attach the piece of tape to the lid.

» **Store the same types of food together.** For example, grains, beans, spices, and other pantry items should be grouped separately. In the freezer, meats in one area, frozen fruits and vegetables in another, and so on.

» **Arrange food in date order.** Take a tip from big families and, if you've stocked up, put items expiring first near the front and items more recently purchased near the back. This saves the time and hassle of looking at the dates; you can just grab and go. The same idea applies to leftovers you plan to eat soon. Put those at eye-level near the front of the shelf, with the "first in" leftovers closest to the front — eat those first or put in the freezer promptly. Keep a running list of what you have stored for a quick update on what's stocked and what needs to be consumed first. Either tape it to the freezer door or slide paper into a plastic page protector and toss right on the top freezer shelf.

Prepping Your Meals, Maybe

You've heard of "meal prepping," but might be on-the-fence about whether it's for you. A straightforward definition of meal prep is preparing foods for meals. Duh. As obvious as that sounds, the scope, extent, and intent of meal prepping can vary widely, but the common benefit of all the iterations is that it provides a benefit that improves your life. For example, meal prepping might help you manage your health, money, or time. Or, all of the above.

After a scroll through social media, "meal prepping" might be speaking to you as the latest, greatest cook-at-home trend of the last decade. If you look at meal prepping in the widest sense, it's been around forever. Just think back to learning about cowboys from the 1800s on cattle drives, who made and carried beef jerky in their packs to provide adequate protein nourishment over the multimonth routes. Or even a grandmother harvesting and canning peaches from her backyard to make pies through the year. Today you see busy mothers preparing big made-ahead freezer meals, grilling enthusiasts making a mega batch of steaks or chicken breast to dole out over the week, and fitness and health enthusiasts portioning up a stockpile of grab-and-go meals in one single-session cooking event to minimize the chances of going rogue through a fast-food drive through later in the week.

Types of meal prep

Meal prepping can mean different things to different people. The key success in meal prep is understanding the different iterations and how to incorporate any or all of the styles to help optimize your daily functioning:

» **Mise en place:** Coined in French culinary circles, this fancy-sounding but basic term simply means to gather and "put in place" exact amount ingredients that will be used for the recipe at hand. Setting up a workspace with ingredients that have been washed, dried, sliced, diced, chopped, strained, and otherwise prepped and measured before jumping into the proverbial fire will prevent many cooking faux pas that could ruin your dish — like realizing you don't have an ingredient or having to stop halfway through to chop an onion — throwing the whole recipe timing off. It's also a good idea to set out the pots and pans and read through the entirety of the recipe's steps before starting.

» **Ingredient prep:** This idea is similar to *mise en place,* but it involves prepping more of the ingredient at once to be stored for handy use later in a variety of recipes — recipes which you may have preplanned or others that you are inspired to make on the fly. Come home from the market and get your specific or generic ingredients ready to go. Wash and dry lettuce and greens; chop celery, carrots, and onions; spiralize zucchini and butternut squash; and toast nuts and seeds. Also consider tasks that take more time on the front end but are worth it for the overall minimized mess, like slow cooking and shredding beef or chicken; making grains ahead; and other tasks you can do in bulk that will save you time during actual recipe making.

» **Make-ahead meals:** Make several meals from a four-to six-serving recipe, such as a big lasagna or pot of stew. Then store the remainder in your fridge or freezer in one-serving portions.

» **Batch prepping and portioning:** Make multiple recipes that you will portion and store in single-serve containers in the freezer and fridge. These recipes can be mixed and matched for variety. For example, grill a big batch of simply seasoned chicken breasts, a variety of vegetables, and a couple of grains. Then, match up the food groups as you see fit and change the flavor profiles with different toppings, sauces, or dressings.

Deciding if the meal-prep lifestyle is for you

More extensive types of meal prepping, such as batch cooking and make-ahead meals, can save you substantial time, money, and worry over what you are going to eat for your next meal. Plus, waste is reduced because you are more thoughtfully creating shopping lists with an efficient use of ingredients that will be consumed and not thrown away. These perks aside, you have to be committed to the process to benefit from the rewards. Do you have the time and temperament to hang around in the kitchen all day and cook? Special equipment may also be required, like a slow cooker and extra freezer-friendly containers. And, don't forget to consider storage issues for meals and the available space in your fridge or freezer.

If you're not a person who embraces leftovers, meal prepping multiple meals of the same variety may not be for you — basically, advance-made meals are glorified leftovers. Batch prepping (like making multiple servings of plain quinoa and freezing in single portion freezer bags) can be useful and provide you shortcut ingredients for your on-demand tastes. The most basic type of meal prep mentioned, *mise en place*, is for everyone and a basic tenant of cooking well.

TIP

Try your hand at meal-prep for the pantry with the do-it-yourself Anything-But-Basic Oatmeal Packets in Chapter 7. These customizable, single-serve packets are better than store-bought — less expensive and they provide total control over ingredients. Plus, the oat packets can be stored on a pantry shelf almost indefinitely and prepared with water when desired with no strain on your fridge space or a strict timeline to consume.

2
Starting the Day Right with Breakfast

Learn how to make the most of your morning meal and why you shouldn't skip it.

Power up with plenty of protein and get a jump-start on your daily fruit and veggie requirements.

Wake up to a preprepped breakfast solution or whip up a 30-minute (or less) dish as the rooster crows.

Enjoy variety in breakfast recipes that will satisfy your preferences and hunger level of the moment, including eggs and meats, oats and grains, waffles and muffins, smoothies and yogurts, plus more!

Chapter **5**

Hearty Eggs and Breakfast Meats

Eggs, bacon, and sausage, oh, my, yes! But why? While eating eggs for breakfast dates back to ancient Rome, throughout much of history anything of substance for breakfast was primarily a necessity of the working class, travelers, or children, who all required more energy to fuel early mornings. Those who could afford to sleep in and skip breakfast certainly did or chose something very light like a grain or pastry and coffee! Breakfast, in some time periods and cultures, was even frowned upon. Can you believe in the Middle Ages, eating any breakfast at all was considered to be a gluttonous sin?

In 1620, English medical writer, Tobias Venner, suggested that a heartier morning meal was important to promote good health. His suggestion was poached eggs, bread, and wine. Still, at the turn of the 20th century, most people were still eating sparsely at the start of the day, if at all. But, enter good–old–fashioned American entrepreneurship. In the 1920s, a public relation and marketing consultant, Edward Bernays, was approached by Beech–Nut Packing Company, manufacturers of many consumer products including pork products. Beech–Nut wanted to push their bacon and the idea of a heavier breakfast, so Bernays worked his marketing magic by getting 5,000 of his doctor acquaintances to support the idea of a more substantial breakfast, such as bacon and egg. The "study" was widely publicized, Beech-Nut's profits rose, and the deliciously inseparable duo of "bacon and eggs," and now classic American breakfast, was born.

Marketing showmanship aside, the primary benefit of eggs and bacon, or other complete proteins for that matter, is that your body is being nourished with plenty of protein that offers a complete amino-acid profile, along with vitamins and micronutrients and adequate fat to keep you feeling satiated until your next meal. All of this is needed for muscle management and immunity to keep your body humming along like it should.

Eggs and breakfast meats are economical choices that won't bust your budget. Plus, you have to appreciate Mother Nature's user-friendly, individual "packaging" of eggs, which is so perfectly matched for single-serve dishes.

TIP

In some recipes, like many of the baked recipes later in the cookbook, you won't need a whole egg. In order to prevent food waste, you have a couple of options. One is to take what you need from a fresh egg and freeze the remainder to thaw out later for another use. Another is to use a liquid whole egg or egg white product available in a pourable carton — use a teaspoon or a cup; it's your call!

Your morning free time (an oxymoron for most) will likely dictate what type of egg and breakfast meat meal will help nourish your best life. Even if you don't have tons of time for scratch cooking, Quick Chilaquiles can be made in less than 15 minutes and will keep you out of the fast-food drive-thru. Mug omelets cook in just 2 minutes in the microwave — you can't even make coffee that quickly! Another option is to make breakfast ahead and keep it in the fridge or freezer — check out the Mix-and-Match Muffin Pan Frittatas. Plus, who says eggs and "breakfast" meats are just for the morning — they make a quick and satisfying supper, too!

Two-Egg Denver Mug Omelet

PREP TIME: 5 MINUTES | COOK TIME: 2 MINUTES | YIELD: 1 SERVING

INGREDIENTS

2 large eggs

Pinch of salt and pepper

2 ounces cooked ham, diced

2 tablespoons finely chopped green bell pepper

2 tablespoons finely chopped white or yellow onion

1 tablespoon shredded cheddar cheese (optional)

Salsa, chopped green onion, or sour cream, for topping (optional)

DIRECTIONS

1 Spray a large 15- to 16-ounce microwave-safe mug with cooking spray.

2 Add the eggs, 2 tablespoons of water, and salt and pepper to the mug; whisk up with a fork.

3 Microwave on high for 40 seconds; remove the mug from the microwave and stir to scramble.

4 Return the mug to the microwave and cook for an additional 30 to 40 seconds, or in 10-second additional increments until cooked through.

5 Embellish with additional toppings, if desired.

NOTE: The deli department is a great place to source small quantities of cooked ham. Also, look for frozen bags of bell pepper and onion mixture. Keep in the freezer, removing just what is needed for the recipe. No waste!

Mix-and-Match Muffin Pan Frittatas

PREP TIME: 5 MINUTES	COOK TIME: 25 MINUTES	YIELD: 3 SERVINGS (2 EACH)

INGREDIENTS

1 teaspoon olive oil

⅔ cup mix-and-match diced vegetables of choice, such as broccoli, cauliflower, white or yellow onions, bell pepper, mushrooms, tomatoes, and/or baby spinach

½ cup precooked meat of choice, such as crumbled bacon, diced leftover steak, pork, or chicken (optional)

6 large eggs

3 tablespoons milk of choice

½ teaspoon salt

½ teaspoon ground black pepper

½ cup shredded cheese of choice, such as cheddar, Monterey jack, Swiss, or feta

DIRECTIONS

1 Place the olive oil in a small skillet and bring to medium heat. Sauté the vegetables for 5 to 8 minutes or until the vegetables are softening. The exact time will depend on the type of vegetables used and size of the pieces. Set aside.

2 Preheat the oven to 350 degrees.

3 Coat six jumbo-sized muffin cups with cooking spray.

4 Divide the cooked vegetables and meat of choice evenly among the muffin cups.

5 Crack the eggs into a large bowl. Add the milk, salt, and pepper; whisk until well combined.

6 Divide the egg mixture evenly among the muffin cups. Sprinkle the cheese on top.

7 Bake for 15 to 18 minutes until just set. Cool on a wire rack for 2 to 3 minutes and then remove from pan. To release the egg frittatas, run a knife around the edge of each muffin cup, and then invert the pan.

8 Store in the fridge for up to 4 days; reheat in the microwave on high for 45 seconds to 1 minute.

VARY IT! You may substitute the jumbo-sized muffin pan with a standard muffin pan, filling 9 wells with the egg mixture in Step 6. Then follow the same baking instructions in Step 7. This will increase serving size to 3 each.

NOTE: Leftovers may be frozen and thawed overnight in the fridge. Then reheat the egg bites in the microwave as directed above.

Quick Chilaquiles

PREP TIME: 5 MINUTES	COOK TIME: 5 MINUTES	YIELD: 1 SERVING

INGREDIENTS

1 cup coarsely crushed tortilla chips (see Note)

2 large eggs

½ cup store-bought tomatillo salsa or salsa verde

⅛ teaspoon salt

⅛ teaspoon ground black pepper

¼ teaspoon ground cumin

4 grape or cherry tomatoes, diced

2 teaspoons diced red onion

2 tablespoons crumbled queso fresco cheese

2 tablespoons Mexican-style crema or sour cream, for garnish

2 teaspoons chopped cilantro, for garnish

DIRECTIONS

1   Preheat the oven broiler or toaster oven to high.

2   Coat an 8-inch, oven-proof skillet with cooking spray and scatter with chips. Turn the temperature to medium-high.

3   In small bowl, whisk the eggs, tomatillo salsa, salt, pepper, and cumin.

4   Pour the egg mixture over the chips in the skillet. Sprinkle with the tomatoes, red onion, and queso fresco. Cook 2 minutes over medium heat, without stirring.

5   Place the skillet under the broiler and cook for approximately 2 more minutes, or until the eggs finish setting up.

6   Slide the chilaquiles out of the skillet with a spatula onto a plate. Remove from the oven and garnish with cream and cilantro.

NOTE: Stale chips work well in this dish. Save remnant chips and crumbs from the bottom of the bag and store in the freezer for this recipe.

Parmesan Egg in a Hole

INGREDIENTS

1 slice quality bread, such as a whole grain or sourdough

2 teaspoons salted butter

1 tablespoon shredded Parmesan cheese, divided

1 large egg

Salt and ground black pepper

DIRECTIONS

1 Use the rim of a glass or biscuit cutter (if available) to press and remove a hole in the center of bread slice.

2 Heat a skillet over medium-low heat and melt the butter.

3 Place bread slice (as well as the punched-out piece) in skillet, pushing them around in the butter a bit to soak it up.

4 Sprinkle half of the Parmesan cheese in the bread hole, straight onto skillet. Quickly crack the egg on top of cheese, being careful not to disturb the yolk. Sprinkle the remaining half of the cheese on top of the egg.

5 Cook the egg until it starts setting up, about 1 minute.

6 Season with salt and pepper before using a spatula to carefully flip toast. Cook another 1 to 2 minutes, until the yolk is cooked to your preference (runny or set) and the bread is golden brown on both sides.

7 Don't forget to flip your cut-out bread piece, too! Serve it on the side as a bonus piece of mini toast!

VARY IT! To make a dairy-free version, substitute olive oil for butter and omit the Parmesan cheese.

Sweet-n-Spicy Bacon

PREP TIME: 5 MINUTES | COOK TIME: 20 MINUTES | YIELD: 1 SERVING

INGREDIENTS

3 slices thick-cut bacon

2 teaspoons brown sugar

⅛ teaspoon ground cayenne pepper

⅛ teaspoon ground black pepper

DIRECTIONS

1 Preheat the oven to 375 degrees.

2 Line a rimmed baking sheet with parchment paper or aluminum foil and place the bacon in a single layer.

3 In a small bowl, toss together the brown sugar, cayenne, and pepper.

4 Bake for 10 minutes; remove from the oven briefly to flip the slices and sprinkle the tops with an even portion of the sugar mixture.

5 Return to the oven and bake an additional 8 to 10 minutes, until the desired level of crispiness is achieved. Transfer onto a plate lined with a paper towel to drain off the excess grease.

VARY IT! To prepare in air fryer, spray the basket with cooking spray. Lay out the bacon and air fry at 350 degrees for 5 minutes. Prepare the sugar mixture as directed. Flip the bacon slices and sprinkle with the sugar mixture. Return to the air fryer for 5 to 8 additional minutes or until suitably crispy. Note that the cooking time will vary significantly by the thickness of bacon, so keep an eye on it to prevent burning.

Crazy Fast Mushroom Swiss Breakfast Quesadilla

PREP TIME: 3 MINUTES | COOK TIME: 7 MINUTES | YIELD: 1 SERVING

INGREDIENTS

1 teaspoon olive oil

3 cups sliced cremini mushrooms

2 large eggs

1 tablespoon milk

⅛ teaspoon salt

⅛ teaspoon ground black pepper

⅓ cup shredded Swiss cheese, divided

1 (10-inch) flour tortilla

Salsa, avocado slices, or sour cream, for topping (optional)

DIRECTIONS

1 Preheat a 10-inch skillet over medium heat.

2 Place the olive oil and mushrooms in the skillet and sauté until the mushrooms are softening and beginning to brown, about 3 minutes.

3 In a bowl, whisk together the eggs, milk, salt, and pepper.

4 Pour the egg mixture into the heated skillet over the mushrooms, swirling around a bit so that the entire pan is coated in the egg mixture. Let cook, untouched, for about 2 minutes until the eggs are setting up on the bottom but still a little wet (but not runny) on top.

5 Sprinkle the top of the egg mixture with half of the cheese. Place the tortilla directly on top of the eggs and mushrooms, pressing down lightly. Carefully flip the entire quesadilla onto the other side, open faced.

6 Sprinkle the quesadilla with the remaining half of the cheese. Cook 1 minute open-faced.

7 Fold the quesadilla in half on top of itself, with the fillings in the middle. Continue to cook a minute or so on each side until the tortilla has become nice and golden brown.

8 Cut in wedges and add toppings, if desired.

VARY IT: Add crumbled bacon, if desired!

Burger Breakfast Salad with Maple Vinaigrette

PREP TIME: 10 MINUTES	COOK TIME: 12 MINUTES	YIELD: 1 SERVING

INGREDIENTS

Burger:

4 ounces lean ground beef

1 tablespoon pure maple syrup

¼ teaspoon dried sage

¼ teaspoon garlic powder

¼ teaspoon onion powder

⅛ to ¼ teaspoon crushed dried red pepper

Vinaigrette:

1 tablespoon olive oil

1 tablespoon pure maple syrup

2 teaspoons apple cider vinegar

2 teaspoons lemon juice, fresh or bottled

Pinch each of salt and ground black pepper

Salad:

2 to 3 cups spring mix lettuce blend

½ small apple, chopped

1 ounce cinnamon-raisin bagel chips, crumbled (optional)

DIRECTIONS

1 Place the ground beef, maple syrup, and seasonings in a bowl and mix together. Form the mixture into a ½-inch thick patty.

2 Heat a nonstick skillet over medium heat and add the patty. Cook for 10 to 12 minutes, flipping once, until the internal temperature reads 160 degrees with an instant read thermometer.

3 Remove the patty from the skillet and allow it to rest for 5 minutes.

4 Meanwhile, make the vinaigrette by whisking together the olive oil, maple syrup, vinegar, lemon juice, salt, and pepper in a bowl.

5 Assemble the salad: place the spring mix on plate, top with the burger, sprinkle with the chopped apple, and drizzle with the desired amount of vinaigrette. If desired, top with crumbled bagel chips.

NOTE: Make an extra patty and keep on hand in the freezer for a quick meal any time of the day.

Small-Batch Sausage Balls

PREP TIME: 15 MINUTES | COOK TIME: 40 MINUTES | YIELD: 6 SERVINGS

INGREDIENTS

¼-pound bulk spicy pork sausage

½ cup all-purpose baking mix (like Bisquick)

1 tablespoon milk

1 cup grated sharp cheddar cheese

DIRECTIONS

1 In a small skillet over medium-high heat, cook the sausage into browned crumbles — approximately 7 to 10 minutes. Drain off any excess fat and let cool 5 minutes.

2 Preheat the oven to 350 degrees and line a baking sheet with parchment paper or aluminum foil. If using foil, spray lightly with cooking spray.

3 Place the baking mix, milk, and cheese in a bowl and mix together; stir in the cooked sausage.

4 With your hands, form the dough into approximately 1-inch balls. Place the balls 2 inches apart on the lined baking sheet.

5 Bake for 20 to 25 minutes until browned and the sausage is cooked through.

NOTE: A great grab-and-go breakfast that can be made ahead, leftovers can be stored for up to 4 days in fridge or frozen for 3 months. Reheat in the microwave for about 15 to 20 seconds, or for a crispier exterior reheat in the oven for 4 to 5 minutes at 350 degrees, or the air fryer at 390 degrees for 2 to 3 minutes

TIP: These sausage balls are also popular as an appetizer.

Presto Pesto Egg Crepes

PREP TIME: 1 MINUTE	COOK TIME: 4 MINUTES	YIELD: 1 SERVING (2 CREPES)

INGREDIENTS

¼ cup liquid egg whites

2 teaspoons prepared pesto

1 teaspoon water

Pinch each of salt and ground black pepper

DIRECTIONS

1 Coat a 6-inch skillet with cooking spray and heat over medium heat.

2 In a bowl, whisk together the egg whites, pesto, water, and salt and pepper with a fork.

3 Pour half of the egg mixture (2½ tablespoons) into the heated skillet and swirl quickly to cover the bottom of the skillet. Keep on the heat for 45 seconds; do not flip.

4 Remove the pan from the heat and let the egg mixture sit in the hot skillet another 45 seconds until set. You will not be flipping it.

5 Use a silicone spatula to gently loosen sides and release the crepe from the skillet.

6 Repeat the process with the remaining 2½ tablespoons of the egg mixture.

VARY IT! Enjoy the crepes as is or spread with a filling of your choice such as cream cheese, guacamole, or hummus. You can also use these crepes as a wrap for deli meats and vegetables.

Two-Egg Prosciutto Cup

PREP TIME: 5 MINUTES	COOK TIME: 16 MINUTES	YIELD: 1 SERVING

INGREDIENTS

2 thin slices of prosciutto

¼ cup fresh baby spinach, chopped

2 large eggs or 4 ounces liquid whole eggs

¼ teaspoon garlic salt

Pinch of ground black pepper

DIRECTIONS

1 Preheat the oven or air fryer to 375 degrees.

2 Line an 8-ounce ramekin with the prosciutto, pressing down on the bottom and up around the sides.

3 Add the chopped spinach on top of the prosciutto.

4 Crack the eggs over the spinach.

5 Bake for 14 to 16 minutes or air fry for 10 to 12 minutes, until the eggs are set or the yolks are the desired consistency.

TIP: For a little extra flavor, try sprinkling a tablespoon of your favorite crumbled or shredded cheese, like feta cheese or aged Parmesan cheese, to the top.

Chapter 6

Filling Waffles, Pancakes, and Mug Muffins

Ready to dig into a feel-good, yet still sensible, sweet breakfast like waffles and pancakes stacked high or a still-warm homemade muffin? Waffles, pancakes, and sweet baked goods are the ultimate in breakfast comfort food. If you were over at Mom's right now, she'd probably be treating you to a breakfast plate that included one of these morning staples.

The convenient thing about making waffles, pancakes, and muffins is that the foundation ingredients are inexpensive and easy to keep stocked in the pantry and fridge. With flour, sugar, and a leavening agent along with eggs, milk, and a little butter or oil, you have the base makings for something worth waking up your appetite. And, most recipes of this type take no more than 30 minutes to make — prep to plate.

Pancakes, waffles, and muffins can be as decadent and over-the-top as you can dream up. How about caramel sauce, chocolate chips, and ice cream added as toppings to the Super-Fluffy Pancake Stack? They can also be a hearty yet healthy meal like the

Muscle-Making Protein powder Waffles. Most recipes accommodate nearly endless variations for toppings or batter mix-ins.

TIP

Most recipes are friendly to certain ingredient swaps to suit your dietary eating preference with minimal effects on the recipe outcome. For example, if all-purpose flour is called for, a gluten-free baking flour that is labeled as a cup-for-cup substitute may be used. Liquid egg whites can be substituted for whole eggs. Or, table sugar can be exchanged for a 1:1 ratio equivalent of granulated sweetener. (I find stevia and monk fruit work the best.)

Remember that breakfast isn't the only meal where pancakes, waffles, and muffins are allowed. There are no rules about what time of day you can eat specific foods, so why not plan to sit down to "brinner" one night this week? The Honey Cornbread Waffles would be amazing topped with a chicken tender and maple syrup. Pancakes, waffles, and muffins are a great way to enjoy a home-cooked meal or side when you are low on supplies and energy. For even less stress, make and freeze a batch or two of your favorite waffles, pancakes, or muffins to rescue you on the most hectic days.

Super Fluffy Pancake Stack

PREP TIME: 5 MINUTES	COOK TIME: 10 MINUTES	YIELD: 2 SERVINGS (4 PANCAKES)

INGREDIENTS

1 cup all-purpose flour or gluten-free flour

1 teaspoon baking powder

½ tablespoon sugar

¼ teaspoon salt

1 large egg

¾ cup milk

2 teaspoons lemon juice

1 tablespoon salted butter, melted

DIRECTIONS

1   In a large bowl, combine the flour, baking powder, sugar, and salt.

2   In a separate bowl, whisk together the egg, milk, lemon juice, and melted butter.

3   Pour the wet ingredients into the dry ingredients and stir well with spoon.

4   Spray a small or medium skillet with cooking spray and heat over medium heat.

5   Ladle a quarter of the batter into the skillet. If there is enough room, add additional batter for a second pancake.

6   Cook until bubbles break on top of the pancake and the edges turn golden brown, about 2 minutes. Flip and cook approximately 1 more minute on other side.

7   Remove the pancake(s) from pan to plate; repeat the process with the remaining batter.

8   Serve with your favorite toppings such as Butter, syrup, whipped cream, or fruit slices, for topping.

9   Store leftover pancakes in the fridge for up to 4 to 5 days and microwave for 30 to 45 seconds to reheat. Also, the pancakes may be frozen for longer storage.

TIP: Don't skip the lemon juice; this is the secret ingredient that makes these pancakes extra fluffy.

Baked Berry Pancake Squares

PREP TIME: 10 MINUTES	COOK TIME: 10 MINUTES	YIELD: 2 SERVINGS (2 PANCAKE SQUARES EACH)

INGREDIENTS

¾ cup all-purpose flour or gluten-free flour

1 tablespoon granulated sugar

½ teaspoon baking powder

¼ teaspoon baking soda

⅛ teaspoon salt

1 large egg

½ cup milk

½ teaspoon vanilla extract

4 teaspoons salted butter, melted but cooled slightly

⅔ cup fresh berries such as blueberries, raspberries, chopped strawberries, or a mixture

Pure maple syrup, whipped cream, or powdered sugar, for topping (optional)

DIRECTIONS

1 Preheat the oven to 425 degrees.

2 In a bowl, whisk together the flour, sugar, baking powder, baking soda, and salt.

3 In a separate bowl or large measuring cup, whisk together the eggs, milk, and vanilla.

4 Add the wet mixture to the dry ingredients and mix until just combined. It's okay if the batter is a little lumpy.

5 Stir in the butter.

6 Spray a 9-inch square pan with cooking spray.

7 Pour the batter into the prepared pan and use back of spoon to spread evenly.

8 Scatter the berries around the top of the pancake batter.

9 Bake for 10 minutes or until set. Remove from the pan and cut into 4 squares.

10 If desired, dress up with special toppings, like maple syrup, whipped cream, or a dusting of powdered sugar.

VARY IT! Substitute nuts and chocolate chips for the berries.

Muscle-Making Protein Powder Waffles

PREP TIME: 5 MINUTES	COOK TIME: 10 MINUTES	YIELD: 2 SERVINGS (2 MINI WAFFLES EACH)

INGREDIENTS

1 large egg plus 1 large egg white, or 6 tablespoons liquid egg whites

¼ cup milk

¼ teaspoon vanilla extract

1 (5.3-ounce) carton Greek yogurt, in flavor of your choice

¼ cup (25 grams) vanilla protein powder (see Note)

½ cup all-purpose flour or gluten-free baking flour

½ teaspoon ground cinnamon

DIRECTIONS

1 In a bowl or large mixing cup, whisk the whole egg and egg white with the milk, vanilla, and yogurt.

2 In a bowl, whisk together the protein powder, flour, and cinnamon.

3 Mix the wet ingredients with the dry ingredients until combined. The mixture may be a little lumpy, and that's okay.

4 Heat a mini or four-square waffle maker according to the manufacturer's instructions and then pour approximately 3 to 4 tablespoons of the batter into the mini waffle iron or all of the batter into a large waffle maker. If you are using a large waffle maker, the batter will not fill from corner to corner, so just pour the batter into the center Greek yogurt, berries, and chopped nuts, for topping (optional) it will spread out into a freeformed circle shape while cooking with the 4 hatch marks going through the center.

5 Cook for several minutes or until the indicator light turns off; waffles should be golden brown on both sides and can be removed easily with a fork.

6 Repeat with the remaining batter, if needed.

7 If desired, serve with healthy-option toppings like Greek yogurt, berries, or chopped fruit, and toasted nuts.

NOTE: Protein powder volume and the scoops that come in containers vary from product to product. Check the nutrition label to see how many grams are in each scoop or use a food scale to accurately measure protein powder.

TIP: To reheat leftovers, microwave in a single layer for 30 seconds (will not be as crispy) or put in air fryer or toaster oven preheated to 350 degrees for about 2 to 3 minutes until crisp.

Honey Cornbread Waffles

PREP TIME: 4 MINUTES | COOK TIME: 6 MINUTES | YIELD: 1 SERVING (2 WAFFLES)

INGREDIENTS

3 tablespoons corn meal

1½ tablespoons all-purpose flour

¼ teaspoon baking powder

Pinch of salt

2 tablespoons milk

1 tablespoon liquid egg

1½ teaspoons canola oil or extra-virgin olive oil

2 teaspoons honey (see Tip)

2 tablespoons Greek yogurt or sour cream

DIRECTIONS

1 In a bowl, mix together the corn meal, flour, baking powder, and salt until combined.

2 In a glass mixing cup, whisk together the milk, liquid egg, oil, honey, and Greek yogurt.

3 Pour the dry ingredients into the wet ingredients and mix until combined.

4 Heat a mini waffle maker according to the manufacturer's instructions and then pour half of the batter into the waffle maker. If using a large waffle maker, pour all the batter in at once to make one larger, round–ish waffle in the center (which you can cut in half later for stacking).

5 Cook for several minutes or until the indicator light turns off; the waffle should be golden brown on both sides and can be removed easily with fork.

6 Repeat for the second waffle, if using the mini waffle maker.

TIP: Makes two waffles, which are yummy with butter and more honey drizzled on top or as the "bread" for a sandwich any time of day!

TIP: Pure maple syrup or date syrup both make good substitutes if you don't have (or don't want to use) honey.

Decadent Double Chocolate Waffle

PREP TIME: 5 MINUTES	COOK TIME: 4 MINUTES	YIELD: 2 SERVINGS (2 MINI WAFFLES EACH)

INGREDIENTS

2 tablespoons unsweetened cocoa powder

1 cup all-purpose flour or gluten-free flour

½ cup granulated sugar

1 large egg

2 tablespoons canola oil

½ cup milk

2 tablespoons mini chocolate chips

Powdered sugar, chocolate syrup, whipped cream, and fruit (optional)

DIRECTIONS

1 In a bowl, whisk together the cocoa powder, flour, and sugar.

2 In a large measuring cup, whisk together the egg, oil, and milk until smooth.

3 Add the wet mixture to the dry ingredients and stir until well combined.

4 Heat a mini or four-square waffle maker according to the manufacturer's instructions and then pour 3 or 4 tablespoons of batter into a mini waffle maker or all of the batter into a large waffle maker.

5 Cook for several minutes until the indicator light turns off. Waffles should be golden brown on both sides and can be removed easily with a fork.

6 Repeat with the remaining batter, if needed.

7 Serve dusted with powdered sugar or other toppings of choice.

TIP: To reheat leftovers, microwave in a single layer for 30 seconds (will not be as crispy) or put in an air fryer or oven preheated to 350 degrees for about 2 to 3 minutes until crisp again.

Maple Pecan French Toast in a Mug

PREP TIME: 5 MINUTES | **COOK TIME: 2 MINUTES** | **YIELD: 1 SERVING**

INGREDIENTS

3 tablespoons milk

1 large egg

1 tablespoon pure maple syrup

¼ teaspoon vanilla extract

¼ teaspoon ground cinnamon

3–5 ounces of day-old French bread, or 2 slices slightly stale sandwich bread (see Tip)

1 tablespoon chopped, unsalted pecans, divided

Pure maple syrup, for serving

DIRECTIONS

1 In a large glass measuring cup, whisk together the milk, egg, maple syrup, vanilla, and cinnamon. Set aside.

2 Spray the inside of a 16-ounce microwave-safe mug or bowl with cooking spray.

3 Tear the bread into bite-sized pieces and put in the mug. Add the pecans to the mug and pour the egg mixture over the top, stirring to combine.

4 Microwave on high for 90 seconds to 2 minutes, or until the egg mixture is set.

5 Serve warm with maple syrup.

TIP: This is a great way to use up the "heels" from a loaf of bread.

Blueberry Mug Muffin

PREP TIME: 3 MINUTES	COOK TIME: 2 MINUTES	YIELD: 1 SERVING

INGREDIENTS

⅓ cup all-purpose flour or gluten-free flour

2 tablespoons brown sugar

¼ teaspoon baking powder

2 tablespoons salted butter, melted and slightly cooled

¼ cup milk

¼ cup fresh blueberries

DIRECTIONS

1 In a 14- to 16-ounce mug, whisk together the flour, brown sugar, and baking powder.

2 Add the melted butter and milk, mixing until the batter is smooth.

3 Gently stir in the blueberries.

4 Microwave on high for 90 seconds to 2 minutes.

5 Enjoy with a spoon right out of the mug.

TIP: Mug cakes cook quickly and often rise and fall like a souffle. Keep your eye on the mug in the microwave, and if it looks like it might overflow, hit the "pause" button for a few seconds before resuming.

TIP: If you would like to remove the muffin from the mug before eating, mix the ingredients in a separate small bowl before transferring to a mug that has been sprayed with cooking spray. Cook as directed.

Lemon Chia Seed Mini Muffins

PREP TIME: 10 MINUTES	COOK TIME: 11 MINUTES	YIELD: 3 SERVINGS (4 MINI MUFFINS EACH)

INGREDIENTS

¾ cup all-purpose flour or gluten-free flour

¼ cup granulated sugar

¾ teaspoon baking powder

¾ teaspoon chia seeds

⅛ teaspoon salt

1 egg white, or 2 tablespoons liquid whole egg

¼ cup milk of choice

1 tablespoon oil, such as canola or extra-virgin olive oil

1 teaspoon lemon zest

2 teaspoons fresh lemon juice (see Tip)

For glaze:

½ cup powdered sugar

1 teaspoon lemon zest

2 teaspoons fresh lemon juice

DIRECTIONS

1 Preheat the oven to 400 degrees. Spray a 12-count mini muffin pan with cooking spray or line with mini paper baking cups.

2 In a bowl, stir together the flour, sugar, baking powder, chia seeds, and salt.

3 In a small bowl, whisk together the egg, milk, oil, lemon zest, and lemon juice.

4 Pour the wet ingredients into the dry mixture and stir until just combined. Divide the batter evenly among the 12 mini muffin cups, filling them about three-fourths full.

5 Bake 9 to 11 minutes, until a toothpick inserted into the center of a muffin pulls clean. Cool 5 minutes in the pan.

6 Make the glaze: Mix together the powdered sugar, lemon zest, and lemon juice. Drizzle over the muffins or dip the tops of muffins into the glaze. Store leftovers in an airtight container.

TIP: This recipe uses the fresh lemon zest and lemon juice from a lemon; you will most likely have extra. Freeze what you don't use in an ice cube tray (mix the zest right into the juice) to thaw out for the next batch.

Monkey Bread

PREP TIME: 5 MINUTES | **COOK TIME: 15 MINUTES** | **YIELD: 2 SERVINGS**

INGREDIENTS

2 pieces of canned jumbo biscuit dough or frozen, uncooked biscuit dough, thawed overnight (see Tip)

1 tablespoon granulated sugar

¼ teaspoon ground cinnamon

2 teaspoons salted butter, melted

DIRECTIONS

1 Preheat the oven to 350 degrees.

2 In a small bowl, mix together the sugar and cinnamon. Toss dough pieces into the sugar mixture until coated.

3 Spray two 10-ounce ramekins with the cooking spray and place half the coated dough inside each ramekin.

4 Sprinkle any remaining sugar mixture over the top of dough.

5 Drizzle with the melted butter.

6 Bake for 15 minutes or until the dough is cooked through. Cool 2 minutes before eating.

TIP: If you want to avoid having leftover canned biscuit dough in the fridge, look for frozen bags of uncooked biscuit dough like Pillsbury Grands! Frozen Biscuits. There are typically a dozen biscuits per bag, and you can easily take out just what you need and store remainders in the freezer for another use or to make additional batches.

Any Season Fruit Dutch Baby

PREP TIME: 5 MINUTES | **COOK TIME: 16 MINUTES** | **YIELD: 1 SERVING**

INGREDIENTS

½ tablespoon salted butter

1 large egg

¼ cup milk

¼ teaspoon vanilla extract

1 teaspoon granulated sugar

¼ cup all-purpose flour

¼ teaspoon ground cinnamon

⅛ teaspoon salt

4-ounce, single-serve diced fruit cup (apple, pear, and peach are great choices; see Tip)

Powdered sugar, for serving

DIRECTIONS

1   Preheat the oven to 400 degrees.

2   Melt the butter in an oven-proof skillet, tilting the skillet or dish to coat the bottom.

3   In a bowl, whisk together the egg, milk, vanilla, and sugar. Next add the flour, cinnamon, and salt, stirring vigorously until combined well and without lumps.

4   Drain the juice from the fruit cup and scatter the diced fruit on top of melted butter in the skillet.

5   Pour the batter over the fruit.

6   Bake for 14 to 16 minutes, until puffed in the center and turning golden brown on the edges.

7   Let cool for 5 minutes before using a spatula to plate. Sprinkle with powdered sugar, if desired.

TIP: Look for convenience fruit cups in the shelf-stable fruit and vegetable aisle of the market. If preferred, ⅓ cup chopped fresh fruit can be substituted.

Chapter **7**

Oatmeals, Cereals, and Toasts with the Most

Being pressed for time in the morning doesn't mean you can't still enjoy a delicious, filling, and healthy breakfast. Quick meals such as oatmeal, whole grain cereals, and loaded toasts can do the job just as well as complicated recipes that take double and triple the time.

Oats make great fuel for champions and help you eat your way to a winning day. Whether soaked, baked, blended, toasted and then turned into granola, oatmeal boasts some mighty fine, health-supporting features including dietary fiber, plant protein, vitamins, minerals, and other important nutrients. Plus, oats are inexpensive and easy to keep on hand in the pantry. Instead of buying premade instant oatmeal packets at the store, which could be laden with sugars and are a little lackluster in flavor, you can make the Anything-But-Basic Oatmeal Packets that are customizable to your tastes and can be toted along to fix in a jiffy anywhere you have access to a microwave.

Although oats are awesome, many other whole grains are available to add variety to your meals. To start the whole grain adventure, try quinoa. Quinoa has been trendy for a while now, but actually it dates back to 15th-century Inca civilization. This ancient grain is really a pseudo seed with an excellent protein profile for plant-based diets as it contains all essential amino acids, making it one of the few complete plant proteins. Quinoa makes a great alternative to oats or rice and can even be cooked together in the same pot, thanks to similar cooking times. Try the Pumpkin Spice Quinoa Oat Bake breakfast casserole that can even be prepped in advance, frozen, and reheated on time-crunched mornings.

Finally, don't dismiss the power of a good piece of toast that has been dressed up with nutritious toppings. To help optimize your health, choose breads that are made with whole grains over more processed and enriched options. It's a simple swap. Another perk of whole grain breads is they tend to hold up better in French toast–type dishes and are more satiating overall. Try the Hip-Pea Avocado Toast, which is loaded with so much vegetable goodness that you can feel righteous all day!

Anything-But-Basic Oatmeal Packets

PREP TIME: 3 MINUTES | COOK TIME: 2 MINUTES | YIELD: 1 SERVING

INGREDIENTS

½ cup old-fashioned rolled oats

2 teaspoons chia seeds

2 teaspoons dried milk (milk powder)

1 teaspoon brown or granulated sugar or 1:1 measurement equivalent sweetener

Pinch of salt

Apple Pie:

2 tablespoons chopped, dried apples

1 tablespoon toasted, chopped walnuts

¼ teaspoon ground cinnamon

Chocolate Cherry Cashew:

2 teaspoons unsweetened cocoa powder

2 tablespoons freeze-dried or dried cherries

2 tablespoons toasted, chopped cashews

Pina Colada:

2 tablespoons chopped freeze-dried or dried pineapple

2 tablespoons toasted, unsweetened shredded coconut

DIRECTIONS

1 To assemble a one-serving oatmeal packet, place the oats, chia seeds, dried milk, sweetener, and salt directly inside a sandwich-sized, zip-top plastic baggie (no need to dirty a bowl).

2 Refer to the recipe and measure in your chosen "mix-ins" (apple pie, chocolate cherry cashew, or pina colada) sealing the baggie and tossing lightly to combine.

3 When you're ready to make the oatmeal, pour the contents of the baggie into a bowl or mug and add ¾ cup water; stir to combine.

4 Microwave on *high* for 90 seconds to 2 minutes, watching vigilantly to ensure the oats don't boil over. If it seems about to overflow, pause cooking for 15 seconds to cool down (and deflate) before resuming.

TIP: With additional ingredients, repeat Steps 1 and 2 however many times you'd like to stockpile additional servings. Sealed, dry packets will last in the pantry for about 2 months.

VARY IT! Get creative and pick your favorite ingredient combos to mix in, based approximately on measurements given previously.

TIP: Toasting the nuts and coconut for these variations is simple! Just add chopped nuts or coconut to a non stick skillet and stir continuously over medium heat for about 2 minutes, or until they turn lightly brown and aromatic.

Banana Bread Baked Oatmeal

PREP TIME: 5 MINUTES | COOK TIME: 25 MINUTES | YIELD: 1 SERVING

INGREDIENTS

½ cup milk of choice

2 tablespoons egg from carton, or 1 fresh egg white

1 tablespoon honey

1 tablespoon salted butter, melted (and slightly cooled)

3 tablespoons mashed banana

½ cup old-fashioned rolled oats

¼ teaspoon baking soda

¼ teaspoon ground cinnamon

Pinch of salt

1 tablespoon toasted, chopped walnuts or pecans

Banana slices and extra walnuts, for topping (optional)

DIRECTIONS

1 Preheat the oven to 350 degrees.

2 In a bowl or glass measuring cup, whisk together milk, egg, honey, melted butter, and mashed banana.

3 Mix in the oats, baking soda, cinnamon, salt, and walnuts until combined.

4 Spray a 16-ounce baking dish or two 6-ounce ramekins with cooking spray and pour in the oatmeal batter (dividing evenly if using two ramekins).

5 Bake for 25 minutes or until set and an inserted toothpick pulls out mostly clean.

6 Serve with toppings, as desired.

VARY IT! Substitute the mashed banana for an equal amount of canned pumpkin puree for Pumpkin Bread Baked Oatmeal.

Cold Brew Overnight Oats

PREP TIME: 2 MINUTES (PLUS 3 HOURS TO CHILL) | YIELD: 1 SERVING

INGREDIENTS

½ cup old-fashioned rolled oats

1 tablespoon chia seeds

1 teaspoon unsweetened cocoa powder

Pinch of salt

⅓ cup cold brew coffee (not concentrate) or cooled coffee

¼ cup almond, coconut, or oat milk

1–2 teaspoons honey

1 tablespoon almond butter

1 to 2 tablespoons milk of choice, for serving

2 teaspoons mini chocolate chips, for serving

DIRECTIONS

1 Place the oats, chia seeds, cocoa powder, and salt into a 12-ounce glass canning jar with lid.

2 Pour in the cold brew, coffee, the milk, and honey; screw on the lid and shake well to combine.

3 Gently stir in the honey and nut butter.

4 Refrigerate at least 3 hours or overnight until the liquid is absorbed.

5 Before eating, stir in a splash of milk to achieve desired consistency, and sprinkle with chocolate chips.

VARY IT! If you're not a coffee fan, try chai tea as a substitute.

Pumpkin Spice Quinoa Oat Bake

PREP TIME: 5 MINUTES	COOK TIME: 45 MINUTES	YIELD: 2 SERVINGS

INGREDIENTS

½ cup milk

3 tablespoons canned pumpkin puree

2 tablespoons egg white from carton

¼ teaspoon vanilla extract

¼ cup steel cut oats

⅓ cup quinoa, rinsed

2 tablespoons brown sugar

½ cup peanut butter powder

¼ teaspoon pumpkin pie spice

¼ teaspoon baking powder

⅛ teaspoon salt

1 tablespoon pepitas

DIRECTIONS

1 Preheat the oven to 375 degrees.

2 In bowl, whisk together ½ cup of water, milk, pumpkin puree, egg white, and vanilla extract.

3 In another bowl, toss together the dry ingredients including steel cut oats, quinoa, brown sugar, peanut butter powder, pumpkin pie spice, baking powder, and salt.

4 Mix the dry ingredients into bowl with the wet ingredients until combined.

5 Spray a 6-inch round cake pan (or baking dish) with cooking spray. Pour in the oat mixture. It will be very watery looking, but the liquid all gets absorbed during baking.

6 Bake for 25 minutes until the top is setting. Remove and sprinkle with the pepitas; don't stir.

7 Return to the pan oven and bake for an additional 15 to 20 minutes, until the middle is set and lightly browning on top.

VARY IT! Save leftover canned pumpkin for future use by freezing it in mini muffin tins. Then pop out the frozen puree and keep in zip-top bag in freezer until needed. Use in smoothies, seasonal coffees, baked goods, and other recipes.

Microwave Cheddar Breakfast Grits

PREP TIME: 1 MINUTE | COOK TIME: 8 MINUTES | YIELD: 1 SERVING

INGREDIENTS

¼ cup yellow corn grits (not instant)

¾ cup whole milk, divided

Pinch of salt

1 tablespoon shredded sharp cheddar cheese

1 tablespoon finely sliced scallions, for garnish (optional)

DIRECTIONS

1 In a 4-cup, microwave-safe bowl, add the grits and most of the milk (reserve 2 tablespoons). Allow plenty of room at the top of the bowl to allow for grits to simmer and rise up without overflowing.

2 Microwave on 50 percent power for 6 to 8 minutes, stopping to stir at the halfway point. If still too thin, cook in additional 30-second intervals on 100 percent power, stirring and checking between.

3 When the grits have thickened, remove and add the remaining milk and the cheese. Stir until the cheese has melted in and the grits are creamy.

4 Top with the sliced scallions and additional cheese, if desired.

TIP: Top with a fried egg and sausage crumbles or bacon to create a super-satisfying meal.

Good Ole Granola

INGREDIENTS

1 tablespoon honey

1 tablespoon natural-style nut or seed butter

½ teaspoon vanilla extract

¼ teaspoon ground cinnamon

Pinch of salt

½ cup old-fashioned, rolled oats

¼ cup raw chopped nuts or seeds of choice

2 tablespoons unsweetened coconut flakes

2 tablespoons dried fruit of choice, or 1 tablespoon chocolate chips

DIRECTIONS

1 Preheat the oven to 300 degrees and line a small rimmed baking pan with parchment paper.

2 In a bowl, add the honey, nut butter, vanilla, cinnamon, and salt and mix well.

3 Stir in the oats, nuts, and coconut flakes into the wet mixture until everything is evenly coated.

4 On the prepared baking pan, spread the mixture onto the pan in even layer.

5 Bake for 12 minutes and then remove from the oven and stir, leaving clumps intact.

6 Return to the oven and bake for about 8 additional minutes until golden brown and aromatic.

7 Remove from the oven and let cool on the pan before tossing in the dried fruit or chocolate chips. Store in an airtight container on the counter or in the fridge for up to 1 month.

NOTE: You can bake this granola in a small toaster oven. Try lowering the rack to the lower one-third of the toaster oven and reducing the temperature to 275 degrees.

TIP: Enjoy your granola over yogurt or ice cream, with milk, over stewed fruit, or just as-is off the baking sheet!

Quick Quinoa Bowl with Apricots and Almonds

PREP TIME: 2 MINUTES	COOK TIME: 8 MINUTES	YIELD: 1 SERVING

INGREDIENTS

⅓ cup dry quinoa

Pinch of salt

2 tablespoons toasted almond slivers

¼ cup almond milk

¼ teaspoon ground ginger

¼ teaspoon ground cinnamon

1 tablespoon brown sugar (or more to taste)

1 to 2 fresh, ripe apricots

DIRECTIONS

1 Rinse the quinoa in a fine-mesh strainer to remove any bitterness.

2 Fill a 2-cup capacity glass measuring cup with ⅔ Cup of water; add the rinsed quinoa and the salt.

3 Microwave on high for 3 minutes; let rest for 2 minutes. Cook another 3 minutes or until all the water is absorbed. Fluff with a fork.

4 While the quinoa is cooking, toast the almond slivers in the oven or in a small skillet for 1 to 2 minutes, until it turns lightly golden brown. Set aside.

5 Stir the almond milk, ginger, cinnamon, and brown sugar into the fluffed quinoa.

6 Dice the apricot(s) and stir into the quinoa; microwave another 1 minute. Top with the toasted almonds.

VARY IT! Substitute the apricots for peaches.

Nostalgic French Toast

INGREDIENTS

1 large egg

3 tablespoons whole milk

¼ teaspoon vanilla extract

4 teaspoons all-purpose flour

4 teaspoons granulated sugar

⅛ teaspoon ground cinnamon

Pinch of salt

2 teaspoons salted butter

2 slices thick sandwich bread, preferably whole grain

Pure maple syrup, for serving (optional)

DIRECTIONS

1 In a shallow bowl, whisk together the egg, milk, vanilla, flour, sugar, cinnamon, and salt.

2 Heat a 12-inch skillet over medium heat; add butter to melt.

3 Dip both sides of one bread slice into the egg mixture, sopping up about half the liquid. Keep the remainder of the egg dip for second slice.

4 Place the dipped bread in the skillet; and immediately place the second slice in the egg dip and quickly sop up the remaining liquids. Place in the skillet next to first slice.

5 Cook both slices 3 to 4 minutes on each side or until golden brown. Slide out onto a plate.

6 Slide the toast onto plate and serve with maple syrup, if desired.

TIP: If you have a smaller skillet, you can make each piece individually and keep the first slice warm by just letting it hang on a plate in the smaller space of the microwave (no actual microwaving). If you have doubled the batch, finished slices can also wait on a baking sheet in an oven preheated to 200 degrees.

Munchy–Crunchy French Toast

PREP TIME: 5 MINUTES	COOK TIME: 8 MINUTES	YIELD: 1 SERVING

INGREDIENTS

6 tablespoons egg from carton, or 1 large egg plus 1 egg white

2 tablespoons half-and-half or whole milk

Pinch of salt

¼ cup frosted cornflakes cereal, crushed

2 tablespoons quick oats (not instant)

2 tablespoons sliced almonds

2 slices brioche, challah, or whole wheat bread

2 teaspoons salted butter

Pure maple syrup, for serving

DIRECTIONS

1 In a shallow bowl, whisk together the eggs, half-and-half, vanilla, and salt.

2 In a separate shallow bowl, toss the cornflakes with the oats and almonds.

3 Dip both sides of one bread slice into the egg mixture, then the cereal mixture. Pat down the cereal coating a bit to help it stick. Repeat for the second slice of bread.

4 Heat a 12-inch skillet over medium heat; add the butter to melt.

5 Place the coated bread in the skillet; cook 3 to 4 minutes on each side or until golden brown.

6 Serve with maple syrup.

VARY IT! Substitute cornflakes for lightly crushed chocolate or fruit-flavored puffed rice cereal.

Strawberry–Almond Yogurt Toast

PREP TIME: 5 MINUTES | COOK TIME: 15 MINUTES | YIELD: 1 SERVING

INGREDIENTS

2 tablespoons of liquid egg (about ½ whisked large egg)

3 tablespoons unsweetened Greek yogurt

2 teaspoons honey

⅛ teaspoon vanilla extract

2 slices hearty bread, preferably brioche, challah, or a denser, baker-style wheat or sourdough

⅓ cup sliced strawberries

1 tablespoon sliced almonds

Powdered sugar and/or mini chocolate chips, for topping (optional)

DIRECTIONS

1 In a small bowl, stir together the egg, yogurt, honey, and vanilla until very smooth. Set aside.

2 Using the back of a spoon or fingers, "smoosh" the bread in the center of each slice to make an indention extending about ⅓- to ½-inch from the edges. (It does not need to be a precise shape.)

3 Place the bread on a baking sheet for the oven or an air fryer basket or tray. Fill the indention with half of the yogurt mixture and top with half of the strawberries and half of the almonds; repeat for the remaining slice of bread.

4 Air fry for 8 to 9 minutes, or bake for 12 to 15 minutes, until the yogurt has a glossy sheen, fruit is caramelizing, and almonds and bread are both turning light golden brown.

5 If desired, sprinkle with powdered sugar and/or mini chocolate chips.

Hip-Pea Avocado Toast

PREP TIME: 5 MINUTES | COOK TIME: 3 MINUTES | YIELD: 1 SERVING

INGREDIENTS

4 ounces ripe avocado, seeded and peeled (about ½ of a large avocado)

¼ cup frozen peas, thawed

2 teaspoons lime juice

1 teaspoon lime zest

¼ teaspoon garlic salt

2 slices hearty whole grain and seed bread

Small handful alfalfa sprouts or pea shoots

1 tablespoon Ranch dressing

2 teaspoons pepitas

DIRECTIONS

1 In a medium bowl, use a fork to mash together the avocado, peas, lime juice, lime zest, and garlic salt. Set aside.

2 Toast the two slices of bread to the desired level of doneness, about 2 to 3 minutes in the toaster oven.

3 Spread the avocado mixture evenly on top of the two slices of toasted bread.

4 Top with the sprouts, drizzle with the Ranch dressing, and sprinkle with the pepitas.

VARY IT! Use a different dressing or choice of seeds or nuts.

Sweet Potato Toast

PREP TIME: 2 MINUTES | COOK TIME: 30 MINUTES | YIELD: 1 SERVING

INGREDIENTS

1 large sweet potato, relatively tubular in shape (approximately ¼ will be used)

Olive oil cooking spray

Salt

DIRECTIONS

1 Preheat the oven to 350 degrees. (if using an air fryer, don't turn it on until prepped and ready to air fry.)

2 Scrub and dry the sweet potato, leaving the skin on.

3 Slice the sweet potato in half lengthwise and then slice two lengthwise planks from one half, about ¼- to ⅓-inch thickness. Reserve the remaining sweet potato for another use or to make more toasts (they reheat well).

4 Place planks onto baking sheet for oven. If using an air fryer, set planks in the air fryer basket or tray. Spray with the olive oil and sprinkle with salt. Flip to the other side and spray with the olive oil and season with salt.

5 Bake in the oven for about 30 minutes, flipping after 15 minutes. Or, air-fry for 10 to 12 minutes at 390 degrees, no preheating. Flip the planks with tongs and air-fry for another 8 to 10 minutes or until both sides are browning and crispy.

6 Remove from the heat and let cool 3 minutes before topping as desired.

TIP: When baking for the crispiest results, use a wire/mesh rack sitting on a sheet pan.

TIP: To reheat cold sweet potato toasts, either air-fry at 390 degrees for 3 minutes or stick them in the pop-up toaster for a cycle on a medium setting (often marked 4 or 5).

NOTE: You can use a smaller sweet potato, but they won't reheat as well in a pop-up style toaster.

VARY IT! Looking for topping ideas? Try simple butter and cinnamon, nut butter, hummus, smashed avocado, cheese spreads like pimento cheese or flavored whipped cream cheese, bacon jam, or any creative topping combos you can dream up. This grain-free toast also works as a lovely side dish for dinner or paired with a salad.

Chapter 8

Healthy Smoothies, Parfaits, and Breakfast Puddings

Smoothies, bowls, parfaits, and puddings are so quick and easy to whip up, making them a life-saver on days when your plate is full with life's responsibilities. In fact, many of the ideas in this chapter will let you hit the snooze button one more time and still make it out the door with a nutritious meal in your belly or a to-go smoothie cup, as the case may be.

Add extra fruit and even vegetables to your day and get it done before the close of morning — that's winning! Smoothies and similar recipes pack wholesome, nutrient-packed ingredients and typically feature multiple servings of produce to get you well on your way to meeting the daily recommended amounts of vital nutrients. Plus, it's easy to swap and customize with the fruits and vegetables you favor; you won't believe that vegetables like spinach and zucchini are blended undiscernibly into the Hidden Spinach Chocolate Smoothie. Try it!

There is also flexibility in how to sweeten this assortment of milk-, yogurt-, chia seed–, and cottage cheese–based recipes. The fruit in these recipes will add natural sweetness, but ingredient lists also suggest honey or pure maple syrup and healthier alternatives to sugar. Another option, and one that helps moderate carbohydrate intake, is to use the sweetener alternative of your choice. Stevia and monk fruit sweeteners are two natural options with few or no calories and carbs.

The no-cook breakfast ideas will keep you cool as a cucumber and lop minutes off the breakfast hour. Who has a full hour, anyway?! If you want to save even more time on morning preparation, then chop, dice, measure, and set out all your ingredients in the fridge the night before. Heck, for smoothies, just load up all the non-frozen ingredients in the blender pitcher and keep it chilled overnight. If you need more time-savings, make your meals ahead. The Chai-Spiced Chia Pudding and Healthy Blueberry FroYo Cups can be made the night before so they are ready to greet you as soon as you stumble into the kitchen.

SWEETENING SMOOTHIES

Smoothies are best made "to taste" when it comes to sweetness. Everyone seems to have a different preference. The sweet level in smoothies can be affected by a number of factors including type of fruit used, ripeness, how much juice is used, and other mix-ins that may be already pre-sweetened like yogurts and sweetened nut milks. If you like to make your smoothie sweeter, honey, molasses, date syrup, maple syrup are all good natural options, but be aware they do add extra calories. Stevia and monk fruit powders, syrups, or liquid drops are naturally sourced ways to add sweetness, while minimizing calories and carbs and keeping you away from controversial and potentially harmful sweeteners such as aspartame and saccharine.

It's best to start with a small amount, a teaspoon or two of the syrups, and just a little packet or two (or a half-dozen drops) of natural sweetener alternatives. Mix the smoothie to completion, including any ice desired (as it's a diluter), and take a sip. Adjust accordingly and sparingly — it's not as easy to take away the sweetness! However, if you do find your smoothie is sickly sweet, you can add ½ teaspoon of apple cider vinegar, lemon, lime, or other acidic juice to counteract the sugary taste.

Blueberry Cheesecake Smoothie

INGREDIENTS

¾ cup milk of choice

⅓ cup whole milk cottage cheese

1 cup frozen blueberries

2 teaspoons honey, or 2 packets sweetener

½ teaspoon vanilla extract

Ice (optional)

1 graham cracker square, crumbled, for topping

DIRECTIONS

1 Pour the milk into a blender and add the cottage cheese, blueberries, sweetener, and vanilla. Blend until smooth.

2 If needed, blend in ice cubes a few at a time, until the desired consistency is achieved.

3 Top the finished smoothie with the crumbled graham cracker square.

VARY IT! Swap the frozen blueberries for frozen raspberries, strawberries, or pitted dark cherries.

Hidden Spinach Chocolate Smoothie

PREP TIME: 5 MINUTES | **YIELD: 1 SERVING**

INGREDIENTS

¾ cup milk of choice

¾ cup fresh baby spinach

2 teaspoons pure maple syrup, or 2 packets sweetener

1 tablespoon natural nut butter (like peanut, almond, or cashew)

2 teaspoons unsweetened cocoa powder

½ cup frozen zucchini

Ice (optional)

DIRECTIONS

1 Pour the milk in a blender and add the spinach, sweetener, nut butter, cocoa powder, and zucchini. Blend until smooth.

2 If needed, blend in ice cubes a few at a time, until the desired consistency is achieved.

VART IT! Instead of spinach, try an equal portion of chopped kale.

Flex–Time Protein Smoothie

PREP TIME: 5 MINUTES | **YIELD: 1 SERVING**

INGREDIENTS

1 cup 2-percent milk

¼ cup 2-percent Greek yogurt, plain or a flavor to complete fruit choices

½ large banana, frozen in 1-inch chunks

2 tablespoons hemp hearts

½ cup chopped fruit (like mango, berries, dark cherries, or peaches), fresh or frozen

Ice, (optional)

Sweetener to taste such as honey, pure maple syrup, or stevia packets (optional)

DIRECTIONS

1 Pour the milk into a blender and add the Greek yogurt, banana, hemp hearts, and fruit. Blend until smooth.

2 If needed, blend in ice, a couple of cubes at a time, until the desired consistency is achieved.

TIP: Need to ensure that you get enough protein each day? Try making this smoothie from day to day by choosing a different fruit for variety. Or try a combination of fruits that total ½ cup combined!

Watermelon Smoothie Bowl

PREP TIME: 10 MINUTES
(PLUS 2 HOURS TO FREEZE)

YIELD: 1 SERVING

INGREDIENTS

1 personal-sized watermelon

2 ounces canned unsweetened coconut milk (see Tip)

½ large banana

Ice (optional)

1 kiwi, peeled and sliced

2 tablespoons shredded unsweetened coconut

¼ teaspoon black sesame seeds, for topping

DIRECTIONS

1 Slice the watermelon in half crosswise and carefully scoop out flesh. Put 2 cups of this chopped-up watermelon in the freezer for 2 hours to overnight. Store the remaining watermelon chunks for another use, but save the scooped-out shell covered in fridge to be used as a bowl later.

2 Freeze the coconut milk in an ice cube tray or small flat container to break up and fit in the blender.

3 Place the frozen watermelon chunks in a blender and add the frozen coconut milk and banana. Blend until smooth.

4 If the watermelon mixture looks thin, blend in ice as needed to thicken it up.

5 Scoop the watermelon mixture into the watermelon-rind bowl.

6 Cut the kiwi slices in half and place around edge of the bowl to resemble the green watermelon skin.

7 Sprinkle the shredded coconut around the edge of the kiwi slices to resemble the white part of rind.

8 Sprinkle the black sesame seeds in the center of bowl to resemble watermelon seeds.

TIP: Don't let the extra coconut milk go to waste; freeze the remaining contents of the can in ice cube trays (or mini muffin tins). Most trays will hold about 1 ounce (2 tablespoons) of coconut milk. Once frozen, transfer the cubes to freezer bags for long-term storage. Pop out what you need to use for smoothies, sauces, and desserts later.

TIP: If your watermelon isn't super sweet, consider adding a sweetener like honey, maple syrup, date syrup, stevia, or monk fruit to taste. Start with just a little and adjust as needed.

Chai-Spiced Chia Pudding

PREP TIME: 5 MINUTES (PLUS OVERNIGHT CHILLING)	COOK TIME: 1 MINUTE	YIELD: 1 SERVING

INGREDIENTS

1 cup unsweetened coconut milk from carton

1 chai tea bag

2 teaspoons honey or 2 sweetener packets

¼ cup chia seeds

Toppings of choice

DIRECTIONS

1 Place the coconut milk in a 12-ounce canning jar and microwave for 1 minute, or until nearly boiling.

2 Add the chai tea bag to the jar and let the tea steep for 5 minutes.

3 Remove the tea bag from the jar, squeezing out any sopped-up liquid back into the jar.

4 Stir in the sweetener and chia seeds. Put the lid on the jar and refrigerate overnight.

5 To serve, sprinkle with the toppings of your choice.

TIP: Try various toppings such as diced fresh or dried fruit; coconut, nuts, or seeds; or nut butters, syrups, or honey.

Blended-Smooth Banana Chocolate Chia Pudding

PREP TIME: 5 MINUTES
(PLUS 3 HOURS TO CHILL)

YIELD: 1 SERVING

INGREDIENTS

¾ cup unsweetened almond milk

1 tablespoon unsweetened cocoa powder

3 tablespoons chia seeds

2 teaspoons honey, pure maple syrup, or 2 packets sweetener

¼ large banana

Greek yogurt, banana slices, and mini chocolate chips/cocoa nibs, for topping (optional)

DIRECTIONS

1 Pour the almond milk into a blender and add the cocoa powder, chia seeds, sweetener, and the banana. Blend for approximately 45 seconds until smooth and the chia seeds are incorporated.

2 Pour the mixture into a 12-ounce glass jar or bowl and chill for at least 3 hours to set up.

3 Top with a dollop of yogurt, banana slices, and mini chocolate chips, if desired.

VARY IT! Make a protein-boosted version by swapping the 1 tablespoon of unsweetened cocoa powder for 1 tablespoon of your favorite protein powder in any flavor.

Healthy Blueberry FroYo Cups

PREP TIME: 10 MINUTES (PLUS 2 HOURS CHILLING)	COOK TIME: 20 SECONDS	YIELD: 2 SERVINGS

INGREDIENTS

1 tablespoon natural peanut butter

1 tablespoon honey, pure maple syrup, or date syrup

½ cup granola

⅔ cup unsweetened Greek yogurt

½ cup fresh or thawed frozen blueberries

DIRECTIONS

1 In a small microwave-safe bowl, heat the peanut butter and honey for 20 seconds or until melted. Stir well to combine.

2 Add the granola to the peanut butter mixture and mix well until everything is coated.

3 Place half of the granola mixture in an 8-ounce ramekin, pressing down lightly with a spoon. Repeat with the remaining granola mixture and another 8-ounce ramekin.

4 In another bowl, mash together the yogurt and blueberries until combined. Some blueberry lumps are fine, even desirable.

5 Pour the yogurt mixture evenly between the two ramekins.

6 Freeze for a minimum of 2 hours or overnight. If frozen overnight, let the ramekins sit on a counter for a few minutes to slightly soften up before eating.

VARY IT! Instead of blueberries, try blackberries or raspberries.

NOTE! Sweeteners that are granulated or powdered, like table sugar or stevia, will *not* substitute well in this recipe. A syrup-consistency sweetener is needed to amplify the stickiness that holds the granola together.

PB&J Cottage Cheese Bowl

PREP TIME: 3 MINUTES YIELD: 1 SERVING

INGREDIENTS

½ cup 2-percent cottage cheese

1 tablespoon natural peanut butter

1 tablespoon all-fruit preserves or jam (any flavor)

1 tablespoon unsalted chopped peanuts

DIRECTIONS

1 Place the cottage cheese in a bowl and drizzle on the peanut butter (see the sidebar) and dollop on the jam.

2 Sprinkle with the chopped peanuts.

3 Eat immediately or make at night and store in the fridge covered for breakfast in the morning.

TIP: If desired, top with chopped fresh fruit to match jam flavor.

DRIZZLING PEANUT BUTTER

If you're having trouble making the perfect peanut butter drizzle, first make sure that you aren't using conventional peanut butter that uses hydrogenated vegetable oil to create a uniform consistency. This stuff will never drizzle! Instead, choose a natural peanut butter consisting of just peanuts and a bit of salt (and sometimes fancy upgrades like cinnamon or other natural flavorings). You'll notice that with jars of natural peanut butter, the peanut oils rise to the top of the peanut solids — elbow grease is needed to mix them back together. Try leaving your jar upside down for a couple of days (to redistribute the oils) before stirring, or using an immersion blender. If your nut butter still won't drizzle gracefully from a spoon, try warming it up in the microwave. Add a tablespoon of peanut butter to a microwave-safe bowl and heat on high for 20 seconds. Stir and heat again for 10 seconds. Repeat in 10-second increments until the nut butter drips delightfully from your spoon.

Banana Cream Breakfast Parfait

PREP TIME: 7 MINUTES	YIELD: 1 SERVING

INGREDIENTS

1 medium banana

¾ cup 2-percent cottage cheese

2 teaspoons honey, or 2 packets sweetener

½ teaspoon vanilla extract

½ cup dairy-free whipped topping, thawed (regular or sugar-free)

7 vanilla wafer cookies, coarsely crumbled

1 tablespoon chopped pecans, for topping

DIRECTIONS

1 Peel and slice the banana. Set aside.

2 Place the cottage cheese, sweetener, and vanilla extract in a blender and blend for approximately 45 seconds or until smooth.

3 Stir in the whipped topping gently with spoon until combined.

4 In a 16-ounce bowl or canning jar, place one-third of the banana slices on the bottom, pour over one-third of the cottage cheese mixture, and top with one-third of the crumbled cookies. Repeat the layers in the same order two more times.

5 Top with the chopped pecans.

VARY IT!: Finish off with extra whipped topping and sprinkle with toffee bits or caramel sauce for a clever dessert!

3

Fueling Up for Lunch

Level up your lunch hour with an easy, homemade dish that tastes better and fresher than most any restaurant, food truck, or deli cart selection.

Save a buck by packing a "brown bag" mid-day meal to avoid delivery fees, tips, and over-priced convenience foods. Make the most of your time by not standing in line, waiting for table service, or twiddling your thumbs on the delivery wait.

Take charge of your nutrition by knowing exactly what you are consuming rather than scarfing down the typical high-calorie, high-fat, high-sodium lunch meal.

Bust out of your lunchtime rut by trying new recipes that include easy-to-make salads, soups, sammies, pizzas, and more.

veggie intake

» Adding protein to salads to create a nourishing, balanced, filling meal

» Whipping up homemade salad dressings in an amount you'll actually be able to finish

» Sweetening your day naturally with a side of fruit salad

Chapter 9

Salads for Every Season

Salads are a super way to add more veggies (and fruit) to your day! In addition to natural flavor and a gratifying crunchy texture, eating fresh, raw produce each day has profound health benefits that can be linked with disease prevention, maintaining a healthy weight, and enjoying abounding energy.

Plus, you get that "big lunch" satisfaction when eating a ginormous plate of leafy greens loaded with other healthy toppings while skirting the drawbacks that come from scarfing down a more calorie-dense option with half the volume. It's a smart way to avoid the post-lunch slump that can cause you to nod off at your desk.

Do ensure that you are getting enough protein in or alongside your salad and not just eating a plate of greens (or what some might jokingly call "rabbit food"). Without adequate protein on your salad such as beef, chicken, eggs, beans, cheese, nuts (or any combination), your energy to go-go-go will not be sustained nearly as long. While vegetables and fruits contain a small amount of protein (a surprise to many), it's almost never enough protein to make a full meal. Experts recommend 20 to 30 grams of protein at each meal and the entree-style salad recipes in this chapter will get you there.

Whip up a protein-packed, meaty "salad" like the Cilantro Lime Chicken Salad and pile on a delicate bed of greens, or even create a roll-up in a large lettuce leaf to maximize veggie intake. Or repurpose last night's leftovers into a mouth-watering midday meal, such as chopping up cold, cooked beef for the Smoked Brisket Kale Salad with Creamy BBQ Dressing.

Of course, salads don't have to be the main feature. Side salads make great side-kicks to a meal, any time of day. Green salad is a go-to, but check out the Festive Winter Fruit Salad with Creamy Chia Seed Dressing to get your fruit fix any time of year.

Cilantro Lime Chicken Salad

PREP TIME: 10 MINUTES | YIELD: 2 SERVINGS

INGREDIENTS

½ cup plain Greek yogurt

1½ teaspoons lime juice

⅛ teaspoon garlic powder

⅛ teaspoon onion powder

Pinch each of salt and ground black pepper

2 tablespoons chopped red onion

2 tablespoons finely chopped fresh cilantro

¼ cup chopped celery

6 ounces chopped or shredded cooked chicken breast

DIRECTIONS

1 In medium bowl, mix together the Greek yogurt, lime juice, garlic powder, onion powder, salt, and pepper.

2 Add the red onion, cilantro, celery, and chicken to the yogurt mixture and stir until combined. Season with additional salt and pepper, if needed.

3 Enjoy sandwiched between bread, in a pita, or on a bed of greens.

TIP: If you don't have precooked chicken in the freezer, use rotisserie chicken for a time-saving shortcut.

Crazy Cobb Salad

INGREDIENTS

1 medium zucchini, spiralized into noodles

3 ounces chopped cooked chicken breast

1 large hard-boiled egg, quartered

2 strips cooked bacon, broken in bite-sized pieces

6 cherry tomatoes, halved

10 baby carrots, quartered lengthwise

2 tablespoons crumbled blue cheese

For Dressing:

1½ tablespoons buttermilk (see Note)

1 tablespoon mayonnaise

1 tablespoon full-fat sour cream

¾ teaspoon minced onion

½ teaspoon dried parsley

¼ teaspoon garlic powder

¼ teaspoon dried dill

⅛ teaspoon salt

⅛ teaspoon ground black pepper

DIRECTIONS

1 On a serving platter, spread out the spiralized zucchini, cutting up any huge strands. If you don't have a spiralizer, use a vegetable peeler to make long ribbons going the length of the zucchini.

2 Use the spirals or ribbons as a bed to arrange the chicken, egg, bacon, tomatoes, and carrots individually. Cobb salads are usually "composed" like this, but if you prefer, you can toss everything together.

3 To make the dressing, whisk all the ingredients in a small bowl and serve with the salad.

NOTE: To avoid purchasing a container of buttermilk that you may not be able to finish, substitute the buttermilk in a recipe for 1½ tablespoons whole milk and ⅛ teaspoon vinegar. Let sit for 10 minutes to sour before using in recipe. For time savings, you may skip making the dressing and substitute your favorite purchased Ranch dressing.

TIP: Save the second serving for another meal by dividing portions equally — one on your plate, one in an airtight storage container or wide-mouth canning jar for a ready-made meal later. It should keep for 2 to 3 days in the fridge if you put salad dressing on the side (or as the bottom layer in a jar salad).

Chicken-Avocado-Berry Salad with Chipotle Strawberry Dressing

PREP TIME: 20 MINUTES	YIELD: 1 SERVING

INGREDIENTS

2 cups salad greens

¼ cup fresh blueberries

¼ cup sliced strawberries

¼ medium avocado, chopped

1 tablespoon pepita seeds

2 tablespoons crumbled queso fresco or feta cheese

3 ounces cooked chicken breast, sliced

For Dressing:

¼ cup chopped fresh strawberries

4 teaspoons honey

1½ tablespoons olive oil

2 teaspoons white wine vinegar

2 teaspoons lime juice

⅛ teaspoon salt

¼ teaspoon chipotle chili powder

DIRECTIONS

1 On a serving plate, create a bed of salad greens. Scatter about the blueberries, strawberries, avocado, pepita seeds, and cheese. Top with the chicken slices.

2 To make the dressing, place the chopped strawberries in a small bowl and drizzle with honey. Stir to combine and let sit for 10 to 15 minutes to macerate.

3 After the strawberries have softened, use a fork to vigorously mash them together.

4 Add the olive oil, vinegar, lime juice, salt, and chipotle chili powder to the strawberry mixture and whisk with the fork until incorporated.

5 Drizzle the dressing over the salad and enjoy!

NOTE: For timesavings, make the dressing first (or even the day before, storing in the fridge) and allow to macerate while preparing the salad ingredients.

TIP: Keep the unused portion of your avocado fresh for a few days in the fridge by one of these two methods. The first method is to keep avocado in its skin, but remove the pit. Then rub the exposed flesh with lemon juice and wrap tightly in plastic wrap. The acids in the lemon juice slow down the browning process. Secondly, you can keep the avocado in skin, remove the pit, and lay flesh-side down into a container filled with a few inches of water. The water creates a barrier to air and stops the avocado from oxidizing.

Smoked Brisket Kale Salad with Creamy BBQ Dressing

PREP TIME: 10 MINUTES | **COOK TIME: 15 MINUTES** | **YIELD: 1 SERVING**

INGREDIENTS

3 ounces frozen corn, thawed

1 teaspoon olive oil

¾ teaspoon Tajín seasoning (see Tip)

2 cups chopped kale

¼ teaspoon dried cranberries

2 tablespoons diced red onion

3 ounces cooked beef brisket

For Dressing:

1 tablespoon nonfat Greek yogurt

1 tablespoon spicy BBQ sauce

1½ teaspoons lime juice

1 teaspoon apple cider vinegar

⅛ teaspoon dried red pepper flakes

2 tablespoons French-fried onion pieces

DIRECTIONS

1 Preheat the oven to 400 degrees.

2 Place the corn on a rimmed baking sheet, drizzle with the olive oil, and season with the Tajín seasoning (or just season with salt and pepper).

3 Roast for 15 minutes or until softened and lightly brown in places. Set aside to cool.

4 Place the kale in a bowl and squeeze with your hands to soften. This "massaging" step helps make the kale more tender.

5 Add the dried cranberries and red onion. Chop or shred the brisket into bite-sized pieces and add to the bowl.

6 To make the dressing, mix the Greek yogurt, barbeque sauce, lime juice, vinegar, and red pepper flakes. Pour the dressing over the salad and toss until everything coated.

7 Top with French-fried onion bits before serving.

VARY IT!: Substitute dried cherries or golden raisins for dried cranberries.

NOTE: Corn may also be roasted in a toaster oven at 375 degrees for 12 to 15 minutes, or pan "toasted" in a nonstick skillet over medium heat for approximately 10 minutes, stirring frequently.

TIP: Tajín is a popular brand of seasoning mix originating from Mexico that is made from dried and ground red chilies, sea salt, and dehydrated lime. It is similar to other chile-lime seasonings, featuring a mildly spicy, citrusy, and piquant profile. Tajín is a quick- and easy-way to add zing to various recipes. It can be used in rubs and marinades, tossed with popcorn, and added as a beloved south-of-the-border way to dress up fresh fruit! In fact, you will probably find Tajín stocked in the produce department, or look for it on the spice aisle.

Speedy Steakhouse Salad with Blue Cheese

PREP TIME:18 MINUTES | COOK TIME: 8 MINUTES | YIELD: 1 SERVING

INGREDIENTS

4 ounces top sirloin steak, 1-inch thickness

2 teaspoons Montreal steak seasoning

2 teaspoons olive oil

2 cups salad greens

6 cherry tomatoes, halved

2 tablespoons finely slivered red onion

2 tablespoons bottled balsamic vinaigrette or preferred dressing

2 tablespoons crumbled blue cheese, for topping

DIRECTIONS

1 Rub both sides of the steak with the Montreal steak seasoning.

2 Pour the olive oil into a skillet and bring to medium-high heat. Add the steak and cook for approximately 3 to 4 minutes on each side for medium-rare doneness (see the sidebar "How do you know when your steak is done?").

3 Remove the steak from heat; let it rest for 5–10 minutes.

4 While the steak is resting, prepare the salad by tossing together the salad greens, tomatoes, and red onion with the vinaigrette.

5 Slice the steak thinly across the grain and add to the top of the dressed salad greens.

6 Sprinkle with the blue cheese and enjoy!

VARY IT! If you don't care for balsamic vinaigrette, creamy blue cheese dressing would make a good substitute.

HOW DO YOU KNOW WHEN YOUR STEAK IS DONE?

Well, that's a personal preference, but using an instant-read meat thermometer to determine doneness is the best way to enjoy perfectly cooked beef. Here are some guidelines to help ensure success:

- **Medium-rare:** Remove from heat at 135 degrees and allow to rest on a plate until 145 degrees

- **Medium:** Remove from heat at 150 degrees and allow to rest on a plate until 160 degrees

- **Well-done:** Remove from heat at 160 degrees and allow to rest on a plate until 170 degrees

To take the most accurate reading, insert the thermometer to the middle of thickest area of meat (horizontally from the side) steering clear of any bones or fat. Remember to remove steaks 5–10 degrees before reaching your ideal internal temperature. Steak will keep "cooking" and temperature rising after it is removed from the heat and allowed to rest for 5–10 minutes.

Chopped Salmon Salad with Tangy Asian Dressing

PREP TIME: 10 MINUTES | COOK TIME: 12 MINUTES | YIELD: 1 SERVING

INGREDIENTS

For Fish:

3 ounces salmon filet, skin on bottom

¼ teaspoon ginger paste (or fresh grated)

¼ teaspoon garlic paste (or fresh grated)

For Salad:

1 cup broccoli slaw mix

½ cup fresh sugar snap peas, coarsely chopped

2 teaspoons red onion, finely chopped

1 cup chopped Romaine lettuce

2 tablespoons chopped fresh cilantro

2 tablespoons slivered almonds, toasted, for serving

2 tablespoons crispy chow mien noodles or wonton strip topping, for serving

DIRECTIONS

1 Preheat the oven to 400 degrees or the air fryer to 390 degrees.

2 Place the salmon on a rimmed baking sheet and rub with the ginger and garlic.

3 Bake for 10–12 minutes or until cooked through and flakey. Air frying goes a little more quickly, so check for doneness at 8 minutes.

4 Remove from the oven or air fryer to cool for 10 minutes. Flake the fish and set aside while preparing the salad.

5 Place the broccoli slaw, snap peas, red onion, lettuce, and cilantro in a bowl. Set aside to make the dressing.

6 Make the dressing by adding all the dressing ingredients in a small jar and shaking until combined.

(continued)

(continued)

For Dressing:

1 tablespoon sesame oil

1 tablespoon rice wine vinegar

1 teaspoon honey

1 teaspoon lime juice

½ teaspoon soy sauce

¼ teaspoon ginger paste (or fresh grated)

¼ teaspoon garlic past (or fresh pressed)

⅛ teaspoon ground black pepper

7 Pour all the dressing onto the lettuce mixture, toss well to coat. Right before serving, add the flaked salmon, almonds, and chow mien noodles and stir gently.

NOTE: This is great way to use up leftover salmon from a restaurant meal. Or, make an extra filet with this recipe, chop it up, and freeze it in an airtight container for up to 4 months. Defrost and toss in the salad!

BROCCOLI SLAW MIX

This recipe utilized a bagged broccoli slaw (sometimes called "power" slaw or "rainbow" slaw) from the produce department for time-saving and to prevent food waste. Various brands differ in their exact contents, but instead of traditional slaw mix with only shredded cabbage and carrots, you get upgrades that may include other veggies like julienned broccoli stalks, shaved Brussels sprouts, bits of kale, and chopped kohlrabi (a bulbous cruciferous veggie sometimes called a German turnip). You won't need to use the whole bag for this recipe, but they will keep in the fridge produce drawer for about a week (see the package "best by" date). Use the remaining slaw mix to spruce up a stir fry or a bowl of ramen, or mix with your favorite bottled dressing for a simple side dish.

South-of-the-Border Egg Salad

PREP TIME: 10 MINUTES | YIELD: 1 SERVING

INGREDIENTS

2 tablespoons salsa

1 tablespoon mayonnaise

⅛ teaspoon onion powder

⅛ teaspoon garlic powder

2 hard-boiled eggs (see Note)

¼ medium avocado, chopped

4 cherry tomatoes, chopped

¼ cup frozen corn, thawed

1 tablespoon chopped red onion

2 tablespoons crumbled queso fresco

DIRECTIONS

1 In a medium bowl, add the salsa, mayonnaise, onion powder, and garlic power; stir with a spatula until combined.

2 Slice the eggs in half and remove yolks from whites. Crumble up the yolks and add to the mayonnaise mixture. Coarsely chop the egg whites and add to the bowl.

3 Add the chopped avocado, tomatoes, corn, red onion, and cheese. Stir gently until everything is evenly coated with the mayonnaise mixture.

4 Enjoy on bread, a green salad, or even stuffed in a large scooped-out tomato.

NOTE: To hard-boil eggs, place the eggs in a small saucepan and cover with 1 inch of water. Bring the water to boil over medium heat and let boil 1 minute. Remove the pan from the heat, cover with a lid, and let sit for 12 minutes. Drain the hot water, fill the pot with ice water, and let it sit for 10 more minutes. Drain the pot again and peel the eggs.

Tortellini Niçoise Salad

PREP TIME: 10 MINUTES	COOK TIME: 10 MINUTES	YIELD: 1 SERVING

INGREDIENTS

¾ cup fresh green beans, trimmed and cut into 1-inch pieces

½ cup sliced fresh zucchini, cut in ¼-inch slices

½ cup cherry or grape tomatoes, sliced in half

2 teaspoons olive oil

½ teaspoon Italian herb seasoning

1 cup refrigerated cheese tortellini, about 24 pieces (see Tip)

1½ ounces pitted black olives, sliced or coarsely chopped

2 tablespoons favorite bottled balsamic vinaigrette

1 to 2 ounces baby lettuce blend

1 tablespoon crumbled feta cheese

DIRECTIONS

1 Preheat the oven to 400 degrees.

2 In a medium bowl, toss the vegetables in the olive oil and Italian seasoning until coated.

3 Spread out the vegetables in single layer on a rimmed baking sheet and roast in the oven for 8–10 minutes, stirring halfway through with a spatula.

4 After cooking, remove the vegetables and let them cool to room temperature.

5 While the vegetables are cooling, prepare the tortellini according to the package directions. After cooking, drain off the hot water and fill the pot back up with cold water and ice to cool the pasta quickly. After 5 minutes, drain the pasta again.

6 Add the cooled vegetables and olives to the pot with tortellini and gently toss with vinaigrette.

7 To serve, add a desired amount of lettuce to a plate. Top with the tortellini mixture and sprinkle with the feta cheese.

TIP: You can freeze the remaining cheese tortellini from the package for another use later. Place the uncooked tortellini in a freezer-proof bag and store in the freezer for up to 3 months.

Chickpea Kale Caesar Salad

PREP TIME: 10 MINUTES YIELD: 1 SERVING

INGREDIENTS

2 cups chopped kale

⅔ cup chickpeas from can, drained and rinsed (see Note)

1 tablespoon shelled, roasted sunflower seeds

⅓ cup precooked quinoa

For Dressing:

1½ tablespoons mayonnaise

⅛ teaspoon garlic powder

¾ teaspoon lemon juice

⅛ teaspoon Dijon mustard

¼ teaspoon Worcestershire sauce

1 tablespoon fine-grated Parmesan cheese

Pinch of ground black pepper

DIRECTIONS

1 Place the chopped kale in a bowl; massage between fists for 60 seconds to soften.

2 Add the chickpeas, sunflower seeds, and quinoa.

3 To make the dressing, use a fork to whisk together all of the ingredients and 1 teaspoon of water. If the dressing seems too thick, add a small amount of additional water, ¼ teaspoon at a time.

4 Add the dressing to the bowl with the kale and other ingredients and stir well to coat.

NOTE: It's personal preference, but if you don't care for the skins on chickpeas, lay them out on a paper towel after draining and rinsing, fold the towel over, and gently roll the chickpeas around until the thin skins slide off. Continue with the recipe as directed.

Green Machine Salad with Lemon Vinaigrette

PREP TIME: 10 MINUTES | YIELD: 1 SERVING

INGREDIENTS

1 cup arugula

1 cup baby spinach

1 ounce pea shoots, broccoli sprouts, or alfalfa sprouts

2 ounces fresh sugar snap peas, halved lengthwise

⅓ cup chopped cucumber

⅓ cup chopped green apple

2 tablespoons shelled pistachios, for topping

For Dressing:

1 tablespoon olive oil

1 tablespoon lemon juice, fresh or bottled

½ teaspoon minced garlic, garlic paste, or garlic powder

¼ teaspoon Dijon mustard

⅛ teaspoon salt

⅛ teaspoon ground black pepper

DIRECTIONS

1 On a plate or in a bowl, toss together the arugula, spinach, and pea shoots.

2 Scatter the top of the salad with the snap peas, chopped cucumber, and green apple.

3 To make the dressing, use a fork to whisk together the olive oil, lemon juice, garlic, mustard, salt, and pepper.

4 Drizzle the dressing over the salad and top with the pistachios.

TIP: If using juice from a fresh lemon, use a zester tool to remove ½ teaspoon of the peel to add to the dressing. This will give a bigger pop of lemon flavor.

Watermelon Feta Mint Salad

PREP TIME: 10 MINUTES	YIELD: 1 SERVING

INGREDIENTS

2 cups chopped watermelon

¼ cup finely slivered red onion

1 tablespoon chopped
fresh mint

2 tablespoons crumbled feta
cheese

2 teaspoons balsamic vinegar

DIRECTIONS

1 In a large bowl, combine the watermelon, red onion, mint, and feta cheese. Toss gently until combined.

2 Drizzle with the balsamic vinegar and serve chilled.

VARY IT! Blue cheese also makes a bold statement.

Festive Winter Fruit Salad with Creamy Chia Seed Dressing

PREP TIME: 10 MINUTES | YIELD: 1 SERVING

INGREDIENTS

½ cup chopped apple, skin on

½ chopped pear, skin on

½ cup grapes, halved

1 seedless tangerine, peeled and segmented

½ kiwi fruit, peeled and sliced

2 tablespoons pomegranate arils (see Tip)

2 teaspoons unsweetened shredded coconut, for topping

For Dressing:

1 teaspoon honey

1 teaspoon white wine vinegar

1 teaspoon olive oil

1 tablespoon unsweetened plain Greek yogurt

½ teaspoon black chia seeds

DIRECTIONS

1 Combine all the fruit (except the shredded coconut) in a bowl.

2 To make the dressing: In a small bowl, whisk together the honey, vinegar, olive oil and yogurt with fork. Stir in the chia seeds.

3 Pour the dressing over the salad and stir to coat evenly. Sprinkle with the shredded coconut.

VARY IT! In the dressing, substitute maple syrup for honey and use a plant-based yogurt to make this salad vegan-friendly.

TIP: Pomegranate arils are the crunchy, juicy edible seeds that are densely packed in this distinctive red fruit. The arils can be labor-intensive to remove from the fruit's inner flesh and likely to stain almost everything they touch, including fingers and cutting boards. A time- and-mess-sparing suggestion is to purchase pomegranate arils in cups from the produce department (usually displayed alongside the cut fruit). In fact, this convenience product is often easier to find than the actual whole fruit, which often only makes a seasonal holiday appearance.

Chapter **10**

Soups for Singles

oup is a fuss-free option for meal time and easy to make ahead and reheat on those days when you're craving a hot, quick meal. Plus, homemade soups can be a great way for both veggie lovers and veggie avoiders to enjoy a serving or more of vegetables diced, chopped, shredded, or pureed and almost hidden in soup.

Some recipes in this soup chapter make a nice-and-tidy, single serving. Others are more generous with two servings or a bit more. You'll quickly discover as a home chef that there is often an economy and efficiency of scale in making multiple servings at once. Sometimes it's a smart move to just chop up and use the whole onion, carton of broth, or whatever rather than having it languish in the fridge for "another day" and end up spoiling. In that case, double or triple the recipe!

Plus, soups, stews, and chilies are some of the best repeat-performance meals around, and even leftover-despisers find it hard to fault them. In fact, many former doubters will freely agree that leftover soups often taste better the next day. That extra time spent in the fridge gives the spices, broths, and flavors more time to mingle and make merry.

THE BENEFITS OF HOMEMADE SOUP

So, if you're looking for a boost in a bowl, make soup! Homemade soups and stews will fill up your body and soul without draining your wallet or stressing out Mother Nature with excess packaging. There are no mystery ingredients like weird preservatives or additives when you throw your own pot of soup together. You have total control over what goes in the pot and how much, which can help you keep to your nutrition goals; this could include eating less salt or fat and more veggies and protein.

However, you can't leave soup in the fridge indefinitely; about 3–4 days is the max for food safety and quality. You can freeze soup in airtight, freezer-proof containers or leak-proof freezer bags. Leave an inch or so of empty space at the top of containers because frozen liquids will expand!

If you need a feel-good boost mentally and physically, the Quick Comfort Chicken Rice Soup will warm your soul and help restore your body. And, if you're looking for a refreshing soup on a hot day, the One-derful Watermelon Gazpacho is sure to treat you right!

WARNING

For safety purposes, do not put the hot soup into the blender; the steam in a blender builds up and can cause the top to pop off and scalding liquid to splatter everywhere. Instead, let the soup cool 5–10 minutes before blending in a traditional blender, only fill the pitcher about half full, remove the center plug on the lid, and lightly cover it with a dish cloth. The only exception is if you have a high-end, high-powered blender that specifically says it can handle hot liquids (usually up to 170 degrees). Alternatively, you can use a stick immersion blender in the pot when the soup is at any temperature.

Easy Creamy Tomato Soup

PREP TIME: 18 MINUTES	COOK TIME: 15 MINUTES	YIELD: 1 SERVING

INGREDIENTS

1 tablespoon salted butter

¼ cup chopped onion

½ teaspoon minced garlic or garlic paste

1 cup vegetable broth

½ teaspoon dried basil leaves

1 medium tomato, or ¾ cup canned diced tomatoes

2 tablespoons unsweetened plain Greek yogurt

DIRECTIONS

1 Melt the butter in a 2-quart saucepot. Sauté the onions over medium-high heat, stirring frequently, for about 4 minutes until softened and beginning to caramelize. Add the garlic and cook for about 30–45 additional seconds, or until fragrant.

2 Reduce the heat to medium; add the broth, dried basil, and tomato and let simmer for about 10 minutes.

3 Remove from the heat and let cool for 5–10 minutes.

4 Stir in the yogurt. Pour the mixture into a blender and process until smooth.

5 If the soup has cooled too much after blending, return to the pot and heat over medium for a couple of minutes or until warmed satisfactorily.

TIP: Try pairing this tangy, creamy tomato soup with the Zesty Tuna Melt Quesadilla (recipe in Chapter 11) for a balanced comfort food lunch.

Cheesy Potato Soup

PREP TIME: 10 MINUTES | COOK TIME: 28 MINUTES | YIELD: 1 SERVING

INGREDIENTS

1 slice uncooked bacon

½ cup chopped white onion

2 tablespoons diced celery

2 tablespoons diced carrots

1 teaspoon minced garlic or garlic paste

1 cup chicken broth

8-to-10-ounce Russet potato (about 1 medium), coarsely chopped

¼ teaspoon salt

¼ teaspoon ground black pepper

½ cup milk

1 teaspoon flour

¼ cup shredded sharp white cheddar cheese

1 tablespoon sliced green scallions, for topping

DIRECTIONS

1 In a 2-quart saucepan over medium-high heat, cook the bacon until crispy, about 4 minutes per side. Remove the bacon to drain on a paper towel; leave the rendered fat in pot.

2 Add the onions, celery, and carrots to pot and sauté in bacon fat on medium-high until tender, about 3 minutes. Add the garlic and cook an additional 30 seconds.

3 Add the broth, potato, salt, and pepper to pot and bring to the boil; reduce heat and simmer, covered, for 10–12 minutes, until the potato is fork-tender.

4 Use a wooden spoon or fork to mash the softened potato into a somewhat smoother consistency.

5 Measure the milk in a spouted mixing cup. Add the flour to a mixing cup and stir until combined.

6 Pour the milk mixture slowly into the simmering soup to thicken it, stirring constantly.

7 Stir in the cheese until it is melted and the soup is heated through, about 2–3 more minutes.

8 Pour into a bowl and serve with the crumbled bacon and sliced scallions on top.

VARY IT! To make this recipe vegetarian, omit the bacon and use olive oil as cooking fat to sauté vegetables.

Very Fast Chicken Verde Soup

PREP TIME: 5 MINUTES | COOK TIME: 5 MINUTES | YIELD: 2 SERVINGS

INGREDIENTS

1 (15-ounce) can chicken broth

1 cup canned fire-roasted, diced tomatoes, undrained

7 ounces salsa verde

½ teaspoon ground cumin

6 ounces cooked chicken breast, chopped

2 ounces fresh spinach, coarsely chopped (about 2 cups)

4 ounces sour cream

Crushed tortilla chips, shredded cheddar cheese, and cilantro, for topping (optional)

DIRECTIONS

1 In a 2-quart pot, add the broth, tomatoes with juices, salsa, cumin, and chicken. Bring to boil over medium–high heat and then turn down to medium and simmer uncovered for 5 minutes.

2 Remove from the heat and stir in the spinach until wilted. Stir in the sour cream until smooth.

3 Pour into a bowl and serve warm with optional toppings.

NOTE: The second portion may be kept, covered, in the fridge for up to 3 days or in an airtight container in the freezer for 3 months.

TIP: Within a week of making this soup, you can use the remaining fire-roasted, diced tomatoes left in the can by adding them to an egg scramble or tossing with olive oil and pasta. Or freeze the remaining portion and store in the freezer for the next time you prepare this soup.

One-derful Watermelon Gazpacho

PREP TIME: 10 MINUTES (PLUS 1 HOUR TO CHILL)	YIELD: 1 SERVING

INGREDIENTS

1 Roma tomato, quartered

¾ cup cubed watermelon, divided

½ cup cucumber, peeled, seeded, and chopped

1 tablespoon minced red onion

½ teaspoon red wine vinegar

1 tablespoon olive oil

⅛ teaspoon red pepper flakes

⅛ teaspoon salt

1 tablespoon feta cheese

DIRECTIONS

1 Place all the ingredients (except ¼ cup of the watermelon and feta cheese) in a blender and pulse on and off until desired consistency is reached, about 30 to 60 seconds.

2 Dice the remaining watermelon into small pieces. Stir it into the gazpacho mixture.

3 Chill for 1 hour.

4 To serve, pour into a bowl and sprinkle with the crumbled feta cheese.

Dressed Up Instant Ramen with Tofu

PREP TIME: 5 MINUTES | COOK TIME: 12 MINUTES | YIELD: 1 SERVING

INGREDIENTS

2 cups vegetable broth

½ cup cremini mushrooms, sliced

½ cup cabbage or kale, shredded

1 teaspoon grated fresh ginger or ginger paste

1½ ounces dry ramen noodles (half a small rectangle package)

3–4 ounces baked tofu, plain or light teriyaki or soy sauce flavor (see Tip)

⅓ cup shredded carrots

1 teaspoon soy sauce

½ teaspoon lime juice

3 tablespoons scallions, greens and whites sliced thinly

½ teaspoon Sriracha (more or less to taste; optional)

DIRECTIONS

1 In a medium saucepan over medium-high heat, bring the broth, mushrooms, and cabbage to a boil. This process should take about 5 minutes. Put the lid on the saucepan to speed it up, but watch to prevent a boil over.

2 Reduce the heat to medium-low and simmer until the vegetables are tender, about 4 minutes.

3 Stir in the ginger and add the ramen noodles, tofu, and carrots. Simmer on medium-low until the noodles soften, about 3 minutes.

4 Stir in the soy sauce and lime juice.

5 Pour into a bowl and sprinkle with the scallions. Serve with Sriracha sauce, if desired.

TIP: Instead of buying baked tofu in the grocery store, try the Crispy Air Fryer Tofu recipe in Chapter 15 for instructions on how to make air-fried tofu that would work beautifully in this recipe.

VARY IT! Substitute 3 ounces of shredded chicken, beef, or pork for the tofu.

Bestie Black Bean Soup

| PREP TIME: 5 MINUTES | COOK TIME: 10 MINUTES | YIELD: 2 SERVINGS |

INGREDIENTS

1 (15-ounce) can black beans

¾ cup vegetable broth

⅓ cup favorite salsa

½ teaspoon chili powder

¼ teaspoon garlic powder

¼ teaspoon ground cumin

2 tablespoons sour cream, divided

2 tablespoons fresh chopped green onion, divided

DIRECTIONS

1 Pour the beans and juice from the can into a blender. Add the broth, salsa, and spices. In a blender, pulse the mixture until it is a coarse puree that is not completely smooth.

2 Transfer the mixture to a 2-quart saucepot and heat over medium-high for about 2 to 3 minutes, or until bubbling.

3 Partially cover the pot with a lid and reduce the heat to medium-low. Simmer the soup for another 7–8 minutes.

4 For one serving, pour half of the soup in a bowl and top with 1 tablespoon of sour cream and 1 tablespoon of green onions.

TIP: When preparing soup, leaving the lid slightly askew gives steam a way to escape and prevents overboiling while also allowing the flavor to develop through a slight reduction without making the soup evaporate too much. If your lid does not sit well, consider investing in a lid with a steam vent or using an inexpensive silicone "lid lifter" designed for this purpose. You also can choose to leave the lid off and keep an eye on the liquid level, adding back in a little more broth or water if too much simmers off.

TIP: The leftover soup may be stored, covered, in the fridge for 3–4 days; or cool and freeze it in an airtight container for up to 3 months.

NOTE: Alternative toppings include cheddar cheese and bacon crumbles.

Quick Comfort Chicken Rice Soup

PREP TIME: 10 MINUTES	COOK TIME: 9 MINUTES	YIELD: 1 SERVING

INGREDIENTS

2 teaspoons olive oil

⅓ cup shredded carrots

¼ cup diced celery

¼ cup diced white onion

¾ teaspoon minced garlic or garlic paste

½ teaspoon ground turmeric

¼ teaspoon ground black pepper

½ teaspoon Italian herb blend

1 (14-ounce) can chicken broth, divided

3½ ounces cooked chicken breast, shredded or chopped

⅔ cup precooked rice (see Tip)

Pinch of salt

DIRECTIONS

1 Pour the olive oil into a small pot and bring to medium heat.

2 Add the carrots, celery, and onions, sauteing for 3 minutes or until softened.

3 Add the garlic, turmeric, pepper, and Italian herb blend. Cook and additional 30–45 seconds, stirring constantly.

4 Add ½ cup of broth to the pot and stir quickly to "deglaze" any stuck-on veggies and spices.

5 Add the remainder of the broth to the pot along with the cooked chicken and rice. Reduce the heat and let simmer for 5 minutes.

6 Season with the salt, adding a bit more salt to taste if needed before serving.

TIP: Use leftover rice or precooked frozen rice of any rice variety (white, brown, wild, and so on). The rice will come back to life almost instantly, and there really isn't a need to cook the recipe longer.

VARY IT! Instead of rice, an equal amount of a cooked grain like quinoa, wheat berry, or farro, or an al dente cooked pasta may be substituted.

Truffled Cauliflower Soup

PREP TIME: 5 MINUTES | COOK TIME: 25 MINUTES | YIELD: 2 SERVINGS

INGREDIENTS

2 teaspoons olive oil

5 cups cauliflower florets, stems removed (about 12 ounces)

2 teaspoons minced garlic

⅛ teaspoon paprika

1½ cups vegetable broth, more if needed, divided

¼ teaspoon ground white or black pepper

¼ teaspoon truffle salt, more to taste

⅓ cup half- and- half

Chopped fresh thyme, for serving (optional)

DIRECTIONS

1 Heat the olive oil in a skillet over medium-high. Add the cauliflower and sauté for 3–4 minutes, or until lightly browned. Add the garlic and paprika and cook an additional 1 minute, stirring constantly.

2 Add ½ cup of broth to the cauliflower in the skillet. Cover the skillet and cook the cauliflower for 10–12 minutes or until tender. Stir as needed.

3 In the skillet, break down the softened cauliflower with a potato masher or fork into a lumpy consistency.

4 Add the remaining broth, pepper, and truffle salt to the skillet. Cover and simmer over medium-low for 5 minutes.

5 Remove the mixture from the heat and let cool 5–10 minutes before pouring into a blender. Let cool in the blender pitcher for 5 minutes. Then blend until smooth, about 30 to 45 seconds.

6 Pour the blended mixture back into the skillet and season with additional truffle salt if needed. If the soup seems too thick, add extra broth, about 2 tablespoons at a time. Warm the soup back up over medium-low for about 4–5 minutes.

7 Pour the soup into bowls and sprinkle with the chopped fresh thyme, if desired.

"Best of Both Worlds" Beef-Mushroom-Quinoa Chili

PREP TIME: 10 MINUTES	COOK TIME: 35 MINUTES	YIELD: 1 SERVING

INGREDIENTS

3 ounces lean ground beef

1 teaspoon olive oil

2 tablespoons chopped white onion

⅓ cup finely chopped mushrooms, white button or cremini

½ teaspoon minced garlic

2 tablespoons uncooked dry quinoa

2 teaspoons Worcestershire sauce

1½ teaspoons chili powder, less if you like a milder flavor

¼ teaspoon ground cumin

2 tablespoons red wine or cooking wine

1 (4-ounce) can tomato sauce

8 ounces beef broth

Salt (optional)

DIRECTIONS

1 Brown the ground beef in a 1-quart pot over medium-high heat for approximately 8 minutes, breaking beef into small crumbles and stirring frequently. Remove the beef from the pot to drain on a paper towel, and pour off the excess liquids from the pot.

2 Pour the olive oil into the pot and add the onion and mushrooms. Sauté on medium-high until softened, approximately 2–3 minutes. Add the garlic and stir for another minute.

3 Add the dry quinoa to this mixture and "toast" in the pot for 2 minutes by stirring constantly with the other ingredients.

4 Add the Worcestershire sauce, chili powder, and cumin and stir quickly for 30–45 seconds to bloom the spices. The bottom of pot may start to look gunky. That's okay; this is all the tasty beef and spice residue.

5 Pour the red wine in the pot to deglaze, stirring around quickly to pull up all the bits.

6 Add the cooked beef along with the tomato sauce and beef broth. Cover with a lid and continue to simmer over medium-low for 20 minutes or until thickened.

7 Season with salt, if needed. Serve warm with your favorite chili toppings.

TIP: Top it, pop it! Make the flavors explode with a variety of toppings put on before serving, such as chopped green scallions, shredded cheese, avocado chunks, chopped fresh cilantro, sour cream (or plain Greek yogurt), and crumbled tortilla or corn chips.

Chapter 11

Sandwiches, Personal Pizzas, and More

S andwiches, pizzas, quesadillas, and more — oh my! These versatile, popular dishes are tried-and-true satisfiers when it comes to lunch-hour dining. Squelch the urge to order take-out because you can most definitely make something much tastier, much healthier, and much more economical at home.

Did you know that on any given day, about one-half (47 percent of Americans, according to a survey conducted by the U.S. Department of Agriculture) report eating at least one sandwich? Perhaps you've had your fill of ham and cheese or peanut butter and jelly sandwiches and are feeling in a rut. It's not difficult to get creative with sandwich making and take your taste buds to the next level. For example, the Roast Beef and Blue Cheese Sliders simply pair deli roast beef with bold blue cheese for an extraordinary eating experience.

Quesadillas and pizzas are also ideal for a solo diner's easy-to-make lunch menu. These items can be customized to your preferences and tweaked to incorporate what's in the fridge at any given moment — melted cheese on a tortilla or pizza crust just seems to pair well with odd bits! You'll quickly become a fan of using tortillas or pita bread as the host for favorite fillings and toppings. Forget about pepperoni pizza on a traditional crust; check out the BBQ Chicken and Corn Tortilla Pizza that you can make super-fast in an air fryer.

Don't assume that if you are on a low-carb diet these sandwich, pizza, and quesadilla options are automatically out of play. The Cucumber "Bun" Club Sandwich is a clever (and crunchy) way to avoid bread and still get that sandwich experience. Also, it's easy to find low-carb (or gluten-free) options at grocery stores today for recipes that use a tortilla or crust.

Artichoke Tomato Pita Pizza

PREP TIME: 2 MINUTES | COOK TIME: 10 MINUTES | YIELD: 1 SERVING

INGREDIENTS

2 tablespoons bottled alfredo sauce or tomato pasta sauce

1 pita bread round

1 marinated artichoke heart, drained and chopped

2 tablespoons chopped sun-dried tomatoes

¼ cup shredded mozzarella cheese

1 teaspoon chopped fresh basil, optional

DIRECTIONS

1 Preheat the oven to 400 degrees.

2 Spread the sauce on top of the pita bread.

3 Scatter around the chopped artichoke and tomatoes.

4 Sprinkle on the mozzarella cheese to cover the top.

5 Bake on the pizza stone, baking sheet, or directly on the oven rack for 8 to 10 minutes or until the cheese is bubbling.

VARY IT! Red onion slivers, chopped spinach, and marinated red peppers are other good additions to this pizza. Get creative and use your imagination.

Philly Cheesesteak French Bread Pizza

PREP TIME: 10 MINUTES | COOK TIME: 20 MINUTES | YIELD: 1 SERVING

INGREDIENTS

1 tablespoon salted butter

½ teaspoon minced garlic

1 (5-inch long) French bread, sliced in half lengthwise

⅓ cup provolone cheese, grated

2 tablespoons American cheese, grated or cut in tiny bits (about 1 wrapped slice)

3 ounces sirloin steak

1 teaspoon olive oil

½ teaspoon minced garlic

⅛ red bell pepper, sliced into thin strips

⅛ green bell pepper, sliced into thin strips

⅛ medium white onion, thinly sliced

3 white button mushrooms, thinly sliced

DIRECTIONS

1 Preheat the oven to 425 degrees.

2 In a small bowl, soften the butter and stir in the garlic. Spread evenly across both halves of the bread.

3 Toss together the cheeses. Sprinkle the tops of bread with a small portion of the cheese mixture, about 1 to 1½ ounces. Reserve the remainder of the cheese for use later.

4 Toast in the oven for 5 minutes or until lightly browned. When done, remove and set aside, keeping the oven preheated.

5 Meanwhile, slice the steak against the grain into very thin strips, approximately 1/8 inch thick. This can be made easier by sticking the steak in the freezer for 15 minutes ahead of time to firm up.

6 Place the oil in a small skillet and cook the steak slices over medium-high until just done, with a little bit of light pink left in the center. This will take only 2 to 3 minutes. Remove the steak from the skillet and set aside.

7 Add the bell peppers, onion, and mushrooms to the same skillet and sauté for about 3 minutes until softened. Remove from the heat and stir the beef back in.

8 Pile up the beef and veggie mixture evenly across the two toasted breads and top with the remaining cheese.

9 Return to the oven for 6 to 8 minutes, until the cheese is bubbling.

VARY IT! Play with the flavors by switching up the Provolone cheese for another option. Try sharp cheddar, Gouda, pepper jack, or Swiss.

BBQ Chicken and Corn Tortilla Pizza

PREP TIME: 3 MINUTES | COOK TIME: 12 MINUTES | YIELD: 1 SERVING

INGREDIENTS

1 (6 to 8-inch) flour tortilla, preferably whole wheat (see Tip)

1½ to 2 tablespoons store-bought barbeque sauce

¼ cup cooked chopped chicken breast

2 tablespoons frozen corn, thawed and patted dry

1 tablespoon chopped red onion

1 tablespoon pickled jalapeño slices

¼ cup mozzarella cheese

DIRECTIONS

1 Preheat the oven to 400 degrees. Place the tortilla on a baking sheet and bake for about 6 minutes, flipping halfway through, until becoming lightly golden brown and crisping. Or preheat an air fryer to 350 degrees and cook the tortilla for 2 to 3 minutes, until starting to become crunchy.

2 Spread the barbeque sauce on the tortilla and scatter about the toppings; sprinkle with the cheese.

3 Return the pizza to the 400-degree oven and cook for an additional 6 to 7 minutes or return it to the 350-degree air fryer and cook for an additional 5 to 6 minutes or until the cheese is bubbling.

4 Slice into wedges and enjoy.

TIP: If using an air fryer for this recipe, make sure you know what size tortilla will fit inside your air-fryer basket before starting.

NOTE: You can also prepare this in the microwave by placing the tortilla on a plate and cooking on *high* for about 1½ to 2 minutes (flipping every 30 seconds). Then add the sauce and toppings and bake at 400 degrees in a traditional or toaster oven for 6 to 8 minutes.

Zesty Tuna Melt Quesadilla

PREP TIME: 5 MINUTES | COOK TIME: 6 MINUTES | YIELD: 1 SERVING

INGREDIENTS

1 pouch tuna fish, about 2½ ounces (liquid drained, if any)

¼ cup diced celery

1 tablespoon sweet pickle relish

2 tablespoons mayonnaise

½ teaspoon lemon juice

⅛ teaspoon Creole seasoning

2 (6-inch) flour tortillas, preferably whole wheat

¼ cup sharp white cheddar cheese

DIRECTIONS

1 To a medium bowl, add the tuna, celery, relish, mayonnaise, lemon juice, and Creole seasoning; stir until combined.

2 Spray a 8-inch skillet with nonstick cooking spray and bring to medium heat. Place one tortilla in the skillet and spread with the tuna mixture to almost the outer edges. Top the tuna with the cheese and the second tortilla.

3 Brown in the skillet for approximately 2 minutes; then flip to cook on the opposite side for approximately 4 minutes until browned and the cheese is melting.

4 Cut into wedges and serve.

VARY IT! Try adding blotted tomato slices between the tuna and cheese layers as a delicious addition.

My Big Fat Greek Hummus Quesadilla

PREP TIME: 2 MINUTES	COOK TIME: 10 MINUTES	YIELD: 1 SERVING

INGREDIENTS

½ teaspoon olive oil

½ teaspoon minced garlic

¼ cup roasted red peppers from jar, diced

1 pepperoncini pepper from jar, diced

⅛ teaspoon Greek seasoning

1 cup baby spinach

¼ cup hummus

1 (10-inch) whole-wheat flour tortilla, or 2 (6-inch) whole wheat flour tortillas

DIRECTIONS

1 Heat the olive oil in a skillet over medium heat. Add the garlic, red peppers, and pepperoncini and sauté for 2 to 3 minutes. Sprinkle with the Greek seasoning.

2 Add the spinach to the pan and sauté for an additional 1 minute. Remove from the heat.

3 Heat another skillet (sized to fit your tortilla) over medium-high heat and spray with nonstick spray.

4 Spread the hummus on one half of the tortilla and top with the spinach mixture. Fold in half and set in the skillet.

5 Cook for 2 to 3 minutes on one side until browned. Flip and cook another 2 to 3 minutes on the opposite side.

6 Transfer to a plate and cut into wedges.

VARY IT! Add 2 ounces of leftover chopped chicken.

TIP: Using a purchased Greek seasoning is convenient, cost-effective, and space-saving. Although you only need ⅛ teaspoon total seasoning for this recipe, you can make your own blend (and save the remainder for other uses) by mixing together 1½ teaspoons dried oregano, 1 teaspoon dried thyme, ½ teaspoon dried basil, ½ teaspoon dried marjoram, ½ teaspoon dried minced onion, and ¼ teaspoon dried minced garlic. Store the seasoning mix in a small, airtight jar.

Roast Beef and Blue Cheese Sliders

PREP TIME: 5 MINUTES   YIELD: 1 SERVING

INGREDIENTS

3 Hawaiian-style pull-apart rolls

2 ounces crumbled blue cheese

1 tablespoon mayonnaise

1 tablespoon plain Greek yogurt or sour cream

Pinch of ground black pepper

3 ounces deli roast beef, sliced thinly

½ cup arugula

DIRECTIONS

1   Slice the rolls into top and bottom halves.

2   In a small bowl, smash together the blue cheese, mayonnaise, Greek yogurt, and black pepper with a fork.

3   To assemble each slider, spread one-third of the cheese mixture on the bottom half of one roll. Next, pile on one-third of the roast beast and one-third of the arugula, then top with the other half of the roll. Repeat for the remaining ingredients.

4   Secure with toothpicks, if needed.

Two-Egg Denver Mug Omelet (Chapter 5)

Blueberry Cheesecake Smoothie (Chapter 8)

Strawberry-Almond Yogurt Toast (Chapter 7)

Green Machine Salad with Lemon Vinaigrette (Chapter 9) and Honey Cornbread Waffles (Chapter 6)

Easy Creamy Tomato Soup (Chapter 10) and Garlic Cheese Sourdough Toast (Chapter 16)

Juicy Bacon-Wrapped Chicken Breast (Chapter 12) and Love 'em Lemon Green Beans (Chapter 17)

Tilapia Fish Tacos with Chile-Lime Sauce (Chapter 14)

**Baked Banana with Oatmeal Cookie Topping (Chapter 19)
and Granola Chocolate Bark (Chapter 20)**

Grilled Cubano

INGREDIENTS

1 Cuban bread or Italian, 6 to 8 inch, sliced lengthwise

1–2 teaspoons yellow mustard

2 teaspoons salted butter, softened

⅛ teaspoon garlic powder

3 ounces Swiss cheese, divided

2 slices Black Forest or honey ham

3 ounces precooked pulled pork roast

6 to 8 thin dill pickle slices

DIRECTIONS

1   In a skillet, over medium heat, place both halves of bread cut side down and toast until lightly golden brown, about 3 to 4 minutes.

2   Remove the bread from pan and spread one side with butter and sprinkle with the garlic powder. Spread the mustard, in the amount to your preference, on the other side.

3   Add half of the cheese to the buttered bread and then layer with the ham, pulled pork, pickles, and the remainder of the cheese and top with the mustard-spread bread slice.

4   Return the sandwich to the skillet at medium heat. Press down on the sandwich with a spatula while toasting in the pan for about 4 minutes or until golden brown on bottom. Alternatively, set a heavy cast-iron skillet on top that will serve the same "smashing" purpose.

5   Flip the sandwich and cook for approximately 4 more minutes in the same manner or until toasted and the cheese is bubbling.

NOTE: If you don't have cooked pulled pork on hand, double up on the deli ham.

Cucumber "Bun" Club Sandwich

PREP TIME: 10 MINUTES | YIELD: 1 SERVING

INGREDIENTS

1 cucumber, approximately 8- to 10-inches long

2 teaspoons mayonnaise

2 slices deli turkey breast

2 slices deli honey ham

2 slices precooked bacon

¼ cup grated cheddar cheese

1 small Roma tomato, quartered and de-seeded

DIRECTIONS

1 Slice the ends off the cucumber and cut in half lengthwise. Use a spoon to scoop out the seeds and some of the flesh to make room for the fillings.

2 Use a spoon or small spatula to spread the mayonnaise inside the hollowed cucumbers.

3 Make a "roll up" by layering 1 slice ham, 1 slice turkey, 1 slice bacon, and half of the cheese, and then rolling tightly. Repeat with the remaining ingredients to make a second roll up.

4 Push one roll up into the hollow of each cucumber. Add the tomato wedges over one side and top with the other.

5 Slice in half crosswise like a traditional sub, if desired.

NOTE: If deli meats are too long to fit in the cucumber "bread," then try rolling up on the short side or cutting to fit, as needed.

Caramelized Onion and Fig Grilled Cheese

PREP TIME: 5 MINUTES	COOK TIME: 33 MINUTES	YIELD: 1 SERVING

INGREDIENTS

2 tablespoons salted butter, divided

½ white or sweet yellow onion, thinly sliced

¾ teaspoon brown sugar

⅛ teaspoon salt

Pinch of ground black pepper

3 dried figs, diced

2 slices Gruyere or Havarti cheese

2 slices sourdough bread

DIRECTIONS

1 Melt 1 tablespoon of the butter in a skillet over medium heat. Add the onions and sauté for about 10 minutes, stirring frequently, until the onions soften and begin to brown.

2 Lower the heat and continue to cook the onions for about 15 to 20 more minutes until they have caramelized and turned a richer shade of golden brown. Watch and stir frequently to ensure that the onions do not burn. In the last 3 minutes of cooking, stir in the sugar, salt, pepper, and figs.

3 Spread the remaining 1 tablespoon butter over one side of the two slices of bread.

4 Heat another skillet or grill pan to medium and add the first slice of bread, buttered side down, and the first slice of cheese. Top with the onion–fig mixture, second slice of cheese, and second slice of bread (buttered side up).

5 Cook for 2 to 3 minutes on each side until the bread is lightly golden brown and the cheese is bubbling.

VARY IT! Pitted and chopped dates make a good substitution for the dried figs.

4

Delicious Dinners

Sit down to more than two dozen, restaurant-inspired dinner recipes that require no reservations or dressing up.

Avoid super-sized, diet-busting restaurant servings and prepare an appropriately sized entree. Customize the ingredients as needed to keep on track with your health and wellness goals.

Discover dinner recipes that perform well as leftovers and can be doubled or meal-prepped for convenience later in the week.

Explore a variety of flavorful protein options including delightful dishes with chicken, beef, seafood, and plant-based options.

Chapter **12**

Chicken Dishes to Cluck About

Toss away the notion that chicken is bland and boring. Actually, it's nothing less than amazing, versatile, and delicious, and it makes a memorable impression if you know how to prepare it properly. It's really not the chicken's fault that most of us get into a recipe rut, preparing the same old chicken dishes over and over on autopilot.

This collection of chicken dinner recipes will jump-start your creativity and tantalize your taste buds with flavor profiles inspired from different corners of the globe, all easily doable for one in your very own home kitchen. From American comfort food-inspired Cheddar Cracker-Crusted Chicken Fingers to Lemony Chicken Piccata with Noodles with Italian flair, you'll definitely find a chicken dish to cluck about.

Another benefit of chicken is that it yields successful, scrumptious results via nearly every conceivable cooking method. Stovetop skillet, air fryer, oven, and slow cooker are the focus in this cooking-for-one curation. Deep-frying is a craving best reserved for eating out elsewhere. (The truth is, it's messy to make!)

Even though I'm all about saving a buck, don't go the trouble of hacking up a whole uncooked chicken to economically get the "parts" for your recipe. Chicken is typically a protein with one of the better price points in the market, even if it's already broken down into a tray of same-portion pieces. Boneless and skinless chicken breasts and chicken thighs are two great cuts to begin your chicken cooking journey with, and you can ask the butcher for just one or two pieces if you don't see the bird packaged up in a smaller amount. Breasts are a little leaner, and thighs are a little more flavorful. If you want to swap a breast for a thigh in any given recipe, typically adopting a strategy of two thighs swapped for one breast (or vice versa).

In this chapter, you'll also learn how to make Small-Batch Slow Cooker Shredded Chicken and several dishes that incorporate the no-fail results. Cooking chicken breasts low and slow all day keeps them moist and juicy and fall-apart tender. You can keep the shredded chicken in the fridge for about 4 days, but if you don't think you'll use it all up by then, it will maintain quality for at least 3 months in the freezer. Just scoop it up into 4- to 6-ounce portions and freeze in individual airtight freezer bags or storage containers to defrost later when needed.

Cheddar Cracker-Crusted Chicken Fingers

PREP TIME: 10 MINUTES | COOK TIME: 16 MINUTES | YIELD: 1 SERVING

INGREDIENTS

1 large egg white, whisked, or 2 tablespoons liquid egg white

½ cup cheddar crackers, coarsely crushed

5–6 ounces raw chicken tenders

½ tablespoon melted salted butter

Prepared honey mustard sauce (optional)

DIRECTIONS

1 Preheat the oven to 425 degrees. Spray a rimmed baking sheet with cooking spray.

2 Add the egg white to a small bowl and spread the cracker crumbs on a separate plate.

3 Dip each chicken tender into the egg white; then roll in the cracker crumbs and place on the baking sheet. Repeat for the remaining tenders.

4 When all the tenders are lined up on a baking sheet, drizzle the tops with the melted butter.

5 Bake 14–16 minutes or until the chicken is no longer pink and reaches 165 degrees when measured in the thickest part of the tender with an instant-read thermometer.

6 If desired, serve with prepared honey mustard sauce for dipping.

NOTE: Those little fish-shaped or small square crackers work great.

Pineapple Chicken Fried Rice

PREP TIME: 15 MINUTES | COOK TIME: 13 MINUTES | YIELD: 1 SERVING

INGREDIENTS

3 ounces chicken breast

1 teaspoon sesame oil

2 teaspoons salted butter, divided

¼ cup finely chopped red onion

½ cup frozen peas and diced carrots blend, thawed

¼ teaspoon minced ginger or ginger paste

¼ teaspoon minced garlic or garlic paste

1 large egg, whisked

1 (4-ounce) cup pineapple tidbits in juices

¾ cup cooked and cooled rice

1 tablespoon soy sauce, or more to taste

1 tablespoon finely sliced green onions, bulb and stalk

Sriracha (optional)

DIRECTIONS

1 Place the chicken in the freezer for 10 minutes to firm up before slicing very thinly across the grain.

2 Heat the sesame oil in a skillet and bring to medium heat.

3 Add the chicken to the skillet and cook quickly, stirring constantly, about 2–3 minutes or until no longer pink. Remove the chicken from the skillet and set aside.

4 Melt 1 teaspoon of butter in the same skillet. Add the onion, peas and carrots mix, ginger, and garlic and cook over medium-high heat for another 2–3 minutes.

5 Use a spoon to scrape the veggies over to one side of the skillet. Add the remaining 1 teaspoon of butter to an open spot in the skillet.

6 When the butter has melted, add the whisked egg and scramble for 2–3 minutes until done.

7 Drain the pineapple and reserve the juice. Add the drained pineapple, cooked rice, and cooked chicken to the skillet. Stir around until incorporated.

8 Drizzle the soy sauce and about 1 tablespoon of the reserved pineapple juice over the fried rice and stir until combined and heated through, about 3–4 minutes.

9 Serve topped with the green onion, Sriracha (if desired), and more soy sauce if needed.

VARY IT! Substitute the vegetables of your choice.

TIP! Cold rice is a must for the best fried rice results. Cold rice grains separate nicely in the skillet and soak up the sauce flavors without becoming gunky and clumpy like hot or warm rice, which is still holding onto a lot of excess moisture. If you are in a pinch and have cooked a fresh batch of rice, spread it out on a rimmed baking sheet and set it in the fridge for 30 minutes to cool off.

Juicy Bacon–Wrapped Chicken Breast

PREP TIME: 5 MINUTES	COOK TIME: 20 MINUTES	YIELD: 1 SERVING

INGREDIENTS

⅛ teaspoon salt

⅛ teaspoon black pepper

⅛ teaspoon sweet paprika

⅛ teaspoon onion powder

⅛ teaspoon garlic powder

6- to 8-ounce skinless, boneless chicken breast

2 slices bacon (not thick cut)

DIRECTIONS

1 Preheat the air fryer to 390 degrees. (See the Note for the oven instructions.)

2 In a small bowl, stir together the salt, pepper, paprika, onion powder, and garlic powder.

3 Starting from one end, snuggly wrap two strips of bacon around the chicken breast. Secure with a toothpick, if needed.

4 Place the chicken in the air fryer and air fry 5 to 6 minutes on each side or until the chicken is cooked through and no longer pink (165 degrees with instant-read thermometer inserted into thickest part of center).

5 Remove the chicken to a plate and let it rest for several minutes before slicing and serving.

NOTE: If you don't have an air fryer, sear bacon-wrapped chicken over medium-high in an oven-safe skillet for 2 minutes on each side; drain off the fat. Finish cooking in a preheated 400-degree oven for 15 to 20 minutes, or until it is cooked through and no longer pink.

Small-Batch Slow Cooker Shredded Chicken

INGREDIENTS

1 1½ pounds chicken breasts

½ cup chicken broth

½ teaspoon onion powder

½ teaspoon garlic powder

½ teaspoon salt

½ teaspoon ground black pepper

DIRECTIONS

1 Place the chicken breasts in a 2-quart slow cooker (or up to 4 quarts). Pour the chicken broth and sprinkle the seasonings over the chicken.

2 Cook on low for 6–8 hours or high for 3 hours.

3 Remove the chicken from the slow cooker and shred with two forks.

4 Season with additional salt and pepper, as needed.

TIP: Save leftovers in the fridge for up to 4 days or keep in airtight freezer container for up to 3 months in freezer.

NOTE: This recipe makes four generous servings. Portion the leftovers to add to salads, sandwiches, soups or some of the chicken recipes in this chapter. Stovetop method: Add the chicken breasts to a 2-quart pot, cover with water or chicken broth, add stated seasonings. Simmer for 15 minutes or until cooked through. Drain off the liquid and shred with a fork.

Green Chile Chicken Casserole

PREP TIME: 10 MINUTES | COOK TIME: 25 MINUTES | YIELD: 1 SERVING

INGREDIENTS

1 tablespoon salted butter

1 teaspoon flour

¼ cup milk

½ teaspoon chicken stock base (concentrate) or ½ chicken bouillon cube, crushed

⅛ teaspoon garlic powder

⅛ teaspoon ground cumin

⅛ teaspoon ground black pepper

3 tablespoons sour cream or plain Greek yogurt

¼ cup green chilies, drained (half of a small, 4-ounce can)

¾ cup precooked shredded or chopped chicken

¼ cup shredded cheddar cheese

¼ cup coarsely crushed tortilla chips

Chopped fresh cilantro and jalapeño slices, for garnish (optional)

DIRECTIONS

1 Preheat the oven to 375 degrees.

2 In a small skillet, melt the butter over medium-low heat and whisk in the flour. Cook for 30 seconds to 1 minute, stirring constantly.

3 With the heat still on, quickly whisk in the milk and the chicken base, stirring until incorporated with the butter mixture. Mix in the garlic powder, cumin, and pepper. Continue to cook until heated and bring to a simmer for 30 seconds to 1 minute.

4 Remove the skillet from heat and stir in the sour cream, green chiles, and shredded chicken. Stir until well combined.

5 Transfer the mixture to an approximate 5-inch square or 6-inch round baking dish. Sprinkle the top with the shredded cheese and crushed chips.

6 Bake for 20 minutes or until heated through and the cheese is bubbling.

7 Remove from the oven and let sit for 5 minutes before topping with chopped cilantro and jalapeño slices, if desired.

TIP: Use the remaining drained green chilies in an egg scramble, simple quesadilla, or even along with juices in the can as part of the cooking liquid for rice or quinoa.

Loaded BBQ Chicken Air-Fried Potato

PREP TIME: 10 MINUTES	COOK TIME: 35 MINUTES	YIELD: 1 SERVING

INGREDIENTS

1 large Russet potato, approximately 10 ounces

½ teaspoon olive oil

⅛ teaspoon garlic salt

3 tablespoons sour cream or plain Greek yogurt

⅛ teaspoon salt

⅛ teaspoon ground black pepper

½ cup shredded or chopped precooked chicken

2 tablespoons store-bought barbeque sauce

2 tablespoons shredded cheddar cheese

2 teaspoons chopped red onion

Pickle wedge (optional)

DIRECTIONS

1 Preheat the air fryer to 400 degrees.

2 Wash and dry the baked potato. Use a fork to make several puncture marks all around. Rub the skin with the olive oil and sprinkle with garlic salt.

3 Air fry the potato for 30 to 35 minutes. Use a fork to pierce through the skin to test for doneness. If it does not feel soft and fluffy to the middle, cook for another 5–8 minutes.

4 Remove the potato from air fryer and let rest for 3–4 minutes.

5 Slice and squeeze the potato open and mix in the sour cream, salt, and black pepper to create a fluffy mashed interior.

6 Place the chicken to the microwave-safe bowl and stir in a BBQ sauce. Microwave on *high* for 30 seconds or until heated through. Pile the chicken on top of the potato.

7 Top with the cheese, red onion, and an optional pickle wedge.

NOTE: To cook the potato in the microwave, follow Steps 1 and 2 and heat in 3-minute intervals (resting 1 minute between each) for two to three rounds, depending on the exact size and density of the potato.

NOTE: To cook a potato in the oven, follow Steps 1 and 2 and place it on a baking sheet and then into a preheated 400-degree oven for 45 minutes or until fork-tender.

Zesty Citrus Cornish Hen

PREP TIME: 5 MINUTES	COOK TIME: 1 HOUR AND 10 MINUTES	YIELD: 1 SERVING

INGREDIENTS

1 medium lemon

1 tablespoon orange marmalade

1 teaspoon soy sauce

½ teaspoon minced ginger or ginger paste

½ teaspoon minced garlic or garlic paste

¼ teaspoon crushed dried red pepper

1 (20- to 24-ounce) Cornish game hen

Salt and pepper to taste

DIRECTIONS

1 Use a zester or paring knife to remove 1 teaspoon of zest from the lemon peel; place in a small microwave-safe bowl. Slice the lemon in half and squeeze out 2–3 tablespoons juice into a bowl. Save the used lemon halves and stick them inside the Cornish hen cavity.

2 In a bowl with the lemon juice, add the marmalade, soy sauce, ginger, garlic, and dried red pepper; stir to combine.

3 Heat the sauce in the microwave on *high* for 20 seconds and stir. Heat for another 15 to 20 seconds until the liquid is reduced some and stir again.

4 Preheat the oven to 350 degrees. Tie the legs of hen together and turn the wing tips under the back.

5 Place the hen breast side up in a small rimmed baking dish. Divide the sauce in half, in two small bowls (one microwave-safe) for food safety. Brush the top of the hen with one portion of the sauce.

6 Bake for 60 to 70 minutes, until juices run clear and the internal temperature is 165 degrees with an instant-read thermometer.

7 Heat the remaining sauce in the microwave on *high* for 30 seconds or until heated. Using a clean spoon, drizzle over the top of cooked hen as a sauce.

Apricot BBQ Chicken Thighs

PREP TIME: 10 MINUTES	COOK TIME: 43 MINUTES	YIELD: 1 SERVING

INGREDIENTS

½ cup store-bought barbecue sauce

1½ tablespoons apricot preserves

1 teaspoon apple cider vinegar

½ teaspoon minced garlic

¼–½ teaspoon hot pepper sauce (optional)

1–2 tablespoons olive oil

2 bone-in, skin-on chicken thighs (about 10 ounces total)

DIRECTIONS

1 Combine the barbeque sauce, preserves, vinegar, garlic and hot pepper sauce (if desired) in a small saucepan and heat over medium heat for about 3 minutes. Set aside.

2 Preheat the oven to 400 degrees.

3 Brush the olive oil on a small, rimmed pan (I use an 8-inch round cake pan) and place the chicken thighs in the center, skin side down. Roast for 20 minutes without the sauce.

4 Remove the chicken from oven briefly to brush with the barbecue mixture. Use tongs to flip the chicken over and brush the sauce on that side too. Return to the oven and bake 15 more minutes.

5 Turn the heat up to 425 degrees and remove the chicken once more to brush with the sauce. Return it to the oven and bake 5 more minutes or until the sauce is browned and the chicken is cooked fully to an internal temperature of 165 degrees.

6 Let the chicken rest for 5–10 minutes before eating.

VARY IT! Switch up the flavor profile with a different type of preserves like pineapple preserves or peach preserves.

Lemony Chicken Piccata with Noodles

INGREDIENTS

2 ounces uncooked thin spaghetti

1 tablespoon salted butter

½ tablespoon olive oil

¼ cup flour or gluten-free blend

6 ounces boneless, skinless chicken thighs (about 2 thighs)

3 ounces chicken stock

2 tablespoons fresh lemon juice

1 tablespoon capers from jar, drained

1 tablespoon white wine or additional chicken broth

1 tablespoon cream or half-and-half

2 teaspoons chopped fresh parsley, for garnish

DIRECTIONS

1 Bring a 2-quart pot of water to a boil and cook the pasta according to the package directions.

2 In a 6- to 8-inch heavy skillet, melt the butter and the olive oil over medium-high heat.

3 Spread the flour out in a shallow dish; place the chicken in the flour and turn so that all sides get a thin coating. Shake off the excess.

4 Gently place the chicken in the heated skillet. Sear on each side until just golden brown, about 4 minutes each side.

5 Lower the heat to medium-low; pour in the chicken stock, lemon juice, and capers. Cover the skillet with the lid and let simmer until the chicken is fully cooked (165 degrees in center), about 4–5 more minutes.

6 When the chicken is fully cooked, transfer to a dinner plate. Keep the sauce in the skillet.

7 Add the wine to the skillet to deglaze (if needed, depending on the skillet size), scraping up any brown bits. Turn off the heat and stir in the cream until incorporated.

8 Add the drained, hot noodles to the skillet and stir around to soak up the sauce.

9 Add the dressed pasta to the plate with the chicken and garnish with chopped parsley, if desired.

VARY IT! Chicken thighs add a lot of flavor, but the recipe also accommodates an approximate 6-ounce boneless, skinless chicken breast if preferred. Also, if you're looking for a lower-carb option to pasta, serve with lightly steamed zoodles (spiralized zucchini) added to the skillet with the sauce to coat before serving.

protein choice

» Discovering a few cuts of beef that will work well with your cooking-for-one routine

» Enjoying flavor experiences inspired from various cultures that appreciate beef

» Meal-prepping a batch of ground beef to minimize cooking efforts on upcoming busy days

Chapter **13**

Beef Dishes That Can't Be Beat

I f you're questioning what's for dinner tonight, how about beef? Beef is a mouthwatering, hearty option that is actually one of Mother Nature's most nutrient-dense proteins, calorie for calorie. It boasts zinc, iron, protein, and other essential vitamins (like B vitamins) and minerals needed for optimal performance. In this chapter, you discover exciting new ways to incorporate lean beef into your diet, including sizzling steak and a roundup of great ground-beef recipes.

Did you know that on average, a 3-ounce serving of cooked lean beef provides only 170 calories with less than 10 grams of total fat, less than 4.5 grams saturated fat, and less than 95 milligrams cholesterol? Plus, you get about 25 grams of muscle-making protein to support strong, lean bodies. There are more than 35 cuts of beef that meet USDA qualifications for being lean. Some of the most popular lean cuts include top sirloin steak, strip steak, tenderloin, and 83 percent lean ground beef.

The *American Journal of Clinical Nutrition* found that following a Mediterranean-style dietary pattern that incorporates fresh lean beef can reduce heart disease risk factors, including total and LDL cholesterol and blood pressure. By incorporating 7 to 18 ounces of cooked, fresh, lean red meat per week (into a diet rich in vegetables, fruits, whole grains, nuts, and beans), individuals can improve their cardiometabolic disease risk factor profile, including high blood pressure, low HDL cholesterol, and diabetes risk.

So there's no reason not to enjoy beef, especially if you love it. Why not treat yourself to a special evening with the Solo Night Strip Steak with Red Wine Mushroom Sauce or load up on more veggies with every bite of beef while enjoying the Mushroom Swiss Beef Zucchini Boats.

When choosing cuts of beef for one, the meat counter can help you out and package up your perfect-sized portion. Sirloin steak, strip steak, and 93 percent lean ground beef are a few excellent beef options for a newcomer to cooking with beef. They are all lower-fat cuts that are still very flavorful. Both sirloin and strip steaks are quite tender for being lean options and don't require marinating to keep them from being chewy. They are also reasonably priced in terms of steak cuts and well suited for a variety of cooking methods, including grilling, pan searing, and slicing to stir fry.

In terms of all-around versatility, ground beef is the champ! Ground beef comes in an array of lean-to-fat rations, and 93/7 is a solid lean choice for browning into crumbles, while beef that's a little less lean, like 80/20, works best to create the most flavorful, juicy burgers.

In this chapter, you'll find instructions for Meal-Prep Southwestern Ground Beef, which can be prepared in advance and used later to create south of the border–inspired meals in mere minutes, like flautas, nachos, taco salads, egg scrambles, and whatever else moves you.

TIP

Leftover cooked ground beef will stay fresh in the fridge for up to 4 days, or divvy it up into single portions and freeze in air tight bags or containers for 3 months and thaw as needed.

REMEMBER

If you buy a 1-pound chub of ground beef and want to store it for later, just stick it in the freezer for 30 minutes to firm up a bit, then use a serrated knife to slice right through the packaging into four, 4-ounce portions. Drop those quartered chub slices into a freezer-safe container and pull one out to use for your burger or ground beef dish when the craving beckons.

Stay-at-Home Big Burger

PREP TIME: 5 MINUTES | **COOK TIME: 12 MINUTES** | **YIELD: 1 SERVING**

INGREDIENTS

6 ounces 80/20 ground beef

1 tablespoon liquid egg product, or 1 egg white

½ tablespoon Worcestershire sauce

1 teaspoon molasses or brown sugar

¼ teaspoon garlic powder

¼ teaspoon salt

⅛ teaspoon cayenne pepper

1 slice cheese (optional)

1 hamburger bun, split

Ketchup, mayonnaise, mustard, pickles/relish, lettuce, tomato, and onion, (optional)

DIRECTIONS

1 In a bowl, mix together the ground beef, egg, Worcestershire sauce, molasses, garlic powder, salt, and cayenne pepper.

2 Form the beef into a slightly flattened ball and then press down with your thumb to create an indention in the center. This will help keep the burger from puffing up while cooking.

3 Heat a grill pan, indoor electric grill, or outdoor grill to approximately 400 degrees. Cook the burger for about 6 minutes on each side, or until the internal temperature reaches at least 160 degrees.

4 Top the burger with cheese during the last 1 minute of cooking, if desired. You can place a lid over the cheese and burger to help it melt faster.

5 Serve on a bun with the condiments of choice.

TIP: If you are looking for a lower-carb option to a hamburger bun, you can wrap the cooked patty in lettuce leaves, use a cauliflower "bun," low-carb alternative bun, or even just place it on a bed of lettuce with all the toppings for a hamburger salad.

Meal-Prep Southwestern Ground Beef

PREP TIME: 5 MINUTES	COOK TIME: 12 MINUTES	YIELD: 4 SERVINGS

INGREDIENTS

1 pound lean ground beef

½ cup finely chopped white or yellow onion

1 teaspoon chipotle chili powder

1 teaspoon ground cumin

½ teaspoon garlic powder

½ teaspoon salt, or more to taste

DIRECTIONS

1 In a large skillet over medium-high heat, brown the ground beef with the onions. Break up the pieces of beef with a wooden spoon and stir frequently, for approximately 7–10 minutes. Drain off any excess fat or use a paper towel to sop it up.

2 In a small bowl, toss together the spices; then sprinkle them over the ground beef. Cook for another 1 to 2 minutes until the spices are becoming fragrant.

3 Let cool and portion into four, 4-ounce servings kept in a freezer-proof zip-top bags or storage containers.

4 Keep in the fridge for up to 4 days or freeze for up to 3 months.

TIP: Store in the freezer and thaw out for easy meals, such as tacos, omelets, queso con carne, and burrito bowls on busy days!

Oven "Fried" Beef Flautas

PREP TIME: 10 MINUTES	COOK TIME: 22 MINUTES	YIELD: 1 SERVING

INGREDIENTS

¼ pound lean ground beef

¼ teaspoon chili powder

¼ teaspoon ground cumin

⅛ teaspoon garlic powder

⅛ teaspoon onion powder

2 (6-inch) flour tortillas

2 tablespoons shredded Monterrey jack cheese

1 tablespoon olive oil

guacamole, sour cream, queso, or salsa (optional)

DIRECTIONS

1 In a small skillet, brown the lean ground beef over medium-high heat for approximately 7 minutes or until it is cooked through and no longer pink. Drain off any excess fat or use a paper towel to sop it up.

2 Sprinkle the spices over the ground beef and cook an additional 1 minute or until the spices become fragrant.

3 Preheat the oven to 425 degrees.

4 Spread out tortillas and divide the beef mixture evenly on top of each tortilla, offset a little to one side from center. Sprinkle 1 tablespoon of cheese over the beef on each tortilla.

5 Starting on the side closest to the beef, roll up one tortilla tightly. Secure with a toothpick, if needed. Repeat for the second tortilla.

6 Place the rolled tortillas seam-side up on a baking sheet and brush with a little of the olive oil. Flip over so that the seam side is resting on the baking sheet. Brush the tops and sides of the rolled tortillas with the remaining olive oil.

7 Bake for 12–14 minutes, flipping once halfway, until golden brown on top and bottom.

8 Remove from the oven and remove any toothpicks, if using.

9 Serve with guacamole, salsa, queso, or sour cream.

NOTE: Save time by using a portion of the Meal-Prep Southwestern Ground Beef recipe in this chapter.

Beefy Loaded Skillet Nachos

PREP TIME: 5 MINUTES | COOK TIME: 18 MINUTES | YIELD: 1 SERVING

INGREDIENTS

¼ pound lean ground beef

¼ teaspoon chili powder

¼ teaspoon ground cumin

⅛ teaspoon garlic powder

⅛ teaspoon onion powder

1½ to 2 ounces corn tortilla chips, divided

¼ cup black beans from can, drained

¼ cup shredded cheddar cheese

1 tablespoon pickled jalapeño slices

1 tablespoon chopped fresh cilantro

Sour cream, guacamole, salsa, pico de gallo, for topping (optional)

DIRECTIONS

1 In a small oven-proof skillet, brown the ground beef over medium-high heat for approximately 7 minutes or until cooked through and no longer pink. Drain off any excess fat or use a paper towel to sop it up.

2 Sprinkle the spices over the ground beef and cook an additional 1 minute or until spices become fragrant. Transfer the cooked beef to a bowl temporarily; keep warm.

3 Preheat the oven to 400 degrees.

4 In the same skillet, layer half of the tortilla chips; scatter around half of the beans, half of the beef mixture, and half of the cheese. Spread out the remaining chips on top of this mixture and layer in the same manner.

5 Bake for 10 minutes or until cheese is bubbling.

6 Remove the nachos and sprinkle with jalapeño slices and chopped cilantro. Serve with toppings such as sour cream, guacamole, salsa, and pico de gallo, as desired.

NOTE: Save time by using a portion of the Meal-Prep Southwestern Ground Beef recipe in this chapter.

Mushroom Swiss Beef Zucchini Boats

PREP TIME: 5 MINUTES	COOK TIME: 45 MINUTES	YIELD: 1 SERVING

INGREDIENTS

1 medium zucchini (about 8 inches)

4 ounces lean ground beef

2 tablespoons chopped white onion

¼ cup chopped cremini or white button mushrooms

½ teaspoon minced garlic

½ tablespoon Worcestershire sauce

¼ teaspoon salt

¼ teaspoon ground black pepper

½ cup grated Swiss cheese (about 2 ounces), divided

DIRECTIONS

1 Trim the ends of the zucchini and cut in half lengthwise; scoop out the pulp, leaving a ½-inch skin. Finely chop the pulp that was removed from the zucchini.

2 In an 8-inch skillet over medium heat, cook the beef, zucchini, pulp, onions, and mushrooms, stirring frequently, until meat is cooked through, about 7 to 10 minutes.

3 Stir in the garlic, Worcestershire sauce, salt, and pepper and cook an additional 30 seconds.

4 Preheat the oven to 350 degrees.

5 Remove from the heat and stir ¼ cup of the cheese into the meat mixture.

6 Divide the meat mixture evenly into the two zucchini shells. Place in a small, rimmed baking dish and sprinkle tops with the remaining ¼ cup of cheese.

7 Bake, uncovered, until zucchini is tender, about 25–35 minutes. Baking time depends on the thickness of the zucchini.

NOTE: If the zucchini halves seem wobbly in the pan, turn them over (before filling) and slice a very thin lengthwise strip off the bottom to help them stand upright.

Orange Beef Stir Fry

PREP TIME: 10 MINUTES | COOK TIME: 6 MINUTES | YIELD: 1 SERVING

INGREDIENTS

1 small orange

1 tablespoon soy sauce

1 tablespoon brown sugar

⅛ teaspoon dried red pepper flakes

½ teaspoon minced ginger or ginger paste

½ teaspoon minced garlic or garlic paste

2 teaspoons sesame oil

4 ounces strip or sirloin steak, sliced across the grain to ⅛-inch thickness (see Tip)

¾ cup snap peas

1 green onion, bulb and stalk sliced thinly

DIRECTIONS

1   Wash and dry the orange; use a zesting tool or microplaner to remove 1 to 2 teaspoons of zest from peel. Use a paring knife to mince strips of zest, if desired. Set aside.

2   Slice the orange in half; squeeze out 3 tablespoons of juice into a small bowl. Add the soy sauce, brown sugar, red pepper flakes, ginger, garlic, and half of the orange zest. Stir to combine and set aside.

3   Place the sesame oil in a small skillet and bring to medium-high heat. Add the steak strips and sear for 2 minutes without turning. Use tongs to flip the strips and cook them on the opposite side for about 2 more minutes until "just" cooked and lightly browned on all sides (but still a tad pink in center). Overcooking in this step will cause tough beef, as it cooks a bit longer in the next step.

4   Reduce the heat to low and add the sauce mixture to skillet. Add the snap peas. Stir to combine and let simmer for approximately 2 minutes until reduced and snap peas are tender-crisp.

5   Sprinkle the sliced green onion and remaining orange zest over the beef and serve with rice, if desired.

TIP: Set the raw steak in the freezer for 10 minutes to firm up for easier slicing.

My Big Fat Greek Meatball

PREP TIME: 10 MINUTES | COOK TIME: 25 MINUTES | YIELD: 1 SERVING

INGREDIENTS

1 egg yolk, or 1 tablespoon liquid egg product

2 teaspoons crumbled feta cheese

¼ teaspoon garlic powder

½ tablespoon Greek seasoning

¼ teaspoon salt

4 ounces lean ground beef

1 tablespoon finely chopped white onion

1 tablespoon plain bread crumbs

1 teaspoon olive oil

DIRECTIONS

1 Preheat the oven to 400 degrees.

2 In a medium bowl, whisk the egg yolk with a fork. Stir in the crumbled cheese, garlic powder, Greek seasoning, and salt.

3 Add the ground beef to the egg mixture and use a spoon or clean hands to mix until combined.

4 Add the onion and breadcrumbs to the bowl and work in until incorporated. Form the beef mixture into a large ball with your hands.

5 Drizzle the olive oil into the center of a small baking dish; set the meatball carefully in the dish.

6 Bake, uncovered, for 20–25 minutes, until the internal temperature reaches 165 degrees.

7 Remove from the oven and let rest for 5 minutes before eating.

TIP: Try this delicious dish featured on a Greek-inspired salad or halved and placed into a pita pocket with greens and veggies and served with tzatziki sauce.

Solo Night Strip Steak with Red Wine Mushroom Sauce

PREP TIME: 5 MINUTES | **COOK TIME: 24 MINUTES** | **YIELD: 2 SERVINGS**

INGREDIENTS

1 (8-ounce) trimmed strip steak

½ teaspoon olive oil

½ teaspoon coarse salt

½ teaspoon coarsely ground black pepper

1 tablespoon olive oil

½ cup sliced white button or cremini mushrooms

½ teaspoon minced garlic

¼ cup dry red wine

3 tablespoons beef broth

1 tablespoon heavy cream

⅛ teaspoon salt

⅛ teaspoon ground black pepper

DIRECTIONS

1 Rub the steak with the olive oil and sprinkle all sides with the salt and pepper.

2 Bring a medium skillet to medium-high heat. Place the steak in the skillet and cook for approximately 11–14 minutes, flipping every couple of minutes. Cook the steak to your preferred degree of doneness — 145 degrees for medium-rare or 160 degrees for medium (remove from the skillet 10 degrees sooner as the steak will continue to cook for several minutes once removed from the heat). Transfer the steak to a platter to rest while making the sauce.

3 Make the sauce in the same skillet used for the steaks; don't wash it. Heat the olive oil in the skillet to medium heat and add mushrooms, cooking for 2–3 minutes until softened.

4 Add the garlic and cook another 30 seconds, stirring continuously.

5 Add the red wine to deglaze the skillet, stirring frequently for about 1 to 2 minutes to incorporate the browned bits in the skillet.

6 Add the broth, heavy cream, salt, and pepper and continue to cook for about 5 more minutes or until the sauce has reduced.

7 Pour the sauce over the steak. Enjoy.

TIP: If you have leftover steak, let it cool and then wrap it in aluminum foil or plastic wrap. Store in the fridge for up to 3 days and use it chopped or sliced on salads or in egg scrambles, paninis, quesadillas, and tacos.

» **Finding a few economical varieties of fish that are tried-and-true recipe performers**

» **Keeping frozen fish, shrimp, and scallops on hand to satisfy seafood cravings at any time**

Chapter **14**

Fish and Seafood Dishes That Make Waves

Preparing fish and seafood from scratch at home can seem extremely intimidating. Due to this fear and the perceived possibility of wasting good money on a recipe fail, you may have avoided cooking fish or seafood other than maybe a prebreaded frozen fish fillet. However, a secret that most not-yet-experienced home cooks aren't privy to (yet) is that preparing fish and seafood is not a hard task, and it's very easy to achieve delicious results with even the simplest ingredients. Plus, when you're cooking for one, you don't have to break down and gut an entire fish. Instead, it's as civilized as grabbing a cleaned and tidy fillet from the seafood counter and throwing it in a pan.

You'll be amazed at how quick, inexpensive, and delicious it can be to incorporate more fish into your diet and avoid the shocking final bill of eating out at a nice seafood restaurant. Making salmon at home is popular for a good reason; it's not hard to find at most grocery stores and it is a great source of omega fatty acids, which are important for good nutrition. Salmon also turns out well through a number of home cooking methods. The Tuscan Pesto Salmon in a Foil Packet is a fancy-sounding yet no-fuss recipe to make on a grill or in the oven. The results are delicious, and the cleanup is a snap.

In terms of white fish, cod and tilapia are both economical and excellent choices that cook easily from fresh or frozen and can be breaded or prepared with little fuss (just some lemon, butter, and garlic) or incorporated into a more creative recipe like the Poached White Fish in Thai Coconut Cream.

Shrimp is another favorite in the seafood department and can find a starring role in your solo meals any day of the week. The Honey Pineapple Shrimp on a Stick is a fun recipe to start with and will really make your taste buds say "Ahoy, matey!". Raw shrimp needs to be shelled and deveined, but that little bit of extra work gives you an almost "really there" coastal eating experience. However, having a bag of frozen, precooked, shelled shrimp on hand in the freezer can make last-minute meals for the single person incredibly easy — like the Shrimp Stir Fry in a Snap.

Lemon Pepper Baked Cod

PREP TIME: 5 MINUTES · **COOK TIME: 25 MINUTES** · **YIELD: 1 SERVING**

INGREDIENTS

1 tablespoon salted butter

2 teaspoons fresh or bottled lemon juice

¼ teaspoon garlic powder

1 (4- to 6-ounce) cod fillet, fresh or frozen

⅛ teaspoon sea salt

⅛ teaspoon ground black pepper

1 teaspoon chopped fresh parsley

DIRECTIONS

1 Preheat the oven to 400 degrees.

2 In a small microwave-safe and oven-proof baking dish (about 5 inches square or not much larger than a piece of fish), melt the butter in the microwave for 15 seconds. Stir in the lemon juice and garlic powder.

3 Place the cod in the center of the baking dish in the butter mixture. Use a small spoon to drizzle some of the butter mixture from the dish over the top of the fish. Season with the salt and pepper.

4 Bake for 15 minutes if fresh, or if the fillet is frozen, for about 20–25 minutes. The fish will be done when it is white, flakey, and registers 145 degrees on an instant-read thermometer.

5 Serve drizzled with baking juices and sprinkled with parsley, if desired.

VARY IT! Spice it up by adding ⅛ teaspoon of dried red pepper flakes, in addition to the black pepper, to the top of fish.

TIP: If using fresh lemon juice in the recipe, reserve a cross-section slice from the lemon before squeezing it and place it on top of the fish fillet before baking. Or use a citrus zester to gather about ½ teaspoon of zest from the peel to sprinkle on the fish.

Honey Pineapple Shrimp on a Stick

PREP TIME: 10 MINUTES | **COOK TIME: 6 MINUTES** | **YIELD: 1 SERVING**

INGREDIENTS

2 tablespoons honey

2 tablespoons pineapple jam

1 tablespoon Sriracha

¼ teaspoon dried red pepper flakes

½ teaspoon minced garlic

1 tablespoon fresh or bottled lime juice

2 teaspoons chopped fresh parsley, divided

9 raw shrimp (16/20), peeled and deveined

9 (1-inch) chunks of fresh pineapple (see Note)

¼ teaspoon ground black pepper

¼ teaspoon salt

DIRECTIONS

1 Soak three bamboo skewers in water for 10 minutes to prevent burning. This step is not necessary if using metal skewers.

2 In a small bowl, mix together the honey, pineapple jam, Sriracha, red pepper, garlic, lime juice, and 1 teaspoon of parsley to make the glaze. Set aside.

3 Heat a grill pan over medium-high heat.

4 Thread the shrimp and pineapple, alternating pieces, onto the bamboo skewers (three shrimp and three pineapple chunks per skewer). Season both sides with the salt and pepper.

5 Place the skewers on the grill pan and cook for 2 minutes without glaze. Flip the shrimp and brush the tops with the glaze and cook 2 more minutes.

6 Flip the skewer again and brush with the glaze uncoated side with the glaze. Cook for 2 more minutes or until firm yet still tender and cooked through.

7 Remove from the heat and brush with the remaining sauce and the sprinkle of parsley.

NOTE: For convenience, purchase precut fresh pineapple from the produce department.

SHRIMP SIZING

Shrimp is measured and sold by the number of shrimp (shown as a range) in 1 pound. They are weighed in shells but without the heads. So, when you see shrimp displayed as "Large 21/30" that means that they are considered larger shrimp and that anywhere from 21 to 30 of them would correspond to a pound. A quick memory tip is that the smaller the count number, the larger the shrimp.

- Colossal: U/10 ("U" stands for under)
- Jumbo: 11/15
- Extra-Large: 16/20
- Large: 21/30
- Medium: 31/35
- Small 36/45

Baked Teriyaki Salmon

PREP TIME: 5 MINUTES (PLUS 20 MINUTES TO MARINATE)	COOK TIME: 15 MINUTES	YIELD: 1 SERVING

INGREDIENTS

3 tablespoons soy sauce

1 tablespoon rice vinegar

1 teaspoon minced garlic or garlic paste

1 teaspoon minced ginger or ginger paste

1 tablespoon olive oil

1 ½ tablespoons brown sugar

¼ teaspoon ground black pepper

1 (6- to 8-ounce) skin-on salmon fillet (see Tip)

½ teaspoon sesame seeds, for garnish (optional)

DIRECTIONS

1 To make the marinade sauce, combine together the soy sauce, vinegar, garlic, ginger, oil, brown sugar, and pepper in a bowl large enough to hold the fillet.

2 Place the salmon fillet in the bowl with the marinade and spoon the marinade over the top. Set in the refrigerator for 15 to 20 minutes, flipping the fish halfway through if not completely submerged in the marinade.

3 Preheat the oven to 400 degrees. Line a small rimmed baking sheet with aluminum foil for easy cleanup.

4 Transfer the salmon to the pan and reserve the marinade.

5 Bake for 12–15 minutes or until the salmon is flaky, cooked through, and has reached an internal temperature of 145 degrees.

6 While the fish is in the oven, microwave the remaining sauce in a bowl in 30-second increments, stirring between, for about 2–3 minutes or until somewhat reduced.

7 Remove the fish from the oven and brush with the reduced sauce. Sprinkle with the sesame seeds, if desired.

TIP: Typically, it's best to cook salmon in the skin. The brown-grey layer between the skin and flesh is the insulating fat and where so much of the beneficial omega fatty acids reside. Additionally, the skin serves as a safety layer between the delicate flesh and a hot pan. After baking, gently insert a spatula between the skin and flesh to release the fillet. And, remember, it's just fine (and good) to eat some of the brown-grey fat that may still be hanging on. If you only have a skinless fillet option, that will still work following the same recipe instructions; just coat the bottom of the pan (or aluminum foil) well with olive oil for an easier release.

Shrimp Stir Fry in a Snap

PREP TIME: 5 MINUTES	COOK TIME: 5 MINUTES	YIELD: 1 SERVING

INGREDIENTS

1 tablespoon soy sauce

1 tablespoon natural-style peanut butter

1 tablespoon bottled lime or lemon juice

1 teaspoon Sriracha, more or less to taste

1 teaspoon sesame oil

1 cup broccoli slaw or rainbow slaw

⅓ cup bean sprouts

¾ teaspoon minced garlic

4 ounces frozen jumbo shrimp, peeled, deveined, and cooked (see Tip)

1 tablespoon chopped peanuts

1 tablespoon chopped fresh cilantro

DIRECTIONS

1 In a small microwave-safe bowl, add the soy sauce, peanut butter, lime juice, and Sriracha (to suit preference for spiciness). Microwave for 10–15 seconds to soften the peanut butter and then stir until combined. Set the sauce aside.

2 Heat the sesame oil in a small skillet over medium heat. Add the broccoli slaw, bean sprouts, and garlic; sauté for 1 minute or until the garlic is fragrant.

3 Add 2 tablespoons of water to the skillet and cook for 2 more minutes, covered, to soften the vegetables.

4 Remove the lid and add the cooked shrimp and sauce, stirring for about 2 more minutes until the shrimp is just heated up and the sauce is starting to bubble.

5 Sprinkle with the chopped peanuts and cilantro and serve warm over prepared rice or noodles, as desired.

TIP: Precooked, frozen shrimp is a quick and easy protein to have on hand for solo meal making. Choose peeled and deveined shrimp with tails on or off depending on your preference. Thaw for about 10 minutes by setting the shrimp in a bowl of cold to room-temperature water (not hot!); refresh the water a few times by draining the old water and adding new. Drain, pat dry, and cook the shrimp as directed.

Tilapia Fish Tacos with Chile-Lime Sauce

PREP TIME: 5 MINUTES	COOK TIME: 12 MINUTES	YIELD: 1 SERVING

INGREDIENTS

6 ounces fresh or thawed tilapia fillet(s)

1 teaspoon olive oil

¼ teaspoon garlic powder

¼ smoked paprika

¼ teaspoon chili powder

¼ teaspoon cumin

¼ teaspoon salt

1 tablespoon mayonnaise

1 tablespoon sour cream or Greek yogurt

1 teaspoon lime juice

1 teaspoon Tajín seasoning (see Tip)

2 to 3 corn or flour tortillas

½ cup broccoli slaw or rainbow slaw

Sliced avocado, crumbled queso fresco, cilantro, pico de gallo, and jalapeño slices, for topping (optional)

DIRECTIONS

1 Preheat the oven to 375 degrees. Spray a small rimmed baking pan or dish with cooking spray. Place the tilapia in the pan and brush with the olive oil.

2 In a small bowl, mix together garlic powder, paprika, chili powder, cumin, and salt. Sprinkle over the fish.

3 Bake for 10–12 minutes or until the fish is white, opaque, and flakey.

4 While the fish is cooking, prepare the chili-lime sauce by mixing together the mayonnaise, sour cream, lime juice, and Tajín.

5 Warm the tortillas for about 10 seconds in a microwave. Remove them from the microwave and fill with equal portions of baked fish, cut into pieces as needed.

6 Top with the broccoli slaw, a dollop of the chili-lime sauce, and any other toppings as desired.

VARY IT! Substitute cod, swai, or other mild white fish.

TIP: Tajín is a popular brand of seasoning mix originating from Mexico that is made from dried and ground red chilies, sea salt, and dehydrated lime. It is similar to other chile-lime seasonings, featuring a mildly spicy, citrusy, and piquant profile. Tajín is a quick-and-easy way to add zing to various recipes. It can be used in rubs and marinades, tossed with popcorn, and added as a beloved south-of-the-border way to dress up fresh fruit! In fact, you will probably find Tajín stocked in the produce department, or look for it on the spice aisle.

Seared Scallops with Bacon Creamed Corn

PREP TIME: 5 MINUTES | COOK TIME: 14 MINUTES | YIELD: 1 SERVING

INGREDIENTS

1 ear corn

2 slices thick center-cut bacon, finely chopped

2 scallions, bulbs and light green stalks, sliced thinly

½ teaspoon minced garlic

¼ teaspoon dried red pepper flakes

¼ teaspoon salt, or more to taste

¼ cup half-and-half

1 tablespoon chopped cilantro

1 teaspoon olive oil

4 ounces sea scallops, fresh or thawed if frozen

1 tablespoon salted butter

DIRECTIONS

1 Husk the corn and shear off the kernels with a sharp knife; set aside.

2 In a small skillet, cook the bacon on medium-high until crisp, about 4 minutes. Transfer the bacon crumbles to a paper towel to drain. Spoon off most of the rendered bacon fat out of the pan, leaving only 1 teaspoon in the skillet. Reserve another 1 teaspoon for use when cooking the scallops.

3 Add the corn, scallions, garlic, red pepper, and salt to the skillet and cook, stirring occasionally for about 6 minutes or until the corn has turned bright yellow. Stir in the cooked bacon crumbles.

4 Remove the skillet from the heat and top with a lid to keep the corn mixture warm while quickly cooking the scallops.

5 Season the scallops with the salt. Place the olive oil and the reserved 1 teaspoon of bacon fat in another small skillet and bring to medium-high heat. Add the scallops to the skillet and cook on one side until a golden-brown crust forms on the bottom, about 3 minutes.

6 Flip the scallops with tongs and add the butter to the skillet. Spoon the melted butter and any pan juices over the top of the scallops and cook for another 45 seconds to 1 minute until firm and the flesh is pearly and opaque.

VARY IT! Substitute basil if you are not a cilantro fan. Also, scallops can be swapped for 4 ounces of shelled and deveined jumbo shrimp; cooking for approximately 3–4 minutes in Step 5 cook.

TIP: Prevent your scallops from becoming tough by taking the skillet off the heat a few seconds early. A scallop will be perfectly cooked when an instant-read thermometer inserted into the center reaches 120 degrees. When the scallops are removed from the heat, they will continue to cook, bringing the internal temperature to a final and ideal temperature between 125–130 degrees.

Poached White Fish in Thai Coconut Cream

PREP TIME: 5 MINUTES	COOK TIME: 15 MINUTES	YIELD: 1 SERVING

INGREDIENTS

1 (6-ounce) fillet fresh or thawed cod or other firm white fish

⅛ teaspoon salt

⅛ teaspoon ground black pepper

1 teaspoon olive oil

¼ cup chopped red onion

½ teaspoon minced garlic

½ teaspoon minced ginger

½ cup canned full-fat coconut milk

1 tablespoon fresh lime juice

1 teaspoon fresh lime zest

2 teaspoons fish sauce

1 teaspoon Sriracha

1 teaspoon brown sugar

½ cup chopped fresh spinach

DIRECTIONS

1 Season the fish with the salt and pepper; set aside.

2 In a small, 6-inch skillet, heat the olive oil to medium high.

3 Add the red onion and sauté for 2 minutes or until softened. Add the ginger and garlic and cook, stirring frequently, for another 1 minute.

4 Add the coconut milk, lime juice, lime zest, fish sauce, Sriracha, and brown sugar to the skillet and bring to a simmer, stirring frequently.

5 After the sauce comes to a simmer for 1–2 minutes, add fish fillets. Cook for around 8–10 minutes until the fish is opaque and flakes easily. Stir the sauce surrounding fish occasionally.

6 Add the spinach and stir around for 30 seconds to 1 minute, until wilted.

7 Serve immediately, spooning the sauce over the top. Serve with rice, if desired.

VARY IT! Cod, haddock, pollock, and halibut are all good, firm white fish selections for this recipe.

NOTE: Don't be confused; not all coconut milks are created equal. This recipe calls for canned coconut milk, a rich and creamy milk made from the meat of coconut that has been strained. It features more fat, more flavor, and a creamier constitution than the coconut milk you find in a carton next to the other refrigerated milk options that you might drink or pour on cereal. Carton coconut milk is manufactured differently and has more water, less fat, a less intense flavor and texture, and often uses various preservatives or additives to extend shelf life. If you try to use carton coconut milk in this recipe, the sauce's flavor and thickness will be drastically affected. However, canned coconut cream (an even higher-fat version of canned coconut milk) may be used as a replacement. But (and this is where it gets confusing semantically) another canned product that sounds similar, cream of coconut, is made with sugar and used for desserts and cocktails. You don't want that — read the labels!

Tuscan Pesto Salmon in Foil Packet

PREP TIME: 10 MINUTES	COOK TIME: 18 MINUTES	YIELD: 1 SERVING

INGREDIENTS

6 ounces vegetable broth

2 tablespoons basil pesto, divided

½ cup instant white or brown rice

1 (6-ounce) salmon fillet

1 tablespoon toasted pine nuts

1 tablespoon chopped sun-dried tomatoes

DIRECTIONS

1 Place the broth in a microwave-safe bowl. Heat in the microwave on high for 2–3 minutes, until very hot — almost boiling. Remove and stir in 1½ tablespoons of pesto and rice. Let sit for 5–10 minutes until most of the water is absorbed.

2 Preheat the oven or grill to 400 degrees. Spread out a heavy sheet of aluminum foil, approximately 18 x 12 inches, and coat it with cooking spray.

3 Lay the salmon in the middle of the foil and season with salt and pepper. Spread the remaining ½ tablespoon of pesto on top of the fish.

4 Spoon the rice mixture around the fillet. Fold the foil over the salmon and rice so that the edges meet. Seal tightly with a ½-inch fold on the top and on both sides. Fold all sides up a second time to seal well, allowing for a bit of extra space for expansion while cooking.

5 Place the foil packet in the oven or on the grill for about 12–15 minutes, until the salmon flakes easily and the rice is tender.

6 To serve, cut a large "X" across the top of the packet with kitchen shears and fold back the foil. For a less fancy presentation, simply unroll the foil! Top with the pine nuts and chopped sun-dried tomatoes.

VARY IT! Add ¾ cup sliced zucchini or about eight asparagus spears (cut in half) to the foil packet if you'd like veggies with your fish.

Chapter **15**

Meatless Meals for Everyone

Whether you are a full-fledged vegetarian, open-minded omnivore, or even a confirmed carnivore, you'll find recipes in this chapter that are sure to satisfy and fill you up with a focus on vegetables and healthy whole grains. Everyone, regardless of their current dietary preference, can benefit from incorporating more vegetables and whole grains into their life — day in and day out. Honestly, it's best if plant-based foods, which can typically be quite voluminous for their lower calorie count, comprise the bulk of your plate with animal products used as nutritionally dense accents to fill in the gaps.

Vegetables and plant-based foods provide energy to keep you active throughout the day and nutrients needed to help you stay strong and healthy. They are wonderfully colorful, versatile, and add an array of textures and tastes to your meal. The Refried Bean–Zucchini Boats offer a big serving of veggies that can't be missed to keep you sailing smoothly and happily until your next meal. And, even if you aren't a fan of such an overt vegetable presence on your plate, the Spinach Alfredo Pasta in a Mug offers all the comfort of a creamy sauce enveloping tender noodles along with a snuck-in serving of spinach that you'll hardly notice.

Choosing whole-grain options over their processed counterpoints, is also a smart decision to support better health. For example, whole-wheat tortillas versus white-flour tortillas or alternative pastas (like quinoa or chickpea pastas) versus traditional flour pasta are great ways to help boost your nutritional intake and meet daily needs for dietary fiber. Look for whole-grain options in breads, buns, and bagels too! The adorable and meal prep–friendly BBQ Meatless Meatloaf Muffins are superfood packed, featuring oats and lentils instead of the traditional ground meats. Definitely not your grandmother's meatloaf, but still surprisingly delicious and juicy, it offers 8 grams of dietary fiber (about 33 percent of your daily need) and more than 21 grams of protein per serving. Oats are a whole grain, and lentils are considered "grain legumes" (also called *pulses*), which are high in fiber and protein.

The recipes in this meatless chapter are all suitable for a lacto-ovo vegetarian diet; however, if you are following a vegan protocol, the dairy ingredients (butter, cheese, and milk) and eggs will need to be swapped with suitable plant-based alternatives (which are becoming easier to source at nearby grocery stores).

Refried Bean–Stuffed Zucchini Boats

PREP TIME: 10 MINUTES | COOK TIME: 28 MINUTES | YIELD: 1 SERVING

INGREDIENTS

1 medium zucchini (about 8 inches)

¼ cup diced white onion

6 grape tomatoes, diced

¼ teaspoon garlic powder

¼ teaspoon ground cumin

½ teaspoon chili powder

½ cup canned fat-free refried beans

2 tablespoons store-bought salsa

¼ cup shredded cheddar cheese

8 pickled jalapeño rings from jar

Sour cream, guacamole, salsa, and fresh cilantro, for garnish (optional)

DIRECTIONS

1 Preheat the oven to 375 degrees.

2 Cut off the ends of the zucchini and slice it lengthwise. Use a small spoon to scoop out the seeds and some flesh in the center, leaving about ¼ inch of flesh around the outside so that the zucchini halves keep their shape during cooking. Finely chop the scooped-out flesh and reserve for later.

3 Lay the halves in a small, rimmed baking pan. If the zucchini halves are noticeably wobbling, slice a very shallow, long strip off the bottom to keep them sitting flat and prevent wobbling.

4 In a small microwave-safe bowl, add the onions, tomatoes, and reserved chopped zucchini from Step 2. Microwave on high for 15–20 seconds until hot and softened. Stir in the garlic powder, cumin, chili powder, beans, and salsa; mix well until evenly combined.

5 Spoon the bean mixture evenly into the two zucchini boats.

6 Bake for 25 minutes or until the zucchini boats are tender. Do not overcook, or they will become mushy.

7 Spread the cheese over the tops of the zucchini boats and line up 4 jalapeño slices on top of each half. Return them to the oven for 2–3 more minutes or until the cheese is bubbling.

8 Serve warm with the optional garnishes, if desired.

VARY IT! Substitute traditional refried beans for refried black beans.

Crispy Air Fryer Tofu

PREP TIME: 35 MINUTES (PLUS 30 MINUTES TO MARINATE)	COOK TIME: 14 MINUTES	YIELD: 1 SERVING

INGREDIENTS

4 ounces extra-firm tofu

1 teaspoon avocado oil or olive oil

1 teaspoon soy sauce, tamari, or coconut aminos

½ teaspoon Sriracha

1 teaspoon corn starch

DIRECTIONS

1 Press the block of tofu by wrapping it in a clean kitchen towel, setting it on plate, and placing a heavy skillet on top for 30 minutes. This squeezes out excess water, ultimately making tofu crispier during cooking.

2 Preheat an air fryer to 390 degrees.

3 In a bowl, combine the oil, soy sauce, and Sriracha. Cut the tofu into bite-sized pieces and add to the bowl, tossing gently to coat. Let it sit for 30 minutes to marinate and absorb flavor. Remove the cubes to a plate and toss it with the cornstarch.

4 Place the coated tofu cubes into an air fryer in a single layer without pieces touching. Air fry for 12–14 minutes, flipping halfway, or until turning golden brown and crispy around the edges.

TIP: You can enjoy this air-fried tofu in a number of ways including topped on a salad, tossed with noodles, rolled in a lettuce wrap, or dipped like "nuggets" into your favorite sauce.

Spinach Alfredo Pasta in a Mug

PREP TIME: 4 MINUTES | COOK TIME: 6 MINUTES | YIELD: 1 SERVING

INGREDIENTS

½ cup uncooked pasta, preferably whole-grain small shells, elbows, or mini bow tie (about 1 ounce)

1 ounce cream cheese (2 tablespoons)

¼ cup milk

½ teaspoon corn starch

2 tablespoons finely shredded Parmesan cheese

½ cup chopped fresh spinach

Salt and pepper, to taste

DIRECTIONS

1 In a large microwave-safe mug, add the pasta and ¾ cup of water. Set the mug on a small plate (in case of overflow) and microwave on high for approximately 3½ minutes or until pasta is tender. If needed, continue to microwave in 30- to 45-second increments until the pasta is tender. The exact time will vary based on the microwave's wattage and the size of the pasta used.

2 When the pasta is tender, remove the mug from the microwave and drain off the excess water.

3 Stir in the cream cheese until it melts. Stir in the milk and cornstarch and then finally add the Parmesan cheese. Microwave for 1 additional minute until the sauce is bubbling and hot; stir well.

4 Stir in the chopped spinach and let it sit for 30 seconds to 1 minute to wilt.

5 Season with salt and pepper and enjoy warm!

NOTE: Use a mug that is a little larger than you think you'll need, as the mixture boils up, and you don't want it to overflow. Watch the cooking process carefully, and if you see that it's going to spill over, stop the microwave to let it cool for a bit, and then resume cooking. Or, transfer the pasta at this time to a larger mug and finish cooking where you left off.

Super Creamy Black Bean Tostados

PREP TIME: 5 MINUTES | COOK TIME: 11 MINUTES | YIELD: 1 SERVING

INGREDIENTS

3 corn tortillas (see Tip)

2 teaspoons salted butter

3 tablespoons finely chopped white onion

1 teaspoon minced garlic

1 cup canned fat-free refried black beans

½ teaspoon cumin

½ teaspoon chipotle chili powder

¼ cup Greek yogurt

1 cup shredded lettuce

9 grape tomatoes, quartered

3 tablespoons crumbled queso fresco

¼ medium avocado, diced

⅓ cup salsa

DIRECTIONS

1 Place the corn tortillas in a single layer on a large microwave-safe plate and microwave on *high*, flipping the tortillas every 30 seconds, until lightly browned and crisp, about 1½ minutes total. Set aside.

2 In a small sauce pan over medium heat, melt the butter.

3 Add the onion and cook for 3–4 minutes until tender. Add the garlic and cook 1 more minute until fragrant.

4 Add the refried beans, mixing together with the onion and garlic mixture. Stir in the cumin and chipotle chili powder until well combined. Heat over medium low for 3–4 minutes until hot.

5 Stir in the Greek yogurt and cook for another 1 minute until warmed.

6 Spread the bean mixture evenly across the three warmed tortillas. If they have cooled, pop them back in the microwave for 10 seconds before topping with the beans.

7 Pile the lettuce on top of the beans along with the tomatoes, queso fresco, and diced avocado. Drizzle with salsa. Enjoy.

TIP: To save a few minutes of prep, use purchased tostado shells.

Broccoli Quinoa Casserole

INGREDIENTS

1 (10-ounce) package frozen chopped broccoli

1 egg plus 1 egg white, or 6 tablespoons liquid egg substitute

¾ cup cooked plain quinoa, (see Tip)

⅔ cup cottage cheese

3 teaspoons whole-wheat flour

¼ teaspoon garlic powder

¼ teaspoon onion powder

¼ teaspoon salt

¼ teaspoon ground black pepper

½ cup shredded Parmesan cheese

DIRECTIONS

1 Preheat the oven to 350 degrees and spray a 1-quart baking dish with cooking spray.

2 Cook the broccoli according to the package instructions; drain and set aside.

3 In a bowl, mix together the eggs, cooked quinoa, cottage cheese, flour, garlic powder, onion powder, salt, and pepper.

4 Fold the slightly cooled broccoli into the quinoa mixture. Transfer to the prepared baking dish.

5 Bake for 25 minutes. Remove and sprinkle the Parmesan cheese over the top and bake for another 5 minutes or until lightly browned.

6 Let cool for 5 minutes before cutting in half to serve.

VARY IT! Frozen cauliflower may be substituted for the frozen broccoli.

TIP: Save time by using cooked quinoa from a pouch found in the rice aisle. Choose a plain "flavor" or, if not available, a variety with mild seasoning that would complement this dish.

BBQ Meatless Meatloaf Muffins

PREP TIME: 5 MINUTES	COOK TIME: 45 MINUTES	YIELD: 2 SERVINGS (2 MINI LOAVES EACH)

INGREDIENTS

½ cup dried brown lentils

¼ cup diced white onion

¼ cup diced white mushrooms

1 teaspoon minced garlic

½ cup quick-cook oats

3 ounces shredded cheddar cheese, divided

2 tablespoons liquid egg substitute

⅓ cup favorite barbeque sauce from bottle, divided

½ teaspoon salt

¼ teaspoon ground black pepper

DIRECTIONS

1 Bring the 1 cup of water to a boil in a small sauce pan. Add the lentils and simmer, covered, for about 25 minutes or until the water is absorbed and the lentils are soft. Drain any excess water in a pan and mash lentils coarsely with a fork.

2 Preheat the oven to 350 degrees. Generously spray four cups of a jumbo muffin pan with cooking spray.

3 Stir in the onion, mushrooms, garlic, and oats until combined well.

4 Stir in most of the cheese, setting aside 2 tablespoons for the topping later. Also stir in the egg substitute, 2 tablespoons of barbecue sauce, salt, and pepper.

5 Spoon the meatless mixture evenly into the prepared muffin pan. The mixture should fill about two-thirds of a muffin cup — no higher.

6 Bake for 15 minutes. Remove from the oven and spread the remaining barbecue sauce and reserved 2 tablespoons of cheese evenly among the tops of the muffins and return them to the oven to cook another 5 minutes.

7 Use a small spatula or knife around the edges to help release the meatless muffins from the pan.

NOTE: Leftovers can be kept in the fridge for up to 4 days or in the freezer in an airtight container for up to 3 months. Double the recipe and meal prep a batch to freeze for easy dinners on busy days.

5
Sides to Swear By

Fill out your plate with an easy-to-prepare and wonderfully flavorful side dish that complements the evening's entree choice.

Create a vibrant, vitamin-packed sidekick to the main course by adding a vegetable or fruit-based side dish.

Discover traditional and new-school options to round out dinner with a serving of whole grains, beans, pasta, or hunk of hearty bread.

Surprise yourself and turn on "creative mode" to switch up the supporting cast of herbs, spices, broths, and other ingredients that nail down the flavor as you see fit!

» that can be made in minutes

» Stocking the pantry with always-on-hand, shelf-stable ingredients for quick side dish recipes

» Elevating your soup, salad, or entree with a warm, comforting bite of bready goodness

Chapter 16

Grains, Beans, and Beyond

Have you struggled at times (or every time!) with what to partner up on your plate with the main dish? Plating a single chicken breast or giant meatball with nothing on the side is boring to say the least, but also often not filling enough to propel you forward for long!

Why not round out your meal with a serving of grains, beans, pasta, or a hunk of hearty bread? This category of food will fill you up and provide energy to get you from nearly any proverbial Point A to Point B in the day. Plus, beans, bread, and grains like rice and quinoa — and I'm even throwing in pasta here — are all pantry staples that can be kept conveniently on hand for last-minute recipe making. From the Creamy Microwave Risotto to Garlicky Browned Butter Noodles or Wonderful Warm Flatbread, you will find a special "basic" side dish that goes fabulously with nearly everything.

One of the keys to success when it comes to making more meals at home rather than eating out constantly is having a variety of grain options that can be stored in the cupboard and stay fresh for long periods of time. Once packages of rice, quinoa, other grains, dried beans, and pastas have been opened, they should be stored in a cool, dry place in a tightly closed container to keep out dust, moisture, pests, and other contaminants. The exact time that grains stay fresh at home can depend, in large part, on how long the package was at the warehouse and store before you purchased it. This means that there are no total guarantees, but the following shelf-life guidelines — from various experts — for common dry grains, beans, and pasta may help:

>> Milled rice (white rice): Almost indefinitely according to USA Rice

>> Whole grain rice (brown rice): 6 months due to oil in the bran layer of grain according to USA Rice

>> Wheat berries, farro, barley, popcorn: 6 months per Whole Grains Council

>> Quinoa, oats, amaranth, teff: 4 months per Whole Grains Council

>> Dried pasta: 2 years

>> Dried beans: at least 1–2 years

TIP

Freeze or refrigerate dry whole grains in airtight bags to double the shelf life.

An assortment of canned beans and pouches of precooked grains, like rice, quinoa, and pasta are also nice to have at the ready for blazing fast meal-making. Canned beans and pouches can last for several years past their "best by" dates if properly stored, but it's good policy to eat within 12–18 months. Use a permanent pen to mark cans and pouches with the date and follow a "first-in, first-out" system (discussed in Chapter 4).

Another option, if you have room, is to batch-cook grains and beans and store in your freezer in airtight freezer storage bags in the portion size you need. Stack them up flat on top of each other for space-saving storage. A quick defrost and reheat in the microwave and you are ready to plate up or add to a recipe. While cooked grains and beans are only considered safe for 3 to 4 days in the fridge, the quality maintains for 3 to 4 months in the freezer and often longer.

Creamy Microwave Risotto

PREP TIME: 7 MINUTES	COOK TIME: 8 MINUTES	YIELD: 1 SERVING

INGREDIENTS

½ tablespoon salted butter

1 tablespoon finely chopped onion

¼ cup arborio rice (no substitutions)

Pinch of garlic powder

Pinch of ground black pepper

½ cup beef or vegetable broth

1 tablespoon dry white wine (or water or additional broth)

3 tablespoons finely chopped mushrooms (approximately 2 white button mushrooms)

1 tablespoon grated Parmesan cheese

Chopped thyme or parsley, (optional)

DIRECTIONS

1 Place the butter and onions in a microwave-safe, oversized mug (20–24 ounces). The mug will look "too big" for the ingredients, but the contents will boil up during cooking.

2 Microwave on *high* for 90 seconds, stopping to stir halfway.

3 Add the rice, garlic powder, pepper, and broth to the butter mixture. Stir and microwave on 50 percent power for 2 minutes, then let rest for 2 minutes. Microwave again at 50 percent power for 2 minutes followed by another 2-minute rest.

4 Stir in the wine and mushrooms. Microwave at 50 percent for another 2-minute session followed by another 2-minute rest.

5 Stir in the Parmesan cheese and herbs, if desired, and heat at 50 percent for 1 more minute.

NOTE: Microwave times can vary by appliance. If the risotto starts to look dry and too much liquid has evaporated, just add another couple of teaspoons of broth or water.

Easy Rice Quinoa Bake

PREP TIME: 2 MINUTES	COOK TIME: 40 MINUTES	YIELD: 1 SERVING

INGREDIENTS

¼ cup medium-grain rice, white or brown

2½ tablespoons dry quinoa, rinsed

⅔ cup vegetable broth

1 teaspoon salted butter

DIRECTIONS

1 Preheat the oven to 400 degrees.

2 Place the rice and quinoa in a 5-inch square baking dish or a dish with similar proportions.

3 Pour the broth into a microwave-safe glass measuring cup or bowl and microwave on high for about 2 minutes, or until boiling.

4 Pour the hot broth over the rice-quinoa mixture. Add the butter; stir to combine.

5 Cover the dish with a lid or aluminum foil tightened around the edges. Bake for 35 to 40 minutes, or until the rice and quinoa are tender.

6 Fluff the grains with a fork, add salt if needed, and enjoy!

VARY IT! Give this dish your signature style by adding 1 tablespoon of chopped fresh herbs or 1 teaspoon of dried herbs. Mix in with the butter before the baking step.

Garlicky Browned Butter Noodles

PREP TIME: 5 MINUTES	COOK TIME: 12 MINUTES	YIELD: 1 SERVING

INGREDIENTS

¼ teaspoon salt, plus more to taste

2 ounces dry spaghetti

1½ tablespoons salted butter

¾ teaspoon minced garlic

1 tablespoon grated Parmesan cheese

¼ teaspoon ground black pepper

DIRECTIONS

1 Fill a medium-sized pot with about 1 quart of water and add the salt. Bring to a boil over high heat.

2 Add the spaghetti and cook for 8–12 minutes, until it is tender but not mushy (or al dente, see the Tip).

3 Reserve 1 tablespoon of the pasta cooking water and drain the remainder from the spaghetti. Set the cooked pasta aside in a bowl.

4 Melt the butter in the same pot. Add the garlic and cook, stirring for about 1 minute or until the butter changes from yellow to tan to light brown in color. Remove from the heat.

5 Add the cooked pasta and pasta water to the pot with the butter. Use tongs or a fork to toss together in the sauce.

6 Sprinkle with the Parmesan cheese, black pepper, and salt to taste, if needed. Toss lightly. Enjoy!

VARY IT! Experiment with a different noodle shape, following the package instructions for designated pasta cooking time.

TIP: *Al dente* is a common cooking term, but what does it really mean? Literally, *al dente* translates "to the tooth" in Italian. But, when it comes to cooking pasta, al dente means that there is a slight bite (or resistance) to the noodle. The pasta is definitely not hard, but it's not a mushy mess either. Finishing your pasta about 2 minutes sooner than the package instructions helps ensure an al dente result and takes into consideration "carryover" cooking (when the heat retained in food keeps it cooking, even though it's been removed from heat).

Garlic Cheese Sourdough Toast

PREP TIME: 2 MINUTES   COOK TIME: 4 MINUTES   YIELD: 1 SERVING

INGREDIENTS

1 slice bakery-style sourdough bread

1–2 teaspoons salted butter

½ teaspoon finely grated garlic

½ teaspoon finely chopped fresh parsley

1½ tablespoons grated mozzarella cheese

1½ teaspoons grated Parmesan cheese

DIRECTIONS

1 Position the oven rack about 8 inches away from the broiler heat element. Preheat on *high*.

2 Spray a small baking sheet with a nonstick spray. Place the bread on the prepared sheet and spread on the butter from edge to edge; then spread on the garlic.

3 Sprinkle with the parsley and cheeses.

4 Broil for 3 to 4 minutes, watching carefully, until the cheese is melted, bubbling, and lightly browned at the edges.

Wonderful Warm Flatbread

PREP TIME: 15 MINUTES	COOK TIME: 8 MINUTES	YIELD: 1 SERVING (2 SMALL FLATBREADS)

INGREDIENTS

½ cup all-purpose flour

½ teaspoon baking powder

¼ teaspoon salt

5½ teaspoons olive oil, divided

½ teaspoon granulated sugar

3 tablespoons cold water

DIRECTIONS

1 In a small bowl, whisk the flour, baking powder, and salt together.

2 Make a well in the center of the flour mixture; add 1½ teaspoons of olive oil, the sugar, and water.

3 Use a rubber spatula to stir the wet ingredients into the flour mixture. If the dough seems dry, add a teaspoon or two of water, as needed.

4 When the dough forms, transfer to a floured work surface and knead 5 to 10 minutes until smooth. Cover with a clean dish cloth and let rest for 10 minutes.

5 Divide the dough into two equal balls and roll each piece in flour. Use a rolling pin (or empty glass) to create a dough circle between ⅛- and ¼-inch thick.

6 Pour 2 teaspoons of olive oil in a skillet and bring to medium heat. When the oil is hot, add a flatbread and cook until golden brown on one side, about 1 to 2 minutes. Then flip and cook the other side for another 1 to 2 minutes.

7 Transfer to a plate, add the remaining 2 teaspoons of olive oil to the skillet, and repeat the cooking process with the second flatbread dough.

TIP: These flatbreads make a great side to your salad or soup and are ideal for personal pizza crusts!

NOTE: If your skillet is large enough, you can also make a single, larger flatbread instead of two smaller ones.

Best Little Pot of BBQ Beans

PREP TIME: 5 MINUTES | COOK TIME: 43 MINUTES | YIELD: 2 SERVINGS

INGREDIENTS

2 slices bacon, chopped

2 tablespoons finely chopped white onion

1 tablespoon finely chopped green bell pepper

½ teaspoon minced garlic

1 (15.5 ounce) can navy or cannellini beans, drained and rinsed

⅓ cup store-bought barbecue sauce

1 tablespoon brown sugar

1 teaspoon yellow mustard

DIRECTIONS

1 Bring a medium pot to medium-high heat and add the chopped bacon. Cook for 5 to 8 minutes, until it becomes crispy. Drain the bacon on a folded paper towel and reserve about 2 teaspoons of the bacon fat in the pot (discard any excess or see Tip to save).

2 Add the onions and bell pepper to the bacon drippings and cook for 4 minutes, stirring frequently, until it is softening. Add the garlic and cook another 1 minute.

3 Add the navy beans, barbecue sauce, brown sugar, and mustard to the pot and stir to combine. Stir in the bacon pieces.

4 Bring to a boil over medium-high heat. Then reduce the heat to medium-low and simmer for 30 minutes, stirring occasionally so that the beans don't stick.

5 Serve warm.

NOTE: Store the leftovers in an airtight container in the fridge for 3 to 4 days or cool and freeze for up to 6 months.

VARY IT! Use your favorite bottled barbeque sauce (sweet, spicy, tangy, smoky) for a personalized flavor experience. Bacon may be omitted for a meat-free dish. Omit Step 1 and, in Step 2, add 2 teaspoons of olive oil to cook the onion and bell pepper.

TIP: Take some advice from a Southerner, save your excess bacon grease! Bacon grease is considered a precious commodity by many and can be used to add a smoky, salty, rich flavor profile to future recipes like vegetable sautés or as a butter substitute in savory baked goods. To safely store bacon grease, strain off small bits of residual bacon by using a fine mesh strainer or coffee filter placed over a glass canning jar and cover with the lid. Keep the bacon grease in the fridge for up to 3 months or the freezer indefinitely. If planning to freeze, let strained drippings come to room temperature, and then pour into ice cube trays to freeze. Pop them out and store in a freezer bag for use as needed.

that produce offers

» Loading your plate with fresh foods that offer a welcomed diversity of vitamins, minerals, dietary fiber, and other important nutrients

» Partaking in an array of tastes and textures that are gifted by Mother Nature herself

Chapter **17**

Fruits and Veggies to Brighten Your Plate

Adding a new veggie or fruit side dish to your meal is like inviting a colorful, intriguing, yet "I'm not sure I'm going to actually like him" character to your party. Maybe you hesitated to extend the invitation but in hindsight are so glad you did because it's love at first bite. Fruits and vegetables really have a lot to offer to an eating experience, including seasonal variety; fresh taste; and lots of vitamins, minerals, antioxidants, and other important nutrients like dietary fiber.

Eating a rainbow not only is good for your body, it can also be fun for your mood! It feels exciting, and I'll go so far as to say adventurous, to visit the produce department and try out new fruits and vegetables. There are some incredibly strange yet wonderful globally sourced fruits and vegetables that are available in many neighborhood markets today! Don't be afraid to talk to your grocery store's produce manager; they are experts in the field, are responsible for sourcing and ordering produce, and can share their expertise to help you pick the best produce from the bunch. Oftentimes, they'll even slice you off a sample!

Obviously, produce doesn't stay safe for eating as long as your pantry shelf staples. That's why it's a smart idea to visit the store a couple of times a week, if possible, to buy fresh produce. You can order for delivery or pickup, but in doing so, you let go of a little control over the quality/size of the fruits and veggies you are procuring. To get the best from an online order, don't be too shy to mention exactly what you want in the "notes" area of your shopping app. For example, "a banana that has no brown spots" or "avocados that are still firm, yet not hard."

Fruits and vegetables are typically best purchased seasonally. However, today we live in a very global economy where you can get almost anything, any time of year. Still, a watermelon is going to be best in the summer! If you see a deal on seasonal produce, stock up if you have the appetite to eat it quickly or to prep and store it. Fruits are easy to freeze. For example, berries can be frozen "as is" and other fruits do better sliced or chopped. In Chapter 21, I recommend blanching vegetables for freezing. Most vegetables can be blanched, with the exception of high-water content vegetables. The process entails prepping veggies into bite-sized pieces, then scalding in boiling water for a couple of minutes. Vegetables are drained and given an ice bath to halt carry-over cooking. Spread the veggies out to dry, then freeze on a baking sheet before ultimately transferring them to a zip-top freezer bag.

REMEMBER

Always wash your produce before eating or cooking for food safety purposes. This includes washing fruits and veggies for eating raw and also for cooking — even when boiling in a pot of water. Some produce, like carrots and potatoes, may require some scrubbing to remove dirt and debris.

Recipes that feature fresh or frozen fruits or veggies can suit nearly any mood or taste preference. If you want a food hug in the comfort zone, try the Best Air Fryer "Baked" Potato, or step outside of your comfort zone and explore the Chile-Spiced Applesauce.

Addictive Roasted Broccoli

PREP TIME: 2 MINUTES   COOK TIME: 18 MINUTES   YIELD: 1 SERVING

INGREDIENTS

10 fresh broccoli florets, approximately the same size

2 teaspoons olive oil

⅛ teaspoon salt

⅛ teaspoon ground black pepper

⅛ teaspoon garlic powder

DIRECTIONS

1 Preheat an air fryer to 380 degrees or an oven to 400 degrees.

2 Place the broccoli florets in a bowl and drizzle with the olive oil; stir to coat. Sprinkle and toss with the salt, pepper, and garlic powder.

3 Air-fry for 8–9 minutes until browning and the edges are becoming crispy. Flip and shake one time in the middle of the air fryer for more even browning. If using an oven, roast for 15 to 18 minutes, flipping with a spatula halfway through cooking.

VARY IT! Spice it up by adding ⅛ teaspoon of crushed dried red pepper or cayenne pepper.

Creamy Cheesy Mashed Cauliflower

PREP TIME: 10 MINUTES | COOK TIME: 10 MINUTES | YIELD: 1 SERVING

INGREDIENTS

8 ounces frozen cauliflower florets

⅛ teaspoon salt

½ ounce cream cheese (1 tablespoon)

2 tablespoons shredded Parmesan cheese

1 teaspoon finely chopped chives

DIRECTIONS

1 Place the frozen cauliflower and the salt in a medium pot and add enough water to cover the cauliflower by 1 inch. Bring to a boil over medium-high heat and cook for 7–10 minutes, until buttery tender. Thoroughly drain the water.

2 Return the boiled cauliflower to the pot and cook over medium-low heat, stirring frequently, for 2–3 minutes to help steam off any excess water that could make the final dish soggy. Be watchful so that it does not burn.

3 Place the cauliflower in a small blender and let it cool for 5 minutes before moving on. Then, add the cream cheese and Parmesan cheese; use the pulse button to process until thick and smooth.

4 Season with salt and pepper. Garnish the top with chopped chives.

VARY IT! Change the flavor profile by swapping the Parmesan cheese for another variety such as pepper jack, blue cheese, sharp cheddar cheese, or your favorite type.

Love 'em Lemon Green Beans

PREP TIME: 3 MINUTES | COOK TIME: 9 MINUTES | YIELD: 1 SERVING

INGREDIENTS

1 teaspoon olive oil

1 teaspoon minced garlic

5 to 6 ounces fresh green beans, trimmed (about 15 green beans)

2 tablespoons vegetable or chicken broth

1 teaspoon salted butter

1 tablespoon lemon juice

1 teaspoon lemon zest

DIRECTIONS

1 In medium skillet, heat the olive oil over medium heat.

2 Add the garlic and green beans; sauté for 2 minutes or until garlic is fragrant.

3 Add the vegetable broth, cover, and steam the green beans for 5–7 minutes or until they are tender but still bright green.

4 Add the butter, lemon juice, and lemon zest; toss to combine until the butter is melted.

5 Season with salt, if needed, and serve warm.

TIP: Toasted slice almonds or toasted pecans are a nice finishing touch!

"Everything Bagel" Brussels Sprouts

PREP TIME: 5 MINUTES | COOK TIME: 35 MINUTES | YIELD: 1 SERVING

INGREDIENTS

6 ounces fresh Brussels sprouts (about 12 sprouts)

2 teaspoons olive oil

¾ teaspoon Everything Bagel seasoning

DIRECTIONS

1 Preheat the oven to 400 degrees.

2 Remove any brown or yellow outer leaves and trim the knobby ends a bit, if excessive. Slice the sprouts in half lengthwise (tip to base).

3 Place the sprouts in a pile on a rimmed baking sheet. Drizzle with the olive oil and sprinkle with seasoning. Toss the sprouts around a bit and then spread them out in a single layer.

4 Roast for about 30–35 minutes, until browned and crispy on the outside and tender inside.

TIP: You can make your own "Everything Bagel" Spice (with extra to use later) by tossing together 1 tablespoon of kosher salt with 2 tablespoons each of poppy seeds, sesame seeds, and dried onion flakes. Store in a small jar in a cool, dark pantry.

VARY IT! Instead of Everything Bagel seasoning, you can use ½ teaspoon of salt and ¼ teaspoon of ground black pepper for a classic taste.

Tiny No-Crust Tomato Sweet Onion Tart

PREP TIME: 10 MINUTES | COOK TIME: 35 MINUTES | YIELD: 1 SERVING

INGREDIENTS

1 medium vine-ripe tomato
(2½- to 3-inch diameter)

1 teaspoon salted butter

¼ cup finely chopped sweet
yellow onion

2 tablespoons liquid egg white,
or 1 whole egg white

Pinch of black pepper

Pinch of salt

1 tablespoon chopped fresh
basil, or ½ teaspoon dried basil

¼ cup plus 1 tablespoon
shredded mozzarella, divided

DIRECTIONS

1 Preheat the oven to 375 degrees.

2 Slice the tomato crosswise into ⅓-inch slices. Pat the slices gently with a paper towel to remove some excess moisture.

3 In a small skillet, melt the butter and sauté the onion until softened, about 3 minutes. Transfer the onion to a bowl and let it cool for 2 minutes.

4 After the onion has cooled slightly, add the egg whites, pepper, salt, basil, and ¼ cup of cheese and stir to combine well.

5 Spray an 8-ounce ramekin with nonstick spray. Layer the ramekin with one tomato slice and a bit of the egg mixture to just cover. Repeat with the remaining tomatoes and egg mixture. Sprinkle the remaining 1 tablespoon of cheese on top. If needed, lightly press down on the tomato stack to compress it into the ramekin (although it will naturally "fall" while baking).

6 Bake for 30 minutes or until the cheese is bubbling and browning in places.

7 Let the tart rest for 5–10 minutes before eating. Serve in the ramekin or use a knife around the sides to release the tart; slip it onto a plate.

VARY IT! Instead of using a medium tomato, substitute ⅔ cup of halved grape tomatoes.

Fast and Fail-Proof Corn on the Cob

PREP TIME: 6 MINUTES	COOK TIME: 2 MINUTES	YIELD: 1 SERVING

INGREDIENTS

1 ear of corn, husk and silks intact

2 teaspoons salted butter

Salt or other seasonings of choice

DIRECTIONS

1   Place the corn on a microwave-safe plate or paper towel and microwave on high for 2–3 minutes.

2   Let the corn cool for 5 minutes in the husk.

3   With a sharp knife, cut off the bottom end of the corn (*not* the top tapered end where the silks show through).

4   Holding the tapered end of the corn, wiggle the ear of corn out of the husk and pull away. The silks will remain inside the husk, but if a few hang on, just pick them away and discard. Use a mitt or oven gloves to protect your hands!

5   Serve hot, rolling in butter, and with your desired seasonings.

VARY IT! Customize your corn cob with a seasoning that speaks to your mood! Try smoked paprika, chili-lime seasoning, Everything Bagel seasoning, Montreal seasoning, or garlic salt.

Best Air Fryer "Baked" Potato

PREP TIME: 2 MINUTES | COOK TIME: 40 MINUTES | YIELD: 1 SERVING

INGREDIENTS

1 large Russet potato
(8 to 10 ounces)

1 teaspoon olive oil

Pinch of salt, more to taste

Pinch of ground black pepper,
more to taste

Pinch of garlic powder

1 tablespoon salted butter

DIRECTIONS

1 Preheat an air fryer to 400 degrees.

2 Make sure that the potato is completely dry after washing. Use a fork to puncture the potato in several areas so that steam can escape while cooking.

3 Rub the skin with the olive oil and sprinkle with the pinches of salt, pepper, and garlic powder.

4 Air-fry for 30–40 minutes or until the outer potato is crisping and you can slip a knife in the center; the flesh will feel soft and tender.

5 Slice the cooked potato lengthwise. Pinch both ends and push toward the middle to open the potato up nicely.

6 Add the butter and season with salt and pepper; if desired, add other toppings.

NOTE: You can bake a potato easily in the oven at 400 degrees for about 1 hour. But that is a time-consuming endeavor that will really heat up your kitchen. Making it in the air fryer offers a convenient (and cooler) option to quickly get a cooked potato on your plate!

Crispy Smashed Baby Potatoes

PREP TIME: 5 MINUTES | COOK TIME: 35 MINUTES | YIELD: 1 SERVING

INGREDIENTS

8 ounces baby potatoes (any color or a blend of small potatoes will work)

½ teaspoon salt, divided

1½ teaspoon olive oil, plus more to oil baking sheet

½ teaspoon garlic powder

⅛ teaspoon ground black pepper

2 tablespoons grated Parmesan cheese

1 tablespoon finely chopped chives

DIRECTIONS

1 Preheat the oven to 425 degrees and rub a baking sheet with olive oil.

2 Place ¼ teaspoon of the salt and the potatoes in a medium pot; fill the pot with enough water to cover the potatoes by 1 inch.

3 Bring the water to a boil over medium-high heat and cook the potatoes until tender, about 10–15 minutes.

4 Drain the water from the potatoes and set the potatoes to dry a few minutes on a clean dish towel.

5 Spread the potatoes on the prepared baking sheet and use the bottom of a measuring cup or glass to smash them down flat, to about ¼-inch thickness.

6 Drizzle with the olive oil and sprinkle with the garlic powder, the remaining ¼ teaspoon of salt, and pepper.

7 Roast in the oven for about 15 minutes or until golden brown and crispy around the edges.

8 Remove them briefly from the oven and sprinkle with the Parmesan cheese. Return them to the oven and bake 5 more minutes. Sprinkle with the chives and serve while still hot.

VARY IT! Replace the Parmesan cheese with nutritional yeast for a dairy-free side dish.

Salted Honey Sweet Potato Fries

INGREDIENTS

1 (8-ounce) sweet potato

1 tablespoon olive oil

2 teaspoons honey

¼ teaspoon coarsely ground Himalayan sea salt, or more to taste

DIRECTIONS

1   Preheat the oven to 400 degrees or an air fryer to 360 degrees.

2   Scrub and dry the sweet potato; peel if desired but it's not necessary. Slice the sweet potato in half lengthwise, and then in half crosswise. Cut each of these sections into approximately ⅓-inch-thick wedges.

3   Place the wedges in a pile on a baking sheet and drizzle with the olive oil. Use your hands or a spoon to ensure that all the wedges are coated and then spread them out into a single layer for even baking.

4   Bake in the oven for 25 minutes or air fry for 8–10 minutes, flipping with a rigid spatula about halfway through. Fries will be done when they are turning crispy, browning on the edges, and soft in the center.

5   Allow to cool for 3–4 minutes and then drizzle with the honey and sprinkle with the salt, to taste.

VARY IT! Instead of honey, drizzle with maple syrup and sprinkle with cinnamon.

Maple-Orange Mashed Sweet Potato

INGREDIENTS

1 medium-large sweet potato (about 10 to 12 ounces)

1 tablespoon salted butter

1 tablespoon fresh orange juice

1 tablespoon real maple syrup

Pinch of ground nutmeg

Pinch of salt (optional)

DIRECTIONS

1 Make sure that the sweet potato is completely dry after washing. Cut into 2-inch cubes.

2 Bring a medium pot of water to a boil over medium-high heat. Add the cubed sweet potatoes and cook until fork-tender, about 15–20 minutes.

3 Drain the water from the pot and place the sweet potatoes in a bowl. Using a fork or potato masher, mash the potatoes to your desired consistency.

4 While the potatoes are still hot, stir in the butter, orange juice, maple syrup, and nutmeg until combined well. Taste and add a pinch of salt, if needed.

VARY IT! For an adult upgrade, mix in a splash of orange liqueur (like Grand Marnier) or bourbon.

Sesame Mushroom Spinach Sauté

INGREDIENTS

1 teaspoon sesame oil

1 cup sliced white button or cremini mushrooms

1 teaspoon minced garlic

3 ounces fresh baby spinach

⅛ teaspoon black pepper

1 teaspoon soy sauce or coconut aminos

½ teaspoon sesame seeds

DIRECTIONS

1 In a large skillet, heat the sesame oil over medium-high heat. Add the mushrooms and sauté until tender, about 2 minutes. Add the garlic and cook an additional 1 minute.

2 Add the spinach to the skillet and stir until wilted, about 2 minutes.

3 Remove from the heat and stir in the pepper and soy sauce.

4 Sprinkle with the sesame seeds before serving hot.

NOTE: As the spinach wilts, the volume decreases tremendously, so add more if you'd like. Leftovers of this dish can always be the filling for tomorrow's omelet.

Chile-Spiced Applesauce

PREP TIME: 1 MINUTE	COOK TIME: 1 MINUTE	YIELD: 1 SERVING

INGREDIENTS

1 teaspoon salted butter

Pinch of ground cayenne pepper, or more to taste

½ cup prepared unsweetened applesauce (see Note)

DIRECTIONS

1 Melt the butter in a small microwave-safe dish for 10–15 seconds.

2 Stir in the cayenne pepper and applesauce. Be careful about the amount of cayenne pepper you use initially; you can add more later.

3 Heat the applesauce mixture in the microwave on high until warm, about 30 seconds.

4 Taste and stir in another pinch of cayenne pepper, if you'd like it spicier.

NOTE: This recipe conveniently uses an individually sized, 4-ounce container of applesauce.

Mediterranean Stuffed Baked Avocado

PREP TIME: 5 MINUTES	COOK TIME: 12 MINUTES	YIELD: 2 SERVING

INGREDIENTS

1 large avocado

1 ounce cream cheese (2 tablespoons), softened

2 tablespoons crumbled feta cheese

1½ tablespoons chopped sun-dried tomatoes

1½ tablespoons chopped marinated artichokes

Pinch of salt

Pinch of black pepper

2 tablespoons store-bought Greek vinaigrette salad dressing

DIRECTIONS

1 Preheat the oven to 400 degrees.

2 Slice the avocado in half lengthwise and carefully remove the pit.

3 In a small bowl, make the filling by mixing together the cream cheese, feta cheese, sun-dried tomatoes, artichokes, salt, and pepper. Divide the mixture to evenly fill the cavities of each avocado half, mounding it up a bit.

4 Bake for 10–12 minutes until the cheese is bubbling and the avocado is warmed through.

5 Remove the avocado from the oven and drizzle with your favorite Greek vinaigrette dressing.

VARY IT! Before stuffing the avocado, if the halves seem wobbly, simply slice a very small edge through the bottom of the peel into the flesh so that it sits flat.

6

Snacks, Desserts, and Nibbles

Make eating between meals better tasting, better for your health, and better on your budget with yummy, do-it-yourself snacks and desserts.

Whip up a savory, salty, or sweet snack in almost no time to satisfy nearly any craving when it hits.

Treat yourself to dessert by making your own — it's a piece of cake! Choose from sweet shop and bakery-inspired desserts that are small-batch (but big enough to share) or portioned just for one, with no guilt.

healthier vibe

» Curbing your "hangries" with savory snacks that offer protein and great taste in every bite

» Munching mindfully with better-for-you snacks than high-processed packaged options at the store

Chapter 18

Savory and Sweet Snacks That Satisfy

S nacking is an important part of life and can boost you both physically and mentally! Whether you're into carefree, recreational noshing or on a focused mission to top off your tank after a workout, good snack choices can help keep your metabolism firing, energy up, and cravings satisfied. From nibbles and noshes including protein-rich Deviled Eggs to Olive Oil and Parmesan Popcorn, there's no need to feel guilty about snacking — just go for it! Also, when you're short on time, patience, or the will to cook yet another meal, a snack like the Charcuterie Stack paired with a piece of fruit or green salad can substitute as a nourishing traditional meal.

Deviled Eggs

PREP TIME: 5 MINUTES | **YIELD: 1 SERVING**

INGREDIENTS

2 hard-boiled eggs, peeled

2–3 teaspoons mayonnaise, to taste

¼ teaspoon Dijon mustard

Pinch of seasoned salt or sea salt

⅛ teaspoon smoked paprika

DIRECTIONS

1 Slice the peeled eggs in half lengthwise.

2 Remove the yolks from the center and place in a small bowl; set the egg whites aside.

3 Add the mayonnaise, Dijon mustard, and seasoned salt to the bowl with the yolks. Mash everything together with a fork until relatively smooth.

4 Spoon the egg yolk filling back into the centers of the egg whites, mounding them up.

5 Sprinkle with the smoked paprika; serve cold.

HARD-BOILED EGGS

Preparing hard-boiled eggs is easy, plus it's smart to have a few on hand for a quick protein snack or as a salad topping. You can boil just one or two eggs, or as many as will sit in a single layer in the pot without overcrowding.

Place the eggs in a saucepot and add enough water to cover by 1 inch. Cover the pot with a lid and bring the water up to a boil over medium-high heat. When the water reaches a full boil, turn off the heat and let the eggs sit in the hot water, with the lid on, for 15 minutes. After 15 minutes, drain the hot water and run the eggs under cool water to stop the cooking. Refrigerate promptly.

Hard-boiled eggs may be stored peeled in the fridge for up to 3 days. For longer storage, keep them in their shells until needed, for up to 7 days.

Classic Snack Mix

PREP TIME: 5 MINUTES	COOK TIME: 3 MINUTES	YIELD: 2½ CUPS

INGREDIENTS

¾ cup Rice Chex cereal

¾ cup Corn Chex cereal

¾ cup plain Cheerios cereal

2–3 tablespoons peanuts, almonds, or mixed nuts

1 tablespoon unsalted butter

1 tablespoon Worcestershire sauce

⅛ teaspoon seasoned salt

⅛ teaspoon onion powder

⅛ teaspoon garlic powder

¼ cup pretzel twists or sticks, broken up a bit

DIRECTIONS

1 Combine all the cereals and nuts in a medium-sized, microwave-safe bowl; set aside.

2 Add the butter to a small, microwave-safe bowl and microwave until melted, about 30 seconds, stopping briefly after 15 seconds to stir it up. Add Worcestershire sauce, seasoned salt, onion powder, and garlic powder then stir to combine. Pour over the cereal and nut mixture and gently stir until evenly coated.

3 Microwave for 45 seconds and then stir well. Microwave for 45 seconds two more times, stirring between each. Add the pretzels and stir to combine, and then microwave 15 more seconds.

4 Spread the snack mix onto a sheet of wax or parchment paper to cool completely. Store in an airtight container or zip-top bag.

NOTE: To prepare in the oven, start the recipe as written through Step 2. Then, pour the snack mix onto a rimmed baking sheet and bake for 30 to 40 minutes in a preheated 250-degree oven, stirring every 10 minutes or so.

VARY IT! Instead of pretzels, replace with ¼ cup of little cheddar fish crackers or oyster crackers. Also, if you like a spicy mix, mix in ⅛ teaspoon of ground cayenne pepper along with the other spices in Step 2.

Easy No-Yeast Giant Soft Pretzel

PREP TIME: 10 MINUTES | **COOK TIME: 20 MINUTES** | **YIELD: 1 SERVING**

INGREDIENTS

¾ cup all-purpose flour

1 teaspoon baking powder

½ teaspoon salt

½ teaspoon granulated sugar

1 tablespoon salted butter, room temperature

⅓ cup milk

2 tablespoons whisked egg (can use liquid egg)

Coarse salt

DIRECTIONS

1 Preheat the oven to 400 degrees. Coat a baking sheet with cooking spray.

2 In a bowl, mix together the flour, baking powder, salt, and sugar.

3 Add the butter to the flour mixture; use a fork to smash up the butter into the flour until pea-sized pieces form.

4 Add the milk and stir until a sticky dough forms.

5 Place the dough on a floured board and knead about 5 or 10 times until combined.

6 With your hands, roll the dough into a 24-inch rope and form it into a pretzel shape about the size of your hand, or 6- x 6-inches. See Figure 18-1 for guidance on shaping the pretzel.

7 Place on the prepared baking sheet and brush the top with the egg mixture. Sprinkle with coarse salt, as desired.

8 Bake for 18–20 minutes, or until it turns golden on top. Let cool 5 minutes before eating. The finished pretzel should be around the same size after baking — just puffier.

VARY IT! Before baking, sprinkle the top of the pretzel with another seasoning like Everything Bagel seasoning, Parmesan cheese, or cinnamon sugar.

Make a 24-inch dough rope and twist as shown.

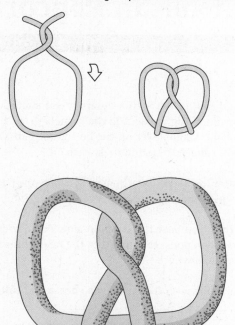

FIGURE 18-1:
Twisting the
pretzel.

After it's cooked as it was at the start, just puffier.

Olive Oil and Parmesan Popcorn

PREP TIME: 1 MINUTE	COOK TIME: 5 MINUTES	YIELD: 3½ CUPS

INGREDIENTS

2 teaspoons olive oil

2 tablespoons popcorn kernels

2 tablespoons grated Parmesan cheese

¼ teaspoon salt, or more to taste

DIRECTIONS

1 Add the oil to 2- to 4-quart metal saucepot and bring it to medium-high heat. Add the kernels to the hot oil so that they form a single layer on the bottom of pan. Cover and give the pot a shake to coat kernels with oil.

2 After the kernels start popping, shake the pan every 15 seconds to help the popcorn cook evenly.

3 When you hear the popping slow down to just 1 or 2 seconds between pops, remove from the heat immediately and pour it into a bowl.

4 Sprinkle with the Parmesan cheese and salt; toss to combine.

VARY IT! Add ¼ teaspoon of Italian seasoning or substitute salt for truffle salt.

Charcuterie Stack

INGREDIENTS

2 large pepperoni slices, cut thin

1 big piece the prosciutto, sliced thin and cut into 2 pieces

1 ounce sharp white cheddar cheese, cut in 2 chunks

1 mini Gouda round, sliced in half

2 to 3 roasted, marinated red pepper slices

2 to 3 pitted black olives (stuffed or plain) from jar or olive bar

2 to 3 dried figs or dried apricots

Buttery round crackers, (or your favorite cracker), for serving

DIRECTIONS

1 Fold the pepperoni in half and then in half again; set aside. Roll up the prosciutto starting on the short end, slice in half through the middle of the roll. You will have four pieces of meat.

2 Thread the meat, cheese, and the remaining ingredients on a bamboo skewer, alternating as desired.

3 Serve with your favorite crackers on the side.

VARY IT! Substitute with any meats, cheese, or antipasto that you prefer!

Small Batch Hummus

PREP TIME: 5 MINUTES YIELD: 2 TO 3 SERVINGS

INGREDIENTS

¾ cup canned chickpeas, drained and rinsed (see Tip)

3 tablespoons olive oil (plus an additional 1 teaspoon for topping)

1½ tablespoons tahini

1 tablespoon lemon juice

½ teaspoon garlic or garlic paste

¼ teaspoon salt

¼ teaspoon ground black pepper

¼ teaspoon smoked paprika

DIRECTIONS

1 Place all the ingredients in a personal-sized blender or mini food processor; process until smooth. If the consistency seems too pasty or thick, blend in 1 teaspoon of water at a time until desired texture is achieved.

2 Transfer the hummus to a serving bowl, drizzle with 1 teaspoon of olive oil, and a sprinkle the paprika.

NOTE: Store the leftovers in an airtight container in the fridge for up to 4 days.

TIP: Extra chickpeas from the can be kept in an airtight container in the fridge for a few days and added to salads, soups, and wraps.

Take a Hike Trail Mix

PREP TIME: 5 MINUTES	COOK TIME: 9 MINUTES	YIELD: 1 SERVING

INGREDIENTS

2 tablespoons raw pecan pieces

2 tablespoons raw cashew halves

1 tablespoon raw sunflower seeds

1 tablespoon raw pumpkin seeds

2 tablespoons raisins

2 tablespoons dried cherries

2 tablespoons dark chocolate chips (see Tip)

⅛ teaspoon ground cinnamon

¼ teaspoon salt

DIRECTIONS

1 Preheat the oven to 250 degrees.

2 Place the pecans and cashews on a baking sheet and toast for 4 minutes. Then add the raw sunflower seeds and raw pumpkin seeds to the baking sheet and toast everything together for an additional 4 to 5 minutes. (The pecans and cashews will have roasted a total of 8 to 9 minutes, and the sunflower and pumpkin seeds for 4 to 5 minutes.) Allow all the nuts and seeds to cool completely.

3 Place the cooled nuts and seeds in a zip-top bag or sealable container with the dried fruit and chocolate chips.

4 Add the cinnamon and salt to the bag; shake to coat. Enjoy.

TIP: If the trail mix will be in the heat, the chocolate chips will melt. You can omit or replace the chocolate chips with mini M&Ms, mini marshmallows, or another dried fruit.

NOTE: If preferred, and to save time, you may use preroasted nuts and seeds.

VARY IT! Make your own custom trail mix creation by exchanging any nut, seed, fruit, or chocolate ingredient with your favorite alternative.

Heavenly Honey-Roasted Peanuts in Air Fryer

PREP TIME: 4 MINUTES	COOK TIME: 7 MINUTES	YIELD: 1 TO 2 SERVINGS

INGREDIENTS

1 teaspoon salted butter

1 teaspoon honey

⅛ teaspoon salt

½ cup raw, shelled peanuts

⅛ teaspoon ground cinnamon

2 teaspoons granulated sugar

DIRECTIONS

1 Preheat an air fryer to 325 degrees.

2 Melt the butter in a small bowl in the microwave (about 10 seconds), and stir in the honey and salt.

3 Add the peanuts to the bowl and stir until coated.

4 Line the air fryer tray with parchment paper. Spread the coated peanuts out on the parchment paper in a single layer.

5 Air-fry for 6 minutes, stirring halfway for more even roasting. The peanuts will be done when they turn golden brown and become aromatic. Watch during the last few minutes to prevent burning, which can happen quickly with sugared nuts.

6 Transfer the peanuts to a shallow dish, spread them around, and let them cool for 5–10 minutes.

7 While cooling, mix cinnamon and sugar together. Toss with the peanuts at the end of their "rest," while they are still slightly warm.

NOTE: Store the leftovers in an airtight container.

VARY IT! Substitute ½ cup of raw almonds, pecans, cashews, or walnuts for the peanuts.

Yogurt Coconut Frozen Grapes

PREP TIME: 10 MINUTES | **YIELD: 1 SERVING**

INGREDIENTS

10 red or green grapes

3 tablespoons vanilla Greek yogurt

2 tablespoons shredded coconut

DIRECTIONS

1 Insert a toothpick into the top of each grape. Place the yogurt in a very small, deep dish (a shot glass works great). Pour the coconut into a little mound on a plate. Line a small baking dish with parchment paper.

2 Use the toothpick to dip each grape into the yogurt, coating about three-fourths of the grape. Then, dip the yogurt-covered grape into the coconut to cover the bottom of the grape.

3 Place each dipped grape on the lined baking dish; repeat the process with the remaining grapes.

4 Freeze for at least 2 hours or until the grapes are frozen solid.

VARY IT! Substitute graham cracker crumbs, crushed cereal, or cookie crumbs for the coconut.

Kettle Corn Just for You

PREP TIME: 2 MINUTES | COOK TIME: 4 MINUTES | YIELD: APPROX. 4 CUPS

INGREDIENTS

2 teaspoons salted butter

2 teaspoons coconut oil

⅛ teaspoon salt

¼ cup brown sugar

3½ tablespoons popcorn kernels (scant under ¼ cup)

DIRECTIONS

1 Add the butter, oil, salt, and brown sugar to a 2-quart microwave-safe bowl with a vented lid.

2 Microwave until the butter and oil are just melted, 15–20 seconds. Stir to combine well and then add the popcorn kernels. Stir again to coat the kernels with the sugar mixture.

3 Place the lid on the bowl; microwave on *high* for about 3 minutes. *Do not* use the "popcorn" function button, if your microwave has one. When the popping slows to 1–2 seconds between pops, remove it from the microwave immediately.

NOTE: Microwave times can vary, so it's important to listen for the popping to slow to avoid a burned result.

VARY IT! Add 2 tablespoons of peanuts with the popcorn kernels during Step 2.

Chocolate-Dipped Dried Apricots

PREP TIME: 2 MINUTES | **COOK TIME: 15 SECONDS** | **YIELD: 1 SERVING**

INGREDIENTS

4 dried apricots

20 dark chocolate chips, divided

1 teaspoon chopped pistachios

DIRECTIONS

1 Arrange the apricots on a microwave-safe plate.

2 Top each apricot with 5 chocolate chips and microwave at 50 percent power for about 15 seconds or until the chocolate softens.

3 Use the tip of a spoon to slightly spread the chocolate around the top of the apricot. While the chocolate is still warm, sprinkle with the chopped pistachios.

4 Set in the fridge for 5 minutes to cool and set the chocolate.

VARY IT! Use white chocolate chips and chopped almonds.

- bite without guilt

» Finding ways to add fruit to your dessert that will help meet some of your daily dietary needs

» Honing cooking and baking skills and enjoying sweet rewards that you don't have to share

Chapter 19

Single-Serve Desserts with Automatic Portion Control

Embrace your favorite sweets in the moment without the worry of being tempted by dozens of cookies, piles of candies, or leftover wedges of pie lying in wait and calling out to you in the middle of the night. Single-serve cookies, cakes, pies, and other desserts offer built-in portion control that hits the mute button on that over-sugared siren song. Baking and making desserts for one can be tricky; scaling down a big recipe creates challenges. Like, how do you divide a single egg by six, or what size pan do I need for such a small amount of batter? This dessert chapter provides measurements, proportions, substitutions, and other recipe tips needed to create personal-sized baked goods and other comforting desserts. From a nostalgic Giant Peanut Butter Cookie that you can bake in a toaster oven to an elegant Roasted Pear with Caramel Pan Sauce, there is something in this chapter to suit every situation and sweet tooth.

Chocolate Java Lava Cake

PREP TIME: 10 MINUTES	COOK TIME: 18 MINUTES	YIELD: 1 SERVING

INGREDIENTS

2 tablespoons salted butter, plus more for greasing dish

¼ cup granulated sugar

¼ teaspoon vanilla extract

2 tablespoons liquid egg from carton

¼ teaspoon espresso powder

1 tablespoon unsweetened cocoa powder

1 tablespoon all-purpose flour

Ice cream or whipped cream, for serving (optional)

DIRECTIONS

1 Preheat the oven to 350 degrees.

2 In a microwave-safe bowl, microwave butter for 30 seconds to melt, stopping half-way through to swirl.

3 Add the sugar, vanilla extract, and egg; mix together.

4 Add the espresso powder, cocoa powder, and flour; mix well.

5 Grease a 6- to 8-ounce ramekin with butter.

6 Pour the batter into the ramekin and bake for 16–18 minutes, or until firm and set at edges but still a little soft and wobbly in the center.

7 Let the cake cool for 3–5 minutes. Use a knife to loosen the edges and invert the cake onto a small plate or eat it from the ramekin.

8 If desired, serve topped with ice cream or whipped cream.

VARY IT! Omit the espresso powder if you are not a fan.

Buttery Cinnamon Tortilla Chips

INGREDIENTS

1 (8-inch) flour tortilla

1 teaspoon salted butter, melted

½ tablespoon granulated sugar

¼ teaspoon ground cinnamon

Honey, for serving

DIRECTIONS

1 Preheat the oven to 350 degrees or an air fryer to 390 degrees.

2 Place the tortilla on a small baking sheet. With a knife or pizza cutter, slice the tortilla into 8 wedges (leave them together in a circular shape for now).

3 Brush the top of the tortilla with the melted butter.

4 In a small bowl, toss together the sugar and cinnamon. Sprinkle over the top of the buttered tortilla.

5 Bake for 10–12 minutes or air-fry for 5 minutes, until it is crispy and the cinnamon sugar is bubbling and sticking.

6 If desired, drizzle with honey before serving.

TIP: Delicious served with ice cream or sweet toppings and sauces like caramel sauce, maple syrup, sweet flavor whipped cream cheese, pineapple bits, or fruit relishes.

Giant Oatmeal Cookie

PREP TIME: 5 MINUTES | COOK TIME: 10 MINUTES | YIELD: 1 BIG SERVING

INGREDIENTS

2 tablespoons salted butter, softened

2 tablespoons brown sugar

2 tablespoons granulated sugar

1 tablespoon liquid egg product

⅛ teaspoon baking soda

⅛ teaspoon ground cinnamon

Pinch of salt

¼ cup all-purpose flour

¼ cup old-fashioned oats

¼ cup raisins

DIRECTIONS

1 Preheat the oven to 350 degrees. Lightly mist a small baking sheet with cooking spray.

2 In a medium bowl, cream the butter and sugars together.

3 Mix in the liquid egg until incorporated.

4 Stir in the baking soda, cinnamon, salt, flour, and oats until a dough forms. Stir in the raisins.

Form the dough into a ball with your hands and set it on the prepared baking sheet. Gently press the dough down with your hands into 4-inch circle approximately.

5 Bake for 10 minutes or until golden brown around the edges. Remove the cookie from the oven and let it rest in pan for 5 minutes.

VARY IT! Swap the raisins for dried cranberries for a twist on the traditional.

NOTE: This cookie is huge and will satisfy even the hungriest of cookie monsters. If it's too large, save the remainder in a zip-top sandwich bag for the next day!

Giant Peanut Butter Cookie

PREP TIME: 5 MINUTES	COOK TIME: 10 MINUTES	YIELD: 1 BIG SERVING

INGREDIENTS

2 tablespoons salted butter, softened

2 tablespoons smooth peanut butter

2 tablespoons brown sugar

2 tablespoons granulated sugar

1 tablespoon liquid egg from carton

⅛ teaspoon baking soda

7 tablespoons all-purpose flour

DIRECTIONS

1 Preheat the oven to 350 degrees. Lightly mist a small baking sheet with cooking spray.

2 In a medium bowl, cream the butter, peanut butter, and sugars.

3 Mix in the liquid egg until incorporated.

4 Stir in the baking soda and flour and stir until dough forms.

5 Form the dough into a ball with your hands. Set it in the center of the prepared baking sheet. Press down to create 5-inch circle approximately. Use a chopstick or skewer to make the traditional "fork" hatch marks.

6 Bake for 9–10 minutes, until the cookie turns golden at edges. Remove the cookie from the oven and let it cool for 5 minutes in the pan.

VARY IT! Almond butter works well in this nostalgic cookie recipe, too!

Giant Pecan Chocolate Chip Cookie

PREP TIME: 5 MINUTES	COOK TIME: 12 MINUTES	YIELD: 1 BIG SERVING

INGREDIENTS

2 tablespoons salted butter, softened

1 tablespoon brown sugar

2 tablespoons granulated sugar

1 tablespoon liquid egg from carton

⅛ teaspoon baking soda

Pinch of salt

6 tablespoons all-purpose flour

1 tablespoon chopped pecans

1 tablespoon mini chocolate chips

DIRECTIONS

1 Preheat the oven to 350 degrees. Lightly mist a small baking sheet with cooking spray.

2 In a medium bowl, cream the butter and sugars together.

3 Stir in the egg until incorporated.

4 Mix in the baking soda, salt, flour, pecans, and chocolate chips.

5 Form a dough ball with your hands or a flipper-style spatula and set it on the prepared baking sheet. Press down on the dough lightly to create 4-inch circle approximately.

6 Bake for 10–12 minutes, until the edges turn golden brown. Remove the cookie from the oven and let it rest on the pan for 5 minutes.

VARY IT! Omit the pecans if you are not a fan.

NOTE: If you are looking to make your giant cookie picture pretty, reserve a couple of the chopped pecans and mini chocolate chips from Step 4 and press them lightly into the top of the shaped cookie before baking.

Chocolate Greek Yogurt Dip with Strawberries

PREP TIME: 3 MINUTES   YIELD: 1 SERVING

INGREDIENTS

1 (5.3-ounce) single-serve carton vanilla Greek yogurt

1 tablespoon unsweetened cocoa powder

2 teaspoons mini chocolate chips

½ cup halved strawberries

DIRECTIONS

1   Open the tub of Greek yogurt. Mix in the cocoa powder until smooth.

2   Stir in the mini chocolate chips.

3   Serve with the halved strawberries for dipping.

VARY IT! Assorted fruit slices, pretzels, or vanilla wafers also go well with this dip.

Baked Banana with Oatmeal Cookie Topping

PREP TIME: 5 MINUTES | COOK TIME: 12 MINUTES | YIELD: 1 SERVING

INGREDIENTS

1 large banana

1½ tablespoons salted butter, melted

⅛ teaspoon ground cinnamon

1 tablespoon brown sugar

2 tablespoons old-fashioned oats

2 tablespoons all-purpose flour

1 tablespoon chopped raisins

1 tablespoon chopped pecans

Ice cream, whipped cream, maple syrup, or caramel sauce, for topping (optional)

DIRECTIONS

1 Preheat the oven to 350 degrees or an air fryer to 390 degrees.

2 Slice the banana in half lengthwise and set aside.

3 In a small bowl, combine the melted butter, cinnamon, brown sugar, oats, flour, raisins, and pecans into a cookie-dough consistency topping.

4 Press half of the mixture gently down onto a banana half to form a crust and place the banana on a baking sheet if baking in the oven or on a small round cake pan if air-frying; repeat with the remaining banana slices and crumb mixture.

5 Bake the banana in the oven for 10–12 minutes or place the coated banana slices in the air fryer basket to cook for 6–7 minutes. The banana will soften and the crumb topping will start to turn golden brown like a cookie.

6 Serve plain or with desired toppings.

VARY IT! Drizzle with chocolate, caramel, or maple syrup for a special presentation.

Apple Walnut Crisp

PREP TIME: 5 MINUTES | **COOK TIME: 30 MINUTES** | **YIELD: 1 SERVING**

INGREDIENTS

1 medium Granny Smith apple, sliced ¼-inch thick slices

2 tablespoons brown sugar

1 teaspoon cornstarch

1 tablespoon chopped walnuts or pecans

⅛ teaspoon ground cinnamon

2 tablespoons old-fashioned oats

2 tablespoons brown sugar

1 tablespoon all-purpose flour

1 tablespoon salted butter, softened

⅛ teaspoon ground cinnamon

Pinch of ground nutmeg

DIRECTIONS

1 Preheat the oven to 375 degrees.

2 In a small bowl, toss the apples with the brown sugar, cornstarch, walnuts, and cinnamon. Arrange in an 8- to 12-ounce ramekin or baking dish. If slices are too long for the ramekin, cut them in half.

3 Use the same bowl to mix together the oats, brown sugar, flour, softened butter, cinnamon, and nutmeg until they form a crumbly mixture.

4 Sprinkle the oats mixture evenly over the apples.

5 Bake for 30 minutes or until the apples are softened and the topping is turning crisp and lightly golden brown.

VARY IT! So delicious served with a scoop of vanilla ice cream.

Roasted Pear with Caramel Pan Sauce

PREP TIME: 5 MINUTES	COOK TIME: 12 MINUTES	YIELD: 1 SERVING

INGREDIENTS

1 tablespoon salted butter

1 medium firm but ripe Bosc pear

4 teaspoons packed brown sugar

1 tablespoon heavy cream

¼ teaspoon vanilla extract

Pinch of salt

DIRECTIONS

1 Cut the pear in quarters lengthwise and remove the core.

2 In a small skillet, melt the butter over medium-high heat.

3 Nestle the pear quarters, with one cut side down, in the skillet and cook about 3 minutes until lightly browned, then reduce the heat to medium and cook an additional 3 minutes. Turn the pear quarters to the other cut side and cook 3–4 more minutes.

4 Add the brown sugar and 1 tablespoon water to the skillet, gently incorporating with a spoon. Turn the pear skin side down and cook, on medium heat, until the sauce is thickened, about 90 seconds.

5 Remove from the heat and stir in the cream, vanilla, and salt.

VARY IT! Add a pinch of ground cinnamon, ground nutmeg, or ground ginger.

Little Lemon Pie with Raspberry Compote

PREP TIME: 10 MINUTES (PLUS 2 HOURS TO CHILL)	COOK TIME: 30 MINUTES	YIELD: 1 SERVING

INGREDIENTS

1 tablespoon salted butter

¼ cup graham cracker crumbs (see Tip)

2 egg yolks

2½ tablespoons fresh lemon juice (about 1 medium lemon)

¼ cup sweetened condensed milk

2 tablespoons frozen raspberries, thawed

1 teaspoon granulated sugar

DIRECTIONS

1 Preheat the oven to 350 degrees.

2 In a 6- to 8-ounce ramekin or 4-inch diameter microwave-safe mini pie pan, melt the butter in the microwave on *high* for 15 seconds. If you are using a metal pie pan, add the butter to the pie pan and stick it in the oven for a minute or two to melt.

3 Add the graham cracker crumbs and then press down to make a crust that covers the bottom and up the sides of the ramekin as far as possible.

4 Bake the crust for 12–15 minutes and then set aside to cool.

5 While the crust is cooling, make the filling by placing the egg yolks and lemon juice in a medium-sized bowl; stir well to combine. Stir in the sweetened condensed milk until incorporated.

6 Let the crust cool for 10 minutes and then pour in the filling. Bake for 15 minutes or until set. Remove the crust and let it cook for about 10 minutes before placing it in the fridge to cool for 2 hours.

7 While the pie is chilling, make the topping by thawing the frozen raspberries in a small microwave-safe bowl. Keep the thawed juices in the bowl and stir in the sugar. Press down with a fork to smash the berries. Microwave for about 45 seconds (in 15-second increments) until thickened into a chunky sauce.

(continued)

(continued)

8 Place the sauce in the fridge to cool along with the pie. To serve, pour the raspberry topping over the cold pie and enjoy!

TIP: Make the graham cracker crumbs by placing two sheets of graham crackers in a zip-top bag and crushing the sheets with a rolling pin. Then measure the crumbs for this recipe.

NOTE: Because this recipe uses two egg yolks, you'll have two leftover egg whites. Save those in the fridge and scramble them for breakfast the next day. Or, freeze them to thaw out later for another recipe.

Chapter **20**

Smaller-Batch Desserts: Sure, Have Another

Hey, there is absolutely no shame in having another bite of your favorite dessert! This chapter features scrumptious, yummy sweet treats that are scaled down from their eye-popping full-sized inspirations to provide a smaller batch and yet still a little something extra for the single baker to share with friends or to keep stashed away for later! From bake-in-a-loaf pan desserts, like Gooey Batter Cake in Loaf Pan and Small-Batch Fudgy Brownies, to a creative and customizable Granola Chocolate Bark, you will have no trouble finding your new favorite goodie to make at home and share at the office or a party. Or gobble it up all by yourself; I'm not judging.

ESSENTIAL SPATULAS FOR YOUR KITCHEN

Not all spatulas perform the same job! But with these three types of spatulas on hand, you should be able to efficiently get the task at hand accomplished.

- **Flipper spatulas** are for turning things over. They have a long handle with a tapered rectangular end that slides easily under food. This spatula can have slots (for flipping juicy or greasy things like sausage patties) or can be solid (for flipping food like pancakes or sliding cookies off the sheet).

- **Spreader spatulas** are for smearing and spreading one food onto another. There are two types of spreader spatulas — straight and offset — and they have slightly different functions. A straight spreader spatula (shaped similarly to a large butter knife) works well for tasks like spreading peanut butter on bread or cream cheese on a bagel, while an offset spatula has a bend in the neck and is designed to keep hands out of food when covering a large, flat area, like spreading icing on a sheet cake.

- **Scraper spatulas** are made for removing soft, sticky food residue (like batters) from the sides of a jar, bowl, or other dish. The handle is long, and the head is typically made from flexible silicone with a rounded and slightly angled edge that makes it much more effective at scraping soft food off a dish than a bulky wooden spoon. The head size and shape can vary a bit depending on an intended extra use such as to scrape and mix or to scrape out of a long, narrow space (like the bottom of a bottle).

Small-Batch Fudgy Brownies

INGREDIENTS

6 tablespoons unsalted butter

½ cup granulated sugar

6 tablespoons, brown sugar

1 large egg, packed or 4 tablespoons liquid egg from carton

½ teaspoon vanilla extract

5 tablespoons all-purpose flour or gluten-free baking blend flour

6 tablespoons unsweetened cocoa powder

⅛ teaspoon salt

¼ cup chocolate chips (optional)

¼ cup chopped pecans or walnuts (optional)

DIRECTIONS

1 Preheat the oven to 350 degrees. Prepare an 8 × 4-inch or 9 × 5-inch bread loaf pan with nonstick cooking spray.

2 Slice the butter, place it in a microwave-safe bowl, and melt it in the microwave, about 20 seconds. Stop and swirl semi-melted butter in the bowl and return to the microwave to continue cooking for about 20 more seconds, or until melted.

3 Add both the sugars to the bowl with the melted butter and stir well. Mix in the egg and vanilla extract.

4 Mix in the flour, cocoa powder, and salt until combined and smooth.

5 Stir in the chocolate chips and/or nuts, if desired.

6 Pour the batter into the prepared pan, spreading the batter evenly across the top with an offset spatula.

7 Bake for 20–30 minutes, depending on the pan size. A toothpick inserted into the center of the brownies should pull mostly clean, not messy with batter.

8 Let the brownies cool completely in the pan before slicing into 6 to 8 pieces.

VARY IT! Customize your brownies with mix-ins. Try the chocolate chips and pecans or walnuts as suggested in the recipe. Or, swap out for between ¼ and ½ cup total mix-ins such as mini M&Ms, toffee bits, crushed peppermint candies, shredded coconut, chopped macadamia nuts, white chocolate chips, peanut butter baking chips, mini marshmallows, or whatever else inspires you!

Gooey Batter Cake in Loaf Pan

PREP TIME: 10 MINUTES	COOK TIME: 50 MINUTES	YIELD: 6 TO 8 SERVINGS

INGREDIENTS

For Crust:

3 tablespoons salted butter, melted

¼ cup granulated white sugar

¼ cup packed brown sugar

1 large egg

¼ teaspoon salt

¾ cups all-purpose flour or gluten-free baking blend flour

1 teaspoon baking powder

For Topping:

4 ounces cream cheese (½ cup), softened (see Tip)

3 tablespoons brown sugar

1 large egg

1 teaspoon vanilla extract

1¾ cup powdered sugar, plus extra for dusting

DIRECTIONS

1 Preheat the oven to 350 degrees. Grease a 9 × 5-inch loaf pan or line with parchment paper.

2 For the crust, mix melted butter with both sugars in a medium mixing bowl. Stir in the egg until well combined. Add the salt, flour, and baking powder; stir until a dough forms.

3 Press the dough into the bottom of the prepared pan to create the crust.

4 In a clean bowl, combine the softened cream cheese, brown sugar, egg, vanilla extract, and powdered sugar; beat until smooth. Pour the topping over the crust. Use a scraper spatula to get every last bit of batter!

5 Bake for 45–50 minutes or until the top is golden brown.

6 Allow to cool completely in the pan. Once cooled, sprinkle the top with the powdered sugar, cut into 6 to 8 pieces, and serve.

NOTE: This dessert is always lovely served with fresh berries on top.

TIP: To soften cream cheese, set it on the counter for an hour until it's needed. Or, place the unwrapped cream cheese on a microwave-safe plate and microwave on low or the defrost setting in 15- to 30-second increments until softened, but not overly warm.

Granola Chocolate Bark

PREP TIME: 5 MINUTES (PLUS 30 MINUTES TO CHILL)	COOK TIME: 2 MIN	YIELD: 6 SERVINGS

INGREDIENTS

¼ cup natural-style peanut butter or almond butter

⅓ cup chocolate chips

½ cup granola

DIRECTIONS

1 Line an 8 × 4-inch or 9 × 5-inch loaf pan with parchment paper.

2 In a small microwave-safe bowl, add the peanut butter and chocolate chips. Microwave on *high* in 30-second intervals, stirring between each, until the chocolate is melted and smooth.

3 Pour the chocolate mixture into the lined loaf pan and gently tap pan on the counter to level it.

4 Sprinkle the granola evenly over the top of the chocolate mixture and press down lightly so that it stays put.

5 Freeze for 30 minutes to 1 hour, or until the bark has firmed up. Slice into 6 pieces and store the leftovers in the refrigerator.

VARY IT! Swap your favorite granola for dried fruit, nuts, or small candy pieces.

TIP: Find the granola recipe in Chapter 7 and make your own. Home-made granola allows you to have more control over the flavor and ingredients in this Granola Chocolate Bark recipe while also making enough granola to have a little extra to snack on later.

Rustic Upside–Down Banana Pecan Cake

PREP TIME: 10 MINUTES	COOK TIME: 35 MINUTES	YIELD: 4 SERVINGS

INGREDIENTS

¼ cup packed brown sugar

1 tablespoon lemon juice, divided

2 teaspoons salted butter

¼ cup pecan halves

1 medium ripe but fairly firm banana, sliced

¾ cup all-purpose flour or gluten-free baking blend flour

¼ cup granulated sugar

½ teaspoon baking soda

½ cup baking powder

⅛ teaspoon salt

2 tablespoons cold butter, cubed

1 large egg, lightly beaten

½ cup plain yogurt

½ teaspoon vanilla extract

DIRECTIONS

1 Preheat the oven to 375 degrees.

2 In 6-inch cast-iron or oven-proof skillet, combine the brown sugar, 1½ teaspoons of the lemon juice, and butter. Heat and stir until the butter is melted, the sugar is dissolved, and the sauce begins to bubble.

3 Remove the skillet from the heat and arrange the pecan halves in a decorative pattern, which will become the top of the cake.

4 Pour the remining 1½ teaspoons of lemon juice into a small bowl; add the bananas and stir, taking care not to mash them. Drain the juice and arrange the bananas in a pattern over the pecans; set aside.

In a medium bowl, combine the flour, sugar, baking soda, baking powder, and salt. Cut in the butter with a fork until the mixture has a crumbly texture. Add the beaten egg, yogurt, and vanilla and stir gently until they are combined. Spoon the mixture over the bananas in the skillet, using a scraper spatula to get every last bit of batter.

6 Bake for 25–30 minutes or until a toothpick inserted in the center pulls clean. Cool the cake for 10 minutes and loosen the sides to invert it on a serving plate, or slice it into 4 wedges and flip onto individual dessert plates for serving.

TIP: If you don't have a 6-inch cast iron skillet, this may also be made in an 8 × 4-inch loaf pan.

Pumpkin Flan for a Few Friends

PREP TIME: 10 MINUTES | COOK TIME: 34 MINUTES | YIELD: 4 SERVINGS

INGREDIENTS

½ cup granulated white sugar

1 large egg, lightly beaten

½ cup canned pumpkin puree

¾ cup evaporated skim milk (see Tip)

⅓ cup packed light brown sugar

½ teaspoon vanilla extract

½ teaspoon pumpkin pie spice

DIRECTIONS

1 Preheat the oven to 325 degrees.

2 In a small saucepan over medium-high heat, combine sugar and ¼ cup of water. Cook, stirring frequently, until the sugar turns a very light amber color, about 3½–4 minutes. Remove the pan from the heat.

3 Use cooking spray to thoroughly coat the inside of four 6-ounce ramekins or a 2-cup capacity shallow baking dish, like a gratin dish. Carefully divide the cooked sugar water mixture evenly among the ramekins.

4 In a bowl, combine the egg, pumpkin puree, milk, brown sugar, vanilla, and pumpkin pie spice. Mix well.

5 Divide the pumpkin mixture among the ramekins and smooth the tops with a spatula.

6 Place the ramekins in a larger baking pan. Pour hot water into the pan to reach halfway up the sides of the ramekins. Carefully place them in the oven on the center rack.

7 Bake until the flans are set and a knife inserted in the centers comes out almost clean, about 30 minutes.

8 Remove the flans from the water bath carefully and let them cool completely. Unmold them onto a dessert plate and serve.

TIP: You can replace the evaporated milk with half-and-half for a richer flavor.

VARY IT! If you don't have pumpkin pie spice, ½ teaspoon of ground cinnamon makes an easy substitution. Or, try a pinch each of cinnamon, nutmeg, allspice, and ginger to make your own pumpkin pie spice.

Nutella Rice Crispy Treats

PREP TIME: 5 MINUTES | **COOK TIME:** 5 MINUTES | **YIELD:** 6 SERVINGS

INGREDIENTS

3 cups unsweetened puffed rice cereal

1 tablespoon unsweetened cocoa powder

3 tablespoons salted butter

3 cups mini marshmallows

6 tablespoons Nutella spread

DIRECTIONS

1 Lightly spray an 8 × 4-inch loaf pan, 6-inch round cake pan, or similar-sized dish with cooking spray.

2 Combine the cereal and cocoa powder in a bowl and toss to combine. Set it aside.

3 Melt the butter over medium heat in a medium pot.

4 Add the marshmallows to the melted butter and stir constantly until melted.

5 Remove the pot from the heat and quickly stir in the Nutella.

6 Add the cereal mixture and stir until completely coated with the marshmallow mixture.

7 Transfer the mixture to the prepared pan and press down with your fingers or a spatula. Let cool for 15 minutes before cutting it into 6 pieces.

NOTE: The key to making these treats successfully is moving quickly before the marshmallow-butter mixture cools off. That's why it's important to have all the ingredients measured out before starting.

7

The Part of Tens

IN THIS PART . . .

Put into place practical strategies that help you make the most of your freezer and save time and money in the process.

Figure out how to store and repurpose leftovers, whether remnants from your meal, scraps in "doggie" bags, or extras you made on purpose.

Chapter 21

Ten Ways to Make the Most of Your Freezer

Freezing food is a good thing when it's properly done. Freezing locks in a food's nutrients, extends the time period of safe storage, allows you to keep "meal starters" on hand for last-minute fixing, saves money by allowing you to stock up on store deals, and reduces waste by giving you a safe shelter for leftovers until you are ready to thaw, reheat, and eat them again.

Open your freezer and what do you see? Maybe just a half-eaten pint of ice cream, a bag of ice, and a bottle of vodka. Or, perhaps you see an about-to-avalanche mountain of mystery containers and unidentified tidbits hoarded because you couldn't bear to throw anything away, but never actually circled back use stuff up because it looks a little weird now. If you've just started down the path to cooking, chances are you haven't given much thought to how your freezer can help make the journey easier and more economical — or you have considered the benefits but just haven't implemented a plan.

It's time to take those good intentions off ice and take the plunge with these ten tips to optimize frozen food storage.

Maximizing Freezer Real Estate

Chances are, you have a small top or bottom freezer, a tandem pairing that came with your refrigerator. This is very suitable for the typical single home cook. Larger chest freezers and stand-alone upright freezers can be very useful if you have the space, budget — and storage needs! But keep in mind that these bigger options aren't always better for the single cook. That's because freezers do a better job of keeping food frozen at the correct temperature when they are kept full but not overpacked. So don't bite off more than you can chew!

Regardless of your freezer's size and style, creating "zones," which are basically food category groupings, is the best way to maximize the amount of available space. Zones will be based on your personal usage and consumption, but may include categories such as fruits and veggies, uncooked meats, cooked grains/ beans, ice cream, little bits, and leftovers. Tidy zones that fill the freezer, without overstuffing it, also help to ensure that frigid air flow keeps circulating around food, maintaining the proper temperature.

Choosing Suitable Storage Containers for the Freezer

Not all containers are created equal when it comes to freezing. The ability in which a freezer storage container has to successfuly keep air out is the key difference between containers in terms of maintaining the long-term quality of their contents. Remember, the air trapped in food packaged up and frozen can eventually cause "freezer burn," an unwanted situation where water evaporates from frozen food rendering it unsightly, dried out, and compromised in taste and texture (although it is actually still edible). Inadequate packaging for the freezer is one of the main factors leading to freezer burn.

A food vacuum sealer is perhaps the most effective method of packaging fresh and precooked items for the freezer and can extend their storage life for a few months or nearly indefinitely. This appliance works by mechanically removing air from the storage bag to create a super air tight seal that hugs snugly around the contents and keeps moisture from escaping. Less expensive pump-style sealers are also available and use your manpower to extract air from the package. (They work like a bicycle hand pump, but in reverse!) Any version of this kitchen helper is a well-worth-it extra to have on hand if you plan on freezing frequently. Look for a model that fits your budget, space, and usage needs.

But an official vacuum sealer isn't an absolute requirement. Plastic storage bags are a very versatile option for storing food in the freezer. They can be made nearly air tight by zipping up the bag most of the way and then sucking out the remaining air by mouth on the bag corner (or with an inserted straw) before sealing completely. Consider this a DIY solution to vacuum sealing — some stubborn air will still remain, but it's better than leaving the bag puffed up.

Zip-top freezer bags are very convenient because they can be smooshed or distributed to lie flat so that the filled bags stack up nicely, conserve space, and thaw out quickly. You may be wondering what the difference is between zip-top bags especially designated for the freezer versus regular zip-top bags. Both can be used in the freezer, but regular bags are made with thin plastic that lets air permeate faster and should be used only for food that will be consumed within a couple days. Otherwise, if food is left in for longer, ice crystals, the first telltale sign of freezer burn, will start showing.

Freezer bags are thicker and less likely to puncture or tear. They are not as inexpensive as regular zip-top storage bags and that makes them tempting to use. But don't do it! The small extra cost more than makes up for itself by preserving the quality of food and preventing food from having to be thrown away. This is because freezer specific bags are also slower to break down or let air permeate through the barrier after long periods of time in the freezer, meaning freezer burn is minimized. Also, freezer bags typically have a designated spot to write down the contents and date, and frugalists can wash them out and use again!

Using glass jars in the freezer can be left to personal preference: Some people swear by the food-quality saving properties of glass canning jars; others say they are prone to crack or break at extreme temperature changes. One way to lessen the chances of breakage is to fill the jars, chill in the fridge to let them more slowly rise to a chilled state before popping them in the freezer. The same goes for plastic storage containers; they can become brittle when frozen and should be prechilled before freezing. Fluids expand when frozen, so for all freezer containers that hold liquids, leave 1 inch of headroom to accommodate the expansion.

Many stores and brands are now offering their meats in vacuum-sealed packaging. This allows you to place the packaging directly in the freezer without any additional prep steps. Please note that plastic-wrapped Styrofoam or plastic supermarket trays will not provide adequate air tight storage. Portion meats or other foods from these into individual servings and place them in a freezer bag or wrap in butcher paper. For meat that you know will be in the freezer for the long haul, you can also vacuum seal or prewrap in plastic wrap before freezer bagging to eliminate almost all air contact.

Naming and Dating to Prevent Mystery Containers

Avoid UFOs (unidentified food objects) by naming and dating all food on a label before sticking it in the freezer. This will help prevent any unfortunate surprises, such as the time I thawed what I thought was leftover chicken stock for a casserole, but it actually was questionable lemon juice. Many brands of freezer zip-top baggies and containers come with a convenient pen-friendly spot to write on the details. Use a permanent marker so that the ink doesn't become smeared and illegible in the icy environment. If there is no official writing spot on my container, I use a piece of masking tape that I adhere to the vessel *before* it becomes cold. For baked items and dry goods, you can just slip in a written piece of paper, like a sticky note. Also, another life-changing tip is to prepare a master list that takes inventory of everything in the freezer. Keeping a master list up to date is a continuous process — mark off food when you remove it to use and write down each new item as you fill the freezer so that you know exactly what is in "stock"! Keep that paper sealed in its own zip-top bag so that it doesn't get soggy and disintegrate in the freezer.

Using "FIFO" Accounting for Your Frozen Food

FIFO stands for First-In First-Out. It is a continuous stock rotation system borrowed from retail and manufacturing industries that can help you optimize your frozen-food storage at home by minimizing waste and maximizing freshness. When prepping food for the freezer, you should mark containers with the dating system you prefer, either the "put in" date or the "use by" date.

Then stack your freezer in the order which the food should be used: food to use first at the top or front of the given food zone, and the food that will last the longest at the bottom or back of the zone. No more finding a possibly decade-old, ice-burned mystery package hiding in the freezer's dark crevasses. FIFO is a continuous process, meaning each time you add a new item to the freezer, you should put it in the correct zone, at the bottom of the stack, which automatically moves up the other food already stored there. Cross off items and add to your master list as you go along.

Plunging into Blanched Produce

Blanching is the best way to get most fresh veggies ready for storage in the freezer. No more running to hide when your neighbor comes over with a bumper crop of broccoli or you overbought on green beans. By taking a few extra minutes to blanch, you stop enzyme actions which can cause loss of flavor, color, and texture in vegetables, and this means that they'll hold up well in the freezer.

To blanch most vegetable (leafy greens and high-water content veggies don't work well), trim and cut them up into bite-sized pieces. Then scald the veggies (submerge into boiling water) or steam them for just a couple of minutes. Immediately afterward, drain the hot water and cover the vegetables with cold water and ice for a couple of additional minutes to halt cooking. After the ice bath, drain the water, and spread out the veggies to dry well. Next, place the veggies in a single layer on a baking sheet and freeze before transferring to zip-top freezer bags — this prevents contents from freezing in one big solid hunk. Fruit doesn't need to be blanched, but it works well to cut up into pieces (like an inch-long hunk of banana or peach slices) and prefreeze on the baking sheet in this same manner, so that later you can just easily grab what you need without having to pry stuff apart.

Freezing Beans and Grains Like a Boss

Preparing grains and beans from scratch can be a time-consuming task, and may not seem worth the effort when you just cooking for yourself. However, if you make a huge pot of grains or beans, the time and effort remain the same, but you've now exponentially increased the yield and your options for on-the-fly, quick meal-making.

Make the whole bag of beans or grains at once, following the directions on the package. Let them cool down in the fridge, and then portion into zip-top freezer bags or containers and stockpile them in the freezer. Thaw what you need in the fridge overnight, and soak a bag in a bowl of hot water for 15 minutes, or use the defrost microwave button for quicker results.

Freezing and Thawing Meats and Fish Safely

Don't try to freeze meat on the Styrofoam meat counter trays that they are sold in. This packaging doesn't offer an adequate air tight seal. Instead, reportion the meat into freezer-proof bags or freezer paper, even wrapping each steak or filet in its own blanket of plastic wrap, before putting it in the outer freezer bag. If you will be prepping a lot of raw meat for the freezer, you may want to consider a home vacuum-sealing machine, which are available in a range of prices and discussed earlier in this chapter.

The safest way to thaw meat, poultry, and fish is to place the freezer bag on a plate in the refrigerator overnight. Do not defrost frozen meats, fish, or poultry at room temperature, or in a bowl of warm or hot water; this can create unwanted bacteria growth. You can also thaw well-sealed packages in cold water (refreshing approximately every 30 minutes to keep food at safe temperatures) or in the microwave using the defrost setting. These two methods require a little more attention than fridge thawing because you need to make sure that they don't become warmer than 40 degrees. When food reaches temperatures greater than 40 degrees, harmful bacteria that may have been present before freezing awaken and can begin to multiply.

Keeping Dairy and Eggs Beyond Their Expiration Date

Dairy products like milk, cheese, and eggs can also be frozen, extending their useability well beyond the date on the carton. Don't try to freeze a whole egg; it will burst. But you can crack open and whisk eggs to freeze in the portions you need. Muffin pans and ice cube trays make good freezing vessels. Many of the recipes in this cookbook call for 1 or 2 tablespoons of egg, which is only a partial egg. Freeze the remainder for another recipe or stay one step ahead and prepare a bunch of 1-tablespoon serving sizes in mini muffin pans. You can do this with whisked egg or liquid egg in the carton. Then simply grab what you need and let it defrost in the fridge — because it's such a small amount, it thaws quickly.

UHT MILK

If you're frustrated that your traditional milk goes sour too fast (about a week after bringing it home from the store), consider purchasing organic milk, which will last a month (or longer unopened). This is because all organic milk goes through a preservation method called *ultra-high temperature* (UHT) treatment that uses extremely high heat for a few seconds rendering it very sterile by killing *all* the bacteria (good and bad), while most regular milk uses a pasteurization process using much lower heat for a longer time to eliminate potentially harmful bacteria, but not all. Since some UHT non-organic milk can be found if you hunt around and all types of UHT milk are shelf-stable (although usually displayed chilled in the United States with some exceptions like the little Horizon brand lunch box cartons and others), you may be wondering why all milk isn't preserved this way. The UHT process makes milk taste a little sweeter or some say "cooked," reduces vitamin content just a tad, and, because it kills both good and bad bacteria, it can't be used for cheesemaking. But, if you go through your milk as slow as a snail, UHT milk will wait and wait for you!

Milk can also be frozen, but the fats separate, which makes the experience a little "off" for drinking. However, thawed frozen milk is perfectly good and usable in baking waffles, muffins, and more. It's a smart, cost-saving way to salvage a big jug of milk that you can't polish off. Leftovers from a batch of whipped cream can be frozen in dollops on a baking sheet and later stored in a zip-top freezer bag. It's a quick and easy way to dress up your desserts for one. Sticks of butter freeze well, as do most hard cheeses. Cut or grate cheese into the portions you'll need later, and then wrap it in cellophane and stick it in a freezer bag.

Saving Herbs in Your Freezer

Herbs really elevate a recipe, especially fresh herbs. Most of us are not fortunate enough to have the space, time, and temperament to tend an herb garden. But purchasing fresh herbs in the produce department is quite pricey, and buyer's remorse hits hard when you realize you've only used a teaspoon of herbs and the remainder has wilted and developed dark spots within days. However, it's very easy to save your investment by freezing fresh herbs. Finely chop a fresh herb like sage, thyme, mint or basil, mix with a small amount of water, broth, or olive oil, and then freeze the mixture in ice cube trays. Once herb cubes have frozen, transfer to zip-top freezer bags and pull them out for use in recipes, as needed.

Knowing That If in Doubt, Throw It Out

If you have any qualms or concerns about the safety of your food, you should cut your losses and toss it away. Don't even fret about the lost expense; it's much more expensive figuratively and literally to get sick. Don't try to thaw and then refreeze food or leave it sitting out on the counter for a few hours. It's often not possible to tell if food has gone into the danger-zone of bacteria-growth based on how it looks, smells, or tastes. Your senses *can* be a good indicator, but not always. Check out the website `www.foodsafety.gov/food-safety-charts/cold-food-storage-charts` for a handy list of cold storage recommendations. You can also purchase an inexpensive freezer thermometer (if your freezer doesn't have a digital display) to help you monitor the interior temperature. Better safe than sorry!

Chapter **22**

Ten Ways to Take Advantage of Leftovers

You're probably feeling a bit skeptical turning the page to this chapter, because who really *loves* leftovers. It's understandable not wanting to eat the same thing over and over again, but savvy home cooks know that leftovers can save the day and are one of the best ways to stick to a food budget, reduce waste, and take a little load off the grind of creating a from-scratch plate of food for every meal daily.

Check out these ten ways to transform leftovers into meals that really hit the spot.

Storing Leftovers Safely

Cooked food like meats, poultry, and seafood and finished recipes like soups, skillets, casseroles, and such can be left at room temperature for a maximum of two hours. However, if you are outside, and the temperature is 90 degrees F or above, that time should be cut in half. When cooked food falls between 40 degrees F and 140 degrees F, it becomes a breeding ground for nasty bacteria that can make you sick. So, stay safe and stick those deviled eggs or pouch of lunchmeat back in the fridge pronto after serving yourself!

These cooked foods aren't the only leftovers than need your attention. Other perishable foods like milk, cheese, and other dairy products; cooked pasta, rice, and veggies; sandwich fixings, salads, and even fruit that has been peeled or cut into are all considered perishable and should abide by the 2-hours rule.

If leftovers have been chilled in a timely manner and packaged in air tight containers, they can remain safe to eat in the fridge for up to 5 to 7 days, and even longer in the freezer. But, if in doubt, always toss it out!

Making Extra on Purpose

Making leftovers on purpose is a viable food strategy. Cook once, eat three or more times! For example, slow cook a couple of pounds of chicken breasts and make that the foundation for the week's meals. Chicken fajitas, chicken and rice, chicken noodle soup, chicken-stuffed barbeque baked potato — you get the idea! What you're not going to use up in a few days, package in single serve portions for the freezer — typically 4 ounces of meat (or a quarter-pound) is considered a serving. The same idea is also smart with beans, rice, and other grains, which are often time consuming and awkward to make in a single serving. Simply scale up the batch to "super-size" and then stock the freezer for a thaw-and-heat side dish or jump-start on an entree recipe.

Giving Scraps and Crumbs a Second Chance as Future Ingredients

Don't look at these bits and pieces as leftovers or trash; reimagine them as useful ingredients for your next meal. You can squeeze out every drop of flavor, value, and nutrition from even the tiniest or scrappiest of scraps of this and that. Crushed tortilla chips salvaged from the bottom of a bag make Migas marvelous or can be tossed atop a salad. Potato peels can be spritzed with oil, sprinkled with salt, and baked for a crispy snack. Cookie and cake crumbs are magical atop a bowl of Greek yogurt, and baby spinach that's nearing the end of its seemingly useful life can be frozen to be reborn later in a smoothie or soup. You are really only limited by your imagination!

Disguising Leftovers in "Kitchen Sink" Casseroles and Stir-Frys

Recipe categories such as casseroles, stir-frys, egg scrambles, omelets, sandwiches, pizzas, and wraps are usually very welcoming to a random, unexpected ingredient. The classic leftover kitchen-sink ingredient of all time may be dark meat turkey; it always seems to remain in excess after a Thanksgiving feast. Or, ham at Easter. Chop these proteins up, or whatever ingredients you have on hand, to create quesadillas, egg scrambles, secret ingredient soups, and more. Do you have a lone stalk of celery, a single egg, a slosh of orange juice that all needs to get used up? Add them to your stir-fry and you can't go wrong. Dinner might sound (and look) like a mishmash, but it will still be mighty tasty!

Making Soup When You're Stumped

Embrace the frugal food hack of grandmothers everywhere, from every nationality and every generation. Make a delicious soup from scraps! Purge the produce bin of its odds and ends, chop and toss them in a big pot, and sauté those scraps in a little olive oil. Then add leftover grains and proteins and enough broth to cover. Sprinkle in various herbs and spices for the flavor profile you prefer. Let those ingredients simmer in the broth for a while — you will magically have soup! If you used the broth that is strained off of your slow cooker chicken or made with a ham hock or soup bone, then you can claim bragging rights as a soup-making super star!

Redefining Traditional Meals

Salad for breakfast, anyone? If you pair it with a banana, all the food groups are represented. Leftover salad is a very unexpected breakfast, but by front-loading your day with veggies, you make solid gains on attaining your daily requirement — and can swagger around self-righteously about it, too! Top the leftover salad greens with a sunny-side up egg and strip of bacon for a more traditional breakfast vibe. Any kind of leftover can be eaten at any time of day. When you cook for yourself, you make the rules. How about leftover pancakes from Sunday morning making a repeat performance for an easy Monday night dinner?

Turning Last Night's Doggie Bag into a Brand-New Meal

Don't be embarrassed to ask for a doggie bag from your dinner out; you paid for it! As long as you've put it in the fridge within two hours, you can give it new life in the next couple of days as a reinvented meal. Chop up your leftover steak and sprinkle it over a green salad with blue cheese dressing or recrisp those burger joint fries in the oven and top with cheese and bacon bits! Even your leftovers made at home can be repurposed — cooked noodles in an omelet, anyone? Try it, so delicious!

Sharing the Excess Bounty with Family and Friends

Realizing there will be leftovers from a recipe is a great excuse to call a buddy or crush to see if that person can join you for dinner. People rarely turn down the offer of being fed! Or, you can package up a plate and deliver it to a neighbor in need, like a homebound elder or single mom with her hands too full to cook for herself. Or, how about mom and dad? If they are in town, show off your cooking talents by delivering a leftover dish in person for them to taste test and give you a pat on the back; they will be so thrilled to see you.

Composting to Clear the Fridge

A final option to get rid of leftovers is to compost. You may think, "I'm just one person in a huge world; why should I even bother to compost?" Composting is the natural process of recycling organic waste into a fertilizer that provides a range of environmental benefits from enriching soil to reducing greenhouse gas emissions. Little actions by lots of people add up to big changes! You can create a compost bin at home or contact your local sanitation department to see if they take food scrap collections or offer pick-up or drop-off subscriptions. More and more municipalities are doing the dirty work for you these days, even providing a special composting bin for pickup. Typically accepted and easily compostable items include fruits, veggies, and eggshells; coffee grinds, tea bags, and nuts/nutshells; bread, grains, and pasta; and flowers and houseplants. Some composting facilities also have the capability to accept meats, fish, and dairy. If you are DIY composter, you can compost whatever you like!

Metric Conversion Guide

Note: The recipes in this book weren't developed or tested using metric measurements. There may be some variation in quality when converting to metric units.

Common Abbreviations

Abbreviation(s)	What It Stands For
cm	Centimeter
C., c.	Cup
G, g	Gram
kg	Kilogram
L, l	Liter
lb.	Pound
mL, ml	Milliliter
oz.	Ounce
pt.	Pint
t., tsp.	Teaspoon
T., Tb., Tbsp.	Tablespoon

Volume

U.S. Units	Canadian Metric	Australian Metric
¼ teaspoon	1 milliliter	1 milliliter
½ teaspoon	2 milliliters	2 milliliters
1 teaspoon	5 milliliters	5 milliliters
1 tablespoon	15 milliliters	20 milliliters
¼ cup	50 milliliters	60 milliliters
⅓ cup	75 milliliters	80 milliliters
½ cup	125 milliliters	125 milliliters
⅔ cup	150 milliliters	170 milliliters
¾ cup	175 milliliters	190 milliliters
1 cup	250 milliliters	250 milliliters
1 quart	1 liter	1 liter
1½ quarts	1.5 liters	1.5 liters
2 quarts	2 liters	2 liters
2½ quarts	2.5 liters	2.5 liters
3 quarts	3 liters	3 liters
4 quarts (1 gallon)	4 liters	4 liters

Weight

U.S. Units	Canadian Metric	Australian Metric
1 ounce	30 grams	30 grams
2 ounces	55 grams	60 grams
3 ounces	85 grams	90 grams
4 ounces (¼ pound)	115 grams	125 grams
8 ounces (½ pound)	225 grams	225 grams
16 ounces (1 pound)	455 grams	500 grams (½ kilogram)

Length

Inches	Centimeters
0.5	1.5
1	2.5
2	5.0
3	7.5
4	10.0
5	12.5
6	15.0
7	17.5
8	20.5
9	23.0
10	25.5
11	28.0
12	30.5

Temperature (Degrees)

Fahrenheit	Celsius
32	0
212	100
250	120
275	140
300	150
325	160
350	180
375	190
400	200
425	220
450	230
475	240
500	260

Index

Brussels sprouts, 210

bulk department, 38–39

Burger Breakfast Salad with Maple Vinaigrette recipe, 67

butcher department, 35–36

buttermilk, 114

Buttery Cinnamon Tortilla Chips recipe, 239

C

cabbage, 133

cake pan, 22

The Calculator Site, 47

can opener, 20

cannellini beans, 204

canning jars, 22

capers, 163

caramel sauce, 244

Caramelized Onion and Fig Grilled Cheese recipe, 149

carrots, 114, 130, 133, 135, 156

cashew butter, 100

cashews, 85, 231, 232

casseroles, 269

categories, for shopping lists, 34–35

cauliflower, 62, 136, 193, 208

celery, 113, 130, 135, 144

cereals, 83–96, 225, 233, 256

chai tea, 87, 103

Chai-Spiced Chia Pudding recipe, 103

challah bread, 93, 94

Charcuterie Stack recipe, 229

Cheat Sheet (website), 4

cheddar cheese

  BBQ Meatless Meatloaf Muffins, 194

  Beefy Loaded Skillet Nachos, 170

  Bestie Black Bean Soup, 134

  Charcuterie Stack, 229

  Cheesy Potato Soup, 130

Creamy Cheesy Mashed Cauliflower, 208

Cucumber "Bun" Club Sandwich, 148

Green Chile Chicken Casserole, 159

Loaded BBQ Chicken Air-Fried Potato, 160

Microwave Cheddar Breakfast Grits, 89

Mix-and-Match Muffin Pan Frittatas, 62

Philly Cheesesteak French Bread Pizza, 142

Refried Beans-Stuffed Zucchini Boats, 189

Small-Batch Sausage Balls, 68

Two-Egg Denver Mug Omelet, 61

Very Fast Chicken Verde Soup, 131

Zesty Tuna Melt Quesadilla, 144

Cheddar Cracker-Crusted Chicken Fingers recipe, 155

cheese, 167. *See also specific types*

cheese grater, 21

cheese tortellini, 122

Cheesy Potato Soup recipe, 130

cherries, 85, 99, 101, 116, 231

chia egg, 48

chia seeds, 80, 85, 87, 103, 104, 126

chicken, 153–163. *See also specific recipes*

chicken broth/stock, 130, 131, 135, 158, 159, 163, 209

Chicken-Avocado-Berry Salad with Chipotle Strawberry Dressing recipe, 115

Chickpea Kale Caesar Salad recipe, 123

chickpeas, 123, 230

Chile-Spiced Applesauce recipe, 218

chives, 208, 214

chocolate, 74, 77, 87, 90, 93, 94, 104, 231, 235, 242, 243, 251, 253

Chocolate Cherry Cashew Anything-But-Basic Oatmeal Packets recipe, 85

Chocolate Greek Yogurt Dip with Strawberries recipe, 243

Chocolate Java Lava Cake recipe, 238

Chocolate-Dipped Dried Apricots recipe, 235

Chopped Salmon Salad with Tangy Asian Dressing recipe, 119–120

chow mein noodles, 119–120

cilantro, 63, 113, 119–120, 131, 159, 170, 181, 182, 183, 189

Cilantro Lime Chicken Salad recipe, 113

cinnamon-raisin bagel chips, 67

Classic Snack Mix recipe, 225

cleaning, 20, 26

club shop memberships, 40–41

cocoa powder, 77, 85, 87, 100, 104, 238, 243, 251, 256

coconut, 85, 90, 102, 126, 233

coconut milk, 87, 102, 103, 184

cod, 177, 182, 184

coffee, 87

colander, 20

Cold Brew Overnight Oats recipe, 87

composting, 270

condensed milk, 247–248

condiments, to have on hand, 42

convenience products, 41–42

conversions, for liquid and dry ingredients, 47

cooking staples, to have on hand, 42

corn, 121, 143, 183, 212

corn meal, 76, 116

corn tortillas/corn tortilla chips, 170, 182, 192

About the Author

Jennifer Fisher is a recipe developer, healthy cooking guide, and creator and personality behind the thefitfork.com, a website helping folks fuel an active lifestyle with easy-to-make, delicious, and nutritious food. Jennifer is a self-taught chef, who started at age 8 and today enjoys cooking for a crowd, cooking for one, and everything in between. She's battled off, spatula to spatula, in numerous cooking competitions and has dozens and dozens of wins to her name. There's probably not an ingredient, cooking method, or appliance Jennifer hasn't tried. In her spare time, she enjoys running obstacle courses, outdoor adventures, participating in fitness races, and having her three young adult sons drop in for a home-cooked meal. She lives in Austin, Texas.

Dedication

To my dearly departed sidekick and crumb-catcher, Lucy, who was arguably a bigger "fit foodie" than me, although she was a "just" a dog.

Author's Acknowledgments

First and foremost, thank you to my amazing and supportive husband of 31+ years and three young adult sons who, through the decades, have been the guinea pigs for all my recipe creations — from blue ribbon dishes to bombs. They have endured hundreds of cold and reheated meals so that I could first photograph the outcome before serving, have been able to deduce my mood for receiving constructive criticism with just a glance, have devoured my successful recipes with such zest that I couldn't help but feel proud, and have always been willing to finish off their plates with an appreciative hug and "thank you," for better or worse. Also a huge hug to my dear parents and forever champions, Pat and Bob Yeargain. Thank you for gifting me my first cookbook in elementary school, letting me have free-range in the kitchen as a kid to do my thing, and for always celebrating my creativity and pouring on your love.

Also, much appreciation to all who have guided me in this cookbook writing process, including senior editor Jennifer Yee for understanding the big picture and providing guidance, For Dummies Coach Vicki Adang for her useful crash course and start-up suggestions for presenting my recipes and knowledge in the Wiley way, project editor Donna Wright whose calm demeanor and attention to detail perfectly complemented my jumping-around body and mind, and also to copy editor Kelly Dobbs Henthorne for her keen eye and spot-on suggestions. Also, I am so appreciative of our recipe tester Rachel Nix for executing each and every dish and written recipe detail to ensure a successful outcome, even if it's your first time in the kitchen. And, finally a big shout-out to our drool-inducing food photographer, Wendy Jo Peterson and to Wiley's amazing production staff.

Publisher's Acknowledgments

Senior Acquisitions Editor: Jennifer Yee

Project Editor: Donna Wright

Copy Editor: Kelly Dobbs Henthorne

Technical Editor and Recipe Tester: Rachel Nix

Photographers: Wendy Jo Peterson and Grace Geri Goodale

Production Editor: Saikarthick Kumarasamy

Cover Image: © fizkes/Shutterstock; Courtesy of Wendy Jo Peterson and Grace Geri Goodale

Take dummies with you everywhere you go!

Whether you are excited about e-books, want more from the web, must have your mobile apps, or are swept up in social media, dummies makes everything easier.

Find us online!

dummies.com

Leverage the power

Dummies is the global leader in the reference category and one of the most trusted and highly regarded brands in the world. No longer just focused on books, customers now have access to the dummies content they need in the format they want. Together we'll craft a solution that engages your customers, stands out from the competition, and helps you meet your goals.

Advertising & Sponsorships

Connect with an engaged audience on a powerful multimedia site, and position your message alongside expert how-to content. Dummies.com is a one-stop shop for free, online information and know-how curated by a team of experts.

- Targeted ads
- Video
- Email Marketing
- Microsites
- Sweepstakes sponsorship

20 MILLION PAGE VIEWS EVERY SINGLE MONTH

15 MILLION UNIQUE VISITORS PER MONTH

43% OF ALL VISITORS ACCESS THE SITE VIA THEIR MOBILE DEVICES

700,000 NEWSLETTER SUBSCRIPTIONS TO THE INBOXES OF *300,000* UNIQUE INDIVIDUALS EVERY WEEK

# of dummies

Custom Publishing

Reach a global audience in any language by creating a solution that will differentiate you from competitors, amplify your message, and encourage customers to make a buying decision.

- Apps
- Books
- eBooks
- Video
- Audio
- Webinars

Brand Licensing & Content

Leverage the strength of the world's most popular reference brand to reach new audiences and channels of distribution.

For more information, visit dummies.com/biz

PERSONAL ENRICHMENT

Staying Sharp
9781119187790
USA $26.00
CAN $31.99
UK £19.99

Facebook
9781119179030
USA $21.99
CAN $25.99
UK £16.99

Guitar
9781119293354
USA $24.99
CAN $29.99
UK £17.99

Investing
9781119293347
USA $22.99
CAN $27.99
UK £16.99

Beekeeping
9781119310068
USA $22.99
CAN $27.99
UK £16.99

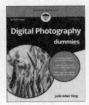

Digital Photography
9781119235606
USA $24.99
CAN $29.99
UK £17.99

Meditation
9781119251163
USA $24.99
CAN $29.99
UK £17.99

Pregnancy
9781119235491
USA $26.99
CAN $31.99
UK £19.99

Samsung Galaxy S7
9781119279952
USA $24.99
CAN $29.99
UK £17.99

iPhone
9781119283133
USA $24.99
CAN $29.99
UK £17.99

Crocheting
9781119287117
USA $24.99
CAN $29.99
UK £16.99

Nutrition
9781119130246
USA $22.99
CAN $27.99
UK £16.99

PROFESSIONAL DEVELOPMENT

Windows 10
9781119311041
USA $24.99
CAN $29.99
UK £17.99

AutoCAD
9781119255796
USA $39.99
CAN $47.99
UK £27.99

Excel 2016
9781119293439
USA $26.99
CAN $31.99
UK £19.99

QuickBooks 2017
9781119281467
USA $26.99
CAN $31.99
UK £19.99

macOS Sierra
9781119280651
USA $29.99
CAN $35.99
UK £21.99

LinkedIn
9781119251132
USA $24.99
CAN $29.99
UK £17.99

Windows 10 All-in-One
9781119310563
USA $34.00
CAN $41.99
UK £24.99

SharePoint 2016
9781119181705
USA $29.99
CAN $35.99
UK £21.99

Fundamental Analysis
9781119263593
USA $26.99
CAN $31.99
UK £19.99

Networking
9781119257769
USA $29.99
CAN $35.99
UK £21.99

Office 2016
9781119293477
USA $26.99
CAN $31.99
UK £19.99

Office 365
9781119265313
USA $24.99
CAN $29.99
UK £17.99

Salesforce.com
9781119239314
USA $29.99
CAN $35.99
UK £21.99

Coding
9781119293323
USA $29.99
CAN $35.99
UK £21.99

dummies.com

dummies
A Wiley Brand

Learning Made Easy

ACADEMIC

Algebra I dummies

Mary Jane Sterling

9781119293576
USA $19.99
CAN $23.99
UK £15.99

Basic Math & Pre-Algebra dummies

Mark Zegarelli

9781119293637
USA $19.99
CAN $23.99
UK £15.99

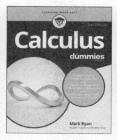

Calculus dummies

Mark Ryan

9781119293491
USA $19.99
CAN $23.99
UK £15.99

Chemistry dummies

John T. Moore, EdD

9781119293460
USA $19.99
CAN $23.99
UK £15.99

Physics I dummies

Steven Holzner, PhD

9781119293590
USA $19.99
CAN $23.99
UK £15.99

1,001 Practice Questions
SAT dummies

Ron Woldoff

9781119215844
USA $26.99
CAN $31.99
UK £19.99

Organic Chemistry I dummies

Arthur Winter

9781119293378
USA $22.99
CAN $27.99
UK £16.99

Statistics dummies

Deborah J. Rumsey, PhD

9781119293521
USA $19.99
CAN $23.99
UK £15.99

2016/2017
ASVAB dummies

Rod Powers

9781119239178
USA $18.99
CAN $22.99
UK £14.99

Includes Online Practice Tests
1,001 Practice Questions
Praxis Core dummies

Carla Kirkland
Chan Cleveland

9781119263883
USA $26.99
CAN $31.99
UK £19.99

Available Everywhere Books Are Sold

dummies.com

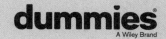

dummies®
A Wiley Brand